The Grass Roots
Cookbook

The Grass Roots Cookbook

JEAN ANDERSON

Times
BOOKS

Manufactured in the United States of America.
Published simultaneously in Canada by
Fitzhenry & Whiteside, Ltd., Toronto

Certain of these chapters previously
appeared in *Family Circle*.

Library of Congress Cataloging in Publication Data

Anderson, Jean, 1929–
    The grass roots cookbook.

    Includes index.
    1. Cookery, American.   I.   Title.
TX715.A56643   641.5′973   77–4472
ISBN 0–8129–0693–4

For D. B. A.

Acknowledgments

I should like to thank, first of all, the Agricultural Extension Service Agents—at both the county and state levels—in Alabama, Arkansas, California, Illinois, Kansas, Maine, Maryland, Massachusetts, Minnesota, Montana, Ohio, Pennsylvania, North Carolina, South Carolina, Texas, Utah, Vermont and Washington for putting me in touch with some of the finest grass roots cooks I have ever met. I should also like to thank the staff at the Mennonite Center in Lancaster County, Pennsylvania, for opening doors in Pennsylvania Dutch country and the staff of the Acadia House Museum in St. Martinville, Louisiana, for making available their resources. Further, I should like to thank the following individuals whose assistance proved invaluable: Anne Lewis Anderson, Chapel Hill, N.C.; Marcelle Bienvenu, New Orleans, La.; Elsie Branden, Garden City, Kans.; Elizabeth L. Buchan, Reidsville, N.C.; Ruth Buchan, New York, N.Y.; Laurie Archer Calkin, Santa Fe, N. Mex.; Mr. and Mrs. Charles H. P. Duell, Charleston, S.C.; Florence J. Flegel, LeRoy, Ill.; Jean Todd Freeman, Hattiesburg, Miss.; Yeffe Kimball, New York, N.Y.; Coleman Lollar, New York, N.Y.; the late Jean May, Charleston, S.C.; Carolyn Mummau, Mt. Joy, Pa.; Margaret Perry of Harrisburg, Pa., and New York, N.Y.; John W. Snyder, New York, N.Y.; Marjorie W. Weaver, Linden, Ala., and Pamela Kobbé, New York, N.Y. (for the expert manuscript typing).

Finally, a very special thanks to Arthur Hettich, editor of *Family Circle*, who recognized the need for a magazine series on "America's Great Grass Roots Cooks," and who has enthusiastically supported the project since its inception in 1973.

Contents

THE MIDWEST

THE PLAINS and SOUTHWEST

Preface

THE purpose of this book, quite simply, is to attempt to do for American cooking what musicologists have for years been doing for American folk music—preserve it from extinction.

Like musicologists who have gone to the source to tape-record unwritten "songs of the people," I have traveled thousands of miles into the hills and heartland of America in an effort to set down before they are lost forever—the old-fashioned regional recipes that have been passed down by word of mouth, from mother to daughter.

Ours is a generation so brainwashed about the glories of instants and mixes, ersatz seasonings and canned soups that we are in serious danger of forgetting the honest flavor of dishes prepared with fresh foods "from scratch." Moreover, in our headlong pursuit of *haute cuisine*, we have forsaken what may be some of the best cooking of all: grass roots American cooking.

You will not find here any quickie casseroles concocted out of potato chips and canned soup. You won't find any imitation fruit gelatins. You won't find a single boxed cake mix or commercial slice-and-bake cooky or an ounce of phony whipped cream dispensed from an aerosol can.

What you will find are soups that begin with a soupbone and bubble lazily on the back of the stove; breads that enable you to get your hands in the dough and feel the life of the yeast respond to your touch; old-time cakes and cobblers filled with fresh fruits; robust stews plumped up with dumplings; vegetables scalloped the long-ago way in butter and cream; delicate shellfish soups and chowders. There are recipes from the Ozarks and Appalachia, from Down East and the Deep South, from Pennsylvania Dutch country, the Pueblos of the Southwest, and the Pacific Northwest.

There are dozens of recipes, representative of nearly every corner (and culture) of America, the sorts of recipes that have been scribbled into margins of dog-eared family receipt books, the sorts that have won many a county or state fair blue ribbon. They come, for the most part, from women well on in years, the last generation to have learned how to cook from their mothers or grandmothers when they were "high enough to reach the dough board."

JEAN ANDERSON

New England
and the
Middle Atlantic States

Mrs. William E. ("Brownie") Schrumpf
of
Penobscot County, Maine

SHE is a little bit of a woman in her early seventies, and she is busier than any two people you can name. Her silvery hair is swept back into a French twist, her lively hazel eyes miss precious little, and when she moves, it is with quick, birdlike steps. "Brownie" seems the perfect nickname.

"My maiden name was Mildred Brown," she explains, "so everyone has always called me Brownie." Brownie is also her pen name; for the past twenty-five years she has been writing a "mostly Down East" cooking column for *The Bangor Daily News*, called "Brownie's Kitchen."

Yes, she *is* Maine born and bred, although she comes from farther south, a dot on the map near Augusta called Readfield Depot, where her father had "a thirty- or forty-acre farm."

"We weren't poor," she says; "we just didn't have any money. We made do with what we had. People under those circumstances today would be on food stamps. It just grieves you to see how people have gotten so lax. We picked wild strawberries, raspberries, and blueberries. We had our own milk. Mother made butter and sold it for twenty cents a pound. Now I pay a dollar thirty-seven. We always killed a couple of pigs every year and smoked hams and bacon and some of the shoulders. But we kept one shoulder for fresh meat, which Mother 'put down,' as we say. We didn't kill beef. But we had clams. And of course Father grew potatoes and apples and raised turnips for the cows, so we always had enough for ourselves. As I look back, I think, 'Golly, we had a good time!'"

We means her older brother, her two younger sisters, her mother and father and grandmother and grandfather, all of whom lived on the farm.

Brownie left the farm when she went to the University of Maine in Orono to study home economics. And this small, green, elm-shaded college town a few miles north of Bangor has been home to her ever since (her husband, whom she met at the University while he was a graduate student in agricultural economics and she an extension worker, died recently).

The Schrumpfs had no children, but, as one close friend said, "All the children in Orono are Brownie's. She's always baking cookies for them."

"I was in the 4-H Club when I was on the farm," Brownie continues. "I won two state championships in canning, and that, I think, was what made me want to go on in food. I won a trip to the State Fair in Bangor, which at that time was a big trip. Of course, high school students today don't think they've been *anywhere* unless they've gone abroad in their junior year."

When did she learn to cook? "When I was tall enough to reach the dough board," she says. "My mother was a good all-round cook. I learned a lot from her. And I learned a lot from a woman I worked for during high school who had summer boarders. She was a real old-fashioned Maine cook, and she paid me, I remember, thirty-five cents a day."

Brownie Schrumpf has always been a worker. After graduation she served for a while as Assistant State 4-H Leader in Maine, but left when she married. "In those days," she says, "women extension workers had to quit if they married."

Quitting, however, didn't mean that Brownie Schrumpf was idle. She doesn't know the meaning of the word. Even today, she is so on top of things that you can't imagine her taking to her rocking chair. Through the years she has been a part-time faculty member in the Home Economics Department at the University, teaching the home ec girls how to can foods and the forestry boys how to cook over campfires. She has been busy all the while giving cooking demonstrations, judging at county and state fairs and, since 1952 or so, writing her Wednesday food column.

Food, she says, is her all-absorbing interest (she has some three-hundred volumes in her cookbook library and, in addition, has collected more than three hundred antique cookie cutters, which she picks up on her travels about the state and about the country).

"I don't pay as much attention to housework as I should," she says. "Just look around." The parlor of her white three-story Victorian house is a cozy clutter of newspapers, magazines and cookbooks. It's the kind of room you feel instantly at home in.

So is the kitchen—old-fashioned compared to the antiseptic, impersonal gleam of today's contemporary kitchens. But it is thoroughly workable and pleasant, done in shades of pink and gray and ivory, and it is, unlike many modern showpiece kitchens, much loved and daily used.

Sea Scallops Chowder

Makes 4 to 6 servings

Mrs. Schrumpf, an old hand at preparing seafood, prefers to make shellfish stews and chowders in the morning, then set them uncovered in the refrigerator until shortly before serving time. That way the flavor of the seafood permeates the liquid. She emphasizes that any seafood stew or chowder must be stored *uncovered*. If not, "some reaction seems to take place that curdles the mixture."

¼ cup butter
1 pound sea scallops, rinsed in cool water, then quartered, or, if very large, diced

1 quart milk
1½ teaspoons salt
⅛ teaspoon cayenne pepper

1. Melt the butter in a large heavy saucepan over moderate heat, add the scallops and sauté gently just until golden—about 4 to 5 minutes. Add the milk, salt and pepper, and heat just until steam rises from top of mixture. Do not allow to boil.
2. Remove from heat, cool 15 minutes—uncovered—then set uncovered in the refrigerator. When ready to serve, heat again *just* until steam rises from the top of the chowder. Ladle into soup bowls and serve.

Oyster Stew

Makes 6 servings

"The ideal proportion for Oyster Stew," Brownie Schrumpf says, "is one pint of oysters to one quart of milk." It is, if your fish market gives you mostly oysters plus the juices they exude. But if the fish man simply dips into a vat of shucked oysters, your pint of oysters may consist largely of juice. So that no one will be gypped when it comes to oysters, we call for them by the dozen rather than by the pint.

2 dozen shucked small oysters and
    their liquor
¼ cup butter

1 quart milk
½ teaspoon salt (about)
⅛ to ¼ teaspoon cayenne pepper

1.   Strain the oyster liquor through several thicknesses of cheese-cloth to remove any grit and bits of shell; reserve. Heat the oysters in the butter in a heavy saucepan over moderately low heat 2 to 3 minutes or until the skirts barely ruffle. Add oyster liquor and set pan off heat.

2.   Meanwhile, bring milk to steaming in a separate large heavy saucepan over moderate heat. Ladle a little of the hot milk into the oysters and stir gently, then stir oyster mixture into hot milk. Season with salt and pepper (starting with ⅛ teaspoon), taste and add more salt and pepper if needed.

3.   Cool the stew—uncovered—for 20 minutes. Set uncovered in re-frigerator and let stand until shortly before serving. Reheat very slowly just until you see steam rising from the surface of the stew. Ladle into soup bowls and serve with oyster or pilot crackers.

New England Clam Chowder

Makes 6 to 8 servings

⅛ pound salt pork, cut in very fine
    dice
2 large yellow onions, peeled and
    sliced thin
6 medium-sized potatoes, peeled
    and sliced thin
1½ cups water

1 pint shucked clams and their liq-
    uor
1 quart milk
1 teaspoon salt
⅛ to ¼ teaspoon cayenne pepper
    (depending upon how hot you
    like things)

1.   "Try out" (render) the salt pork in a large heavy kettle over moderately high heat until most of the fat has been released and the dice have cooked down to crisp brown bits. With a slotted spoon, re-move brown bits to paper toweling and reserve.

2.   In the drippings, sauté the onions and potatoes about 5 minutes until golden. Add water, cover and simmer 10 to 12 minutes or until

potatoes are tender. Strain the clam liquor through several thicknesses of cheesecloth and add to the kettle along with the clams. Heat 2 to 3 minutes—no longer. Remove from heat.

3. In a large saucepan, heat milk just to the steaming point. Ladle a little of the hot milk into the chowder mixture, then add the remainder, stirring gently. Season with salt and pepper, taste, then adjust if necessary.

4. Cool mixture—uncovered—about 30 minutes; then set uncovered in the refrigerator and let stand until about 10 minutes before serving time. Reheat very slowly just until steam rises from top of chowder; do not boil. Stir in reserved salt pork, ladle into soup plates and serve.

Parsnip Stew

Makes 6 to 8 servings

"A dish we had a lot on the farm was Parsnip Stew," says Brownie Schrumpf. "Really it's more of a chowder because it has potatoes and onions and milk in it. I remember that, just before serving the stew, my mother would take some common crackers—you know what they are? they're hard and dry, more like beaten biscuit than anything I can think of—well, Mother would soak the common crackers in milk, then add them to the Parsnip Stew. And if someone came along and was asked to stay to supper, she'd put in a little more milk."

⅛ pound salt pork, cut in small dice
2 large yellow onions, peeled and sliced thin
2 large parsnips, peeled and sliced thin
4 large potatoes, peeled and sliced thin

2½ cups water
6 cups (1½ quarts) milk
2 teaspoons salt
¼ teaspoon pepper
1½ cups crumbled common crackers, water biscuits or beaten biscuits softened in ⅔ cup milk

1. Render (or "try out," as Brownie Schrumpf says) the diced salt pork in a medium-sized heavy kettle over moderately high heat until most of the fat has cooked out of the pork, leaving crisp brown bits. With a slotted spoon, remove crisp salt pork to paper toweling and reserve.

2. Stir-fry the onions, parsnips and potatoes in the drippings about 5 minutes until golden and lightly browned. Add water, reduce heat so that it simmers gently, cover and cook 30 to 40 minutes until vege-

tables are very tender. Watch kettle closely and, if vegetables threaten to scorch, add a bit more water.

3.   Add milk, salt and pepper, and heat, uncovered, just to the simmering point. Do not allow milk to boil.

4.   Just before serving, stir in the reserved browned salt pork and the milk-softened crackers. Ladle into soup bowls and serve.

Steamed Maine Lobster

Makes 4 servings

If you know lobster only as it is prepared at restaurants, you have probably never tasted one properly cooked, because most restaurants, alas, boil or broil lobster until it is dry and rubbery. The flesh of a perfectly cooked lobster is moist, sweet, and velvety-tender. Brownie Schrumpf prefers to steam lobster, and, she says, "eighteen to twenty minutes is long enough." She produces, in the words of one of our taste-testers, "absolutely the best lobster I ever put in my mouth."

Water (about 2 quarts)
4 live (and lively!) lobsters weighing about 1½ to 1¾ pounds each

1 cup melted butter, skimmed of milk solids
2 lemons, quartered

1.   For steaming the lobsters, you'll need 2 giant kettles (about 4 gallons each), fitted with racks (cake or steamer racks work well). Pour water into each kettle to a depth of 1 inch. Bring to a boil over moderately high heat.

2.   Add the lobsters to the kettles (two to each) by grasping around the back and lowering head-first onto the racks. As soon as the water returns to the boil, cover kettles snugly and begin timing the steaming. Eighteen minutes will produce a "just done" lobster with unusually soft meat still slightly transparent; in 20 minutes the meat firms up slightly and turns milk-white.

3.   Remove lobsters from kettle with tongs and discard pegs in claws. Place lobsters on their backs on a large cutting board (and have ready plenty of paper towels to sop up juices); split the underside of each lobster from head to tip of tail, using a sturdy, sharp knife. Bend the two sides backward slightly so the lobsters will lie flat, then serve with small ramekins of melted butter and lemon quarters. Be sure to put out lobster crackers and picks, plenty of napkins and a plate or bowl for the shells.

Lobster Rolls

Makes 6 servings

"I always put lemon juice on lobster meat and marinate it in the refrigerator overnight," says Brownie Schrumpf. "Gives a lobster salad more flavor." And to make Lobster Rolls, she adds, she "piles a slew of lobster salad" into buttered hamburger buns.

3 cups cooked, cubed lobster meat
2 tablespoons lemon juice
½ cup diced celery
2 tablespoons finely grated onion (optional)
1 teaspoon salt
⅛ teaspoon cayenne pepper
½ cup mayonnaise
6 hamburger buns
6 tablespoons butter
6 crisp lettuce leaves

1. Toss the lobster meat with the lemon juice, cover and refrigerate overnight. Next day add celery; onion, if you like; salt, pepper, and mayonnaise; and toss well to mix. Re-cover and let marinate several hours in the refrigerator.

2. To assemble the Lobster Rolls, spread hamburger buns well with butter, lay in a lettuce leaf, then mound the chilled lobster salad into the buns. Serve for a light lunch or supper.

Oven-Poached Salmon with Egg Sauce

Makes 6 to 8 servings

"We always have salmon on the Fourth of July. I don't know why; it's just a custom that goes back. We also have green peas—because they're coming in—and parsleyed potatoes." Mrs. Schrumpf's favorite way to prepare salmon is to oven-poach it, then serve it with Egg Sauce.

3 pounds fresh salmon, in one piece
4 cups water (about)

Egg Sauce:
6 tablespoons butter
4 tablespoons flour
1⅔ cups salmon cooking liquid
Juice of 1 lemon
3 hard-cooked eggs, peeled and minced
1½ teaspoons salt
⅛ to ¼ teaspoon cayenne pepper (depending upon how hot you like things)

1. Wrap the salmon in cheesecloth, set on a rack in a shallow baking pan and pour in water to a depth of 1 inch. Cover pan snugly with aluminum foil. Set in a moderate oven (350°) and bake for about 1 hour or until fish flakes at the touch of a fork.

2. *For the egg sauce:* Melt the butter in a small saucepan, blend in flour and let mellow over moderate heat about 3 minutes. Add salmon cooking liquid (from the baking pan) and heat, stirring constantly, until thickened and smooth. Stir in remaining ingredients and let sauce mellow over moderately low heat while you prepare the salmon for serving.

3. Remove cheesecloth wrapping from salmon, then carefully peel away and discard skin. Slide a small sharp knife along central backbone, lift off top half of salmon, then pull out and discard backbone. Replace top half of salmon on lower half, garnish platter with lemon wedges and parsley. Pass Egg Sauce separately.

Stifled Beef

Makes about 6 servings

"We didn't raise beef on the farm," Mrs. Schrumpf says. "And we didn't buy much beef either." Whenever there was beef, it was usually a soupbone, "which cost about a quarter," or stew meat, which was made into something called Stifled Beef, a robust but frugal fricassee.

2 pounds boned beef chuck, cut in ½-inch cubes
2 teaspoons salt
¼ teaspoon pepper
¾ cup *unsifted* all-purpose flour

3 to 4 tablespoons lard (*hog* lard)
1 large yellow or Spanish onion, peeled and cut in very slim wedges
1¼ cups water

1. Dredge the beef cubes, a few at a time, by shaking in a brown paper bag in a mixture of the salt, pepper and flour. Brown the dredged beef, about a third of the total amount at a time, in a large heavy kettle in the lard over moderately high heat. As beef browns, remove to paper toweling to drain. In the same kettle, sauté the onion about 5 minutes until limp and lightly browned.

2. Return beef to kettle, add water, scraping up browned bits on bottom of kettle, reduce heat so that water simmers gently, cover, and

cook slowly about 1 to 1½ hours or until beef is tender. Uncover and, if gravy seems thin, let simmer uncovered about ½ hour longer.

3. Taste for salt and pepper and add a little more of each, if needed, then serve with boiled, peeled potatoes.

Maine-Style Scalloped Potatoes

Makes about 6 servings

Like many Maine farmers, Mrs. Schrumpf's father grew potatoes. "Mostly we would have them boiled or parsleyed," she says. "But sometimes we would scallop them." Here's the recipe she grew up on. The trick to scalloping potatoes successfully, according to Mildred Schrumpf, is to keep the oven heat very low. "The milk must not boil," she points out, "or it may curdle."

6 large all-purpose potatoes, peeled and sliced very thin
2 large yellow onions, peeled, sliced thin and separated into rings
1½ teaspoons salt
¼ teaspoon pepper
4 tablespoons flour
4 tablespoons butter
2½ cups milk (about)

1. Layer half the potatoes into a well-buttered 9- × 9- × 2-inch baking dish, cover with half the onion rings, sprinkle with half the salt, pepper and flour, then dot with half the butter. Make a second layer precisely the same way, ending up with flour and butter. Pour in milk just until it is visible in the potatoes—it should not cover them.

2. Bake uncovered in a slow oven (300°) for about 1¾ to 2 hours or until potatoes are nicely browned on top.

Boiled Potatoes with Vinegared Onions and Sour Cream

Makes 6 servings

"They came out a few years ago and said something *new* to do with sour cream was to serve it on potatoes. Good heavens! I was brought up on potatoes and sour cream, and so was my mother!"

6 large potatoes, boiled in their
    skins until tender, then peeled
2 cups chopped yellow or Spanish
    onions

⅓ cup cider vinegar
1 cup sour cream, at room tempera-
    ture
Salt and pepper to season

1. Pile the hot potatoes in a large bowl. Combine onions and vinegar and mound into a small bowl. Spoon the sour cream into a third
bowl and set out the salt and pepper shakers.

2. The way to eat the combination is largely a matter of preference.
Some people will take potatoes, quarter and mash them slightly, top
with the vinegared onions, a big gob of sour cream, then salt and
pepper. Others will salt and pepper the quartered potatoes, slather
on the sour cream, then "chase" each bite of potato with a spoonful of
vinegared onion (this is the sequence Brownie Schrumpf prefers).

Apple Froth with Custard Sauce

Makes 6 to 8 servings

This unpretentious fruit dessert is two hundred years old at least, according to Mrs. Schrumpf. "We used to have Apple Froth a lot when
I was a girl," she says. "And I know a lady today who uses it as a
cake filling. Oh, that is gorgeous."

6 medium-sized apples, cored but
    not peeled (use a variety that
    will cook down to mush, such as
    Red Delicious)
1 tablespoon lemon juice
Pinch of ground nutmeg (optional)
3 large egg whites

½ cup sugar

Custard Sauce:
1½ cups milk
3 tablespoons sugar
Pinch of salt
3 large egg yolks, lightly beaten
1 teaspoon vanilla

1. Bake the apples uncovered (with no additional liquid in pan)
in a moderate oven (350°) for 1 hour. Remove from oven, lift apples
from pan and cool until easy to handle. Halve apples, then scoop all
pulp into a large, *deep* bowl. Add lemon juice and, if you like, the
nutmeg. Beat hard with an electric mixer until fluffy. Add the egg
whites, one at a time, beating hard after each addition until light and
frothy. (Caution: Mixture spatters, so adjust beater speed accordingly.) Very slowly add the sugar, again beating hard, until mixture
mounds softly. Cover and refrigerate 5 to 6 hours before serving.

2. *For the custard sauce:* Heat milk with sugar and salt in a small heavy saucepan over moderately low heat just long enough to scald the milk; do not boil. Mix a little of the hot milk into the egg yolks, then stir back into milk. Reduce heat to low and cook, stirring constantly, until mixture is thickened and leaves a thin custard-like film on a metal spoon. Remove from heat, stir in vanilla, then cool 20 minutes at room temperature. Set uncovered in refrigerator and chill until ready to use.

3. To serve, spoon apple mixture into dessert dishes and top each portion with a ladling of custard sauce.

Down East Strawberry Shortcake

Makes 6 servings

There's nothing fancy about this old-fashioned Strawberry Shortcake, but, my, it is good. Mrs. Schrumpf says that her mother sometimes made it with the wild strawberries that she, her sister and brothers used to gather.

3 pints fresh ripe strawberries, washed and hulled
½ to ⅔ cup sugar (depending upon tartness of berries)
¼ cup butter, softened to room temperature

Shortcake:
2 cups sifted all-purpose flour
3 teaspoons baking powder
½ teaspoon salt
2 tablespoons sugar
⅓ cup butter or margarine
1 egg, lightly beaten
½ cup milk (about)

1. Halve or quarter the berries, place in a large bowl, sprinkle with sugar and let stand several hours at room temperature.

2. *For the shortcake:* Combine flour, baking powder, salt, and sugar in a large mixing bowl. Cut in butter with a pastry blender until mixture is the texture of coarse meal. Fork in beaten egg well, again until mixture is uniformly crumbly. Add milk gradually, mixing briskly with a fork just until dough holds together (you may not need quite ½ cup of milk). Spoon dough onto an ungreased baking sheet and shape into a rectangle about ½ inch thick.

3. Bake the shortcake in a hot oven (425°) for about 12 minutes or until nicely dappled with brown. Cool about 20 minutes before cutting. Meanwhile, crush the strawberries lightly with a potato masher.

4. To serve, cut shortcake in large squares, split each and butter well. Sandwich the split shortcakes together with berries and pile more berries on top of each portion.

Blueberry Buckle

Makes 8 to 10 servings

Maine is almost as famous for its blueberries as for its lobsters and potatoes. And old-time Down East cooks like Brownie Schrumpf know enough different ways to prepare them to keep the family from being bored during the midsummer blueberry season. The Blueberry Buckle below, a sort of three-layer cobbler, is genuinely old. For best results, use fresh blueberries or those you have frozen yourself (*unthawed*). Commercially frozen blueberries are packed in too much sugar to produce an entirely successful buckle.

½ cup butter, margarine, or vegetable shortening
½ cup sugar
1 egg, lightly beaten
2 cups sifted all-purpose flour
2½ teaspoons baking powder
½ teaspoon salt
½ cup milk

1 pint fresh blueberries, washed and stemmed

Topping:
½ cup sugar
½ cup flour
¾ teaspoon ground cinnamon
½ cup butter or margarine

1.   Cream butter and sugar until light; beat in egg. Sift together the flour, baking powder and salt and mix in alternately with the milk, beginning and ending with dry ingredients.

2.   Spread batter across bottom of a well-greased 9- × 9- × 2-inch baking pan. Cover with blueberries.

3.   *For the topping:* Mix sugar with flour and cinnamon, then cut in butter until mixture is uniformly crumbly. Scatter topping evenly over blueberries.

4.   Bake in a moderately hot oven (375°) for 1 to 1¼ hours or until buckle is puffed and nicely browned. Remove from oven and cool the buckle upright in its pan for 10 to 15 minutes before cutting into squares and serving. You can, if you like, top with drifts of whipped cream or scoops of vanilla ice cream, although the buckle certainly doesn't need either.

Blueberry Fungi

Makes 6 to 8 servings

This blueberry dessert, according to Mrs. Schrumpf, comes from the French-Canadian immigrants up in Aroostook County, Maine. You might try serving it as we did, topped with gobs of sour cream.

8 slices firm-textured white bread
4 tablespoons butter or margarine
  (at room temperature)

1 quart fresh blueberries, washed
  and stemmed
1 cup sugar

1. Spread each slice of bread well with butter—one side only—then arrange four slices, buttered sides up, in a well-buttered 9- × 9- × 2-inch baking dish. Spoon half the blueberries on top and sprinkle with ½ cup of the sugar.
2. Arrange remaining slices of bread, buttered sides up, on top of blueberries, cover with remaining blueberries and sprinkle with remaining ½ cup of sugar. With a potato masher, press blueberries on top firmly, crushing slightly.
3. Bake uncovered for about 40 minutes in a moderate oven (350°). Remove from oven and again press surface with potato masher, crushing berries. Return to oven and bake 10 to 20 minutes longer, until blueberries have a syrupy consistency and are bubbly.
4. Remove from oven and cool 20 to 30 minutes before serving. Spoon into dessert dishes and top, if you like, with cream, ice cream or sour cream.

Steamed Chocolate Pudding

Makes 4 to 6 servings

"Steamed puddings were for Thanksgiving and Christmas and nothing else," Brownie Schrumpf says. Few people bother to make them anymore—a pity, because they are not difficult to prepare; they are easier, in fact, than most cakes, and conveniently steam unattended on top of the stove. You will need, of course, a steamed-pudding mold if you plan to make the recipe below. Molds are obtainable in kitchen departments of most fine department stores and in specialty kitchen shops.

1 square (1 ounce) unsweetened chocolate
3 tablespoons butter
1 egg
½ cup sugar
1 cup sifted all-purpose flour

1 teaspoon cream of tartar
½ teaspoon baking soda
Pinch of salt
½ cup milk
1 teaspoon vanilla

1. Melt chocolate and butter in a small, heavy butter-warmer over low heat. Meanwhile, beat egg and sugar well. Mix in melted chocolate mixture.

2. Combine flour with cream of tartar, soda, and salt and add alternately to chocolate mixture with milk, beginning and ending with dry ingredients. Beat after each addition just enough to mix. Stir in vanilla.

3. Pour into a well-oiled 6-cup steamed-pudding mold and snap on cover. Lower onto a rack in a large kettle containing about 1 inch of boiling water. Cover kettle and steam for 1 hour exactly.

4. Remove pudding from steamer and cool upright on a wire rack for about 10 minutes (cover should still be on pudding mold).

5. Uncover mold, loosen pudding by running a thin-bladed knife around edges and central tube, then invert pudding on a dessert plate. Cut into wedges and serve warm with sweetened whipped cream or, better still, with Foamy Sauce (recipe follows).

Foamy Sauce

Makes about 2 cups

2 eggs, separated
1 cup sugar

1 tablespoon milk
1 teaspoon vanilla

1. Place egg whites and 1 tablespoon of the sugar in a small mixing bowl. Beat egg yolks with the remaining sugar, milk and vanilla in a second small bowl until very thick and pale—about 5 minutes of beating with an electric mixer set at highest speed.

2. Whip the egg whites to stiff peaks, then fold into beaten yolk mixture so that no streaks of white or yellow remain. Serve over Steamed Chocolate Pudding. Also delicious over angel-food cake.

Lill's Blueberry Gingerbread

Makes one 9- × 9- × 2-inch loaf

"Lill," explains Mrs. Schrumpf, "was our hired girl on the farm, and this is the way she made gingerbread. It's a *light* gingerbread—three tablespoons of molasses only." For best results, make the gingerbread with fresh blueberries. If you must use frozen blueberries, thaw them first, drain them well, then pat dry on paper toweling.

2 cups sifted all-purpose flour
1 teaspoon ground cinnamon
½ teaspoon ground ginger
½ teaspoon salt
½ cup butter, margarine, or vegetable shortening
1 cup plus 3 tablespoons sugar

1 egg
1 teaspoon baking soda dissolved in 1 cup buttermilk or sour milk
3 tablespoons molasses
1 cup fresh blueberries, washed, stemmed and patted dry on paper toweling

1. Sift the flour, cinnamon, ginger, and salt onto a piece of waxed paper and set aside.
2. Cream the butter with 1 cup of the sugar until light and fluffy; beat in the egg.
3. Add the sifted dry ingredients alternately with the soda-buttermilk mixture, beginning and ending with the dry. Stir in molasses, then fold in blueberries.
4. Spoon batter into a well-greased-and-floured 9- × 9- × 2-inch baking pan. Sprinkle the remaining 3 tablespoons of sugar evenly on top.
5. Bake in a moderate oven (350°) for 45 to 50 minutes or until loaf begins to pull from sides of pan and is springy to the touch. Cut in large squares and serve.

Mrs. Willard Lourie
of
Bennington County, Vermont

"KIDS nowadays don't live the way we used to," says Mrs. Willard Lourie of West Rupert, Vermont. She takes a break from peeling beets, settles into a straight-backed chair at the big lace-covered dining table and begins reminiscing about the early 1900s, when she was a girl.

"My mother," she continues, "would put supper on the table, and we kids either ate it or we didn't. Nowadays mothers *ask* their children what they want for supper. To me, that's not right. I think the mother should plan the food."

Mary Lourie planned the meals when her own five children were growing up. And she plans them still, whether there will be two to eat, or ten, or twenty.

Widowed twelve years ago, she lives alone now in the trim white clapboard farmhouse where she went to keep house in 1924 as an eighteen-year-old bride. But her life is scarcely lonely. People are constantly dropping by to sit a spell in the big red-and-white kitchen.

Mary Lourie is surrounded by family, her side of the family (the Wilsons) as well as the Louries. There are four sons and a daughter, nine grandchildren and one great-grandchild, not to mention six brothers and sisters. Most live in West Rupert, a maple-shaded, church-steepled mountain valley village in Bennington County, Vermont, and none lives more than an hour away by car.

"Before the grandchildren reached their teens and got busy," she says, "there would be fifteen here every Sunday." And they could count on plenty of old-fashioned Yankee food—usually roast chicken, but sometimes Chicken Stew and Dumplings or New England Boiled Dinner—all of it made from scratch, right down to the breads.

Breads are what Mary Lourie remembers best making as a child, no doubt because a loaf she baked at the age of twelve went all the way to a state 4-H judging and won. "I wish I still had that recipe," she says.

Not that Mary Lourie is one to cook by recipe—written recipe, that is. Particular favorites are dishes her mother taught her—or her father's sister, or the 4-H Club. "I expect I learned the most about cooking from my aunt and my 4-H Club leader."

Mary Lourie's trial-by-fire in the kitchen came early, when she was about ten or twelve. Her mother, who ran a boarding house in West Rupert, was laid up with blood poisoning. And her younger brothers and sisters all had scarlet fever. So it was up to Mary, the oldest child, to cook and clean and run the house singlehanded.

How did she do it? "I managed," she says with typical Yankee reserve.

She also managed well as a dairy farmer's wife, although she had been a town girl. "We only had about an acre of ground," she says, "but my father—he was a barber—always kept a cow and pigs and chickens. Besides, before Willard and I were married, my brother and I used to get his cows in whenever he was busy haying. Willard's farm, you see, was just up the road."

So Mary Lourie knew how to milk a cow when she married, how to tend pigs and chickens. "We were up every morning about four-thirty," she remembers, "and when the children came along, they were up at four-thirty, too, to eat breakfast with us. I always tried to get my chores done in the morning so that I'd be free to run errands for Willard."

She also raised broilers for market, sold eggs, helped up at the sap house at sugaring-off time and kept a vegetable garden behind the house (she still does). At butchering time it was her job to smoke the hams, can or corn the beef, lay the fried pork down in stone crocks. "Taking care of the meat was women's work," she explains.

For Mary Lourie, however, women's work was *often* done, leaving time for other interests. For thirty-nine years she served as a 4-H Club leader, for thirty-five as a home demonstration club member and leader (she is presently Crafts Chairman), and all the while she has been deeply involved in the local Congregational church.

Although four of her sons now run the dairy farm (500 acres and 100 Ayrshires), Mary Lourie is hardly idle. Almost any day you drop by you'll find her bustling about the garden or sewing room or kitchen. She may be putting up beet relish or canning green beans or tomatoes or cream-style corn (her output this year totaled nearly 100 quarts).

She may be making a whopping batch of Rolled Molasses Cookies, stirring up a johnnycake or fixing a casserole for a church supper—with plenty of energy to spare.

"I can't believe I'm a grandmother," she says, "let alone a *great*-grandmother. I certainly don't *feel* like a grandmother. We used to think of grandmothers as tottery old gray-haired ladies in long skirts."

That may be the image. But that's not Mary Lourie.

Chicken Stew and Dumplings

Makes 8 to 10 servings

Hens, Mrs. Lourie will tell you, are too tough to roast or fry. So she simmers them into soups and stews, then tops them with dumplings. "There has to be plenty of gravy, too," she adds.

1 hen or stewing chicken (about 6½ pounds), stripped of excess fat
3 quarts cold water
2 medium-size yellow onions, peeled and cut in slim wedges
2 large celery stalks, cut in 1-inch chunks
2 large carrots, peeled and cut in 1-inch chunks
1 bay leaf, crumbled
3 teaspoons salt (about)

¼ teaspoon pepper (about)
1 recipe Old-Timey Dumplings (recipe follows)

Chicken Gravy:
3 cups chicken broth (reserved from stewing the chicken)
1 cup milk
¼ cup water
8 tablespoons flour
Salt and pepper to season and, if you like, a pinch or two of sage or poultry seasoning

1. Place hen, neck and giblets in a very large heavy kettle. Add water, onions, celery, carrots, bay leaf, salt and pepper, cover and simmer about 2 hours or until hen is tender.

2. Remove hen, neck and giblets from broth and cool; meanwhile, refrigerate the broth. Peel skin from chicken and discard; remove meat from carcass and cut in large chunks. Strip as much meat as possible from neck; mince the giblets.

3. Remove kettle of broth from refrigerator and skim off fat; measure out and reserve 3 cups broth for making gravy. Return kettle of broth to moderate heat, add chicken meat and giblets and bring to a simmer. Taste for seasoning and add more salt and pepper, if needed.

4. Prepare Old-Timey Dumplings as directed, drop by rounded tablespoonfuls onto bubbling broth, cover and boil 12 minutes.

5. *For the gravy:* While the dumplings cook, bring reserved chicken broth to a simmer in a medium-sized saucepan. Meanwhile, shake milk, water and flour briskly in a jar to make a smooth paste. Pour gradually into broth, whisking all the while, until thickened and smooth. Season to taste with salt, pepper, and, if you like, sage or poultry seasoning. Turn heat to lowest point and let gravy mellow while the dumplings finish cooking.

6. To serve, ladle dumplings into large soup plates and top with kettle vegetables and chunks of chicken. Pass the gravy separately.

Old-Timey Dumplings

Makes 8 to 10 servings

"Just drop these dumplings into chicken stew, cover them, and they'll puff right up," says Mrs. Lourie. She also likes to add these to New England Boiled Dinner. "I don't use them in *place* of potatoes but in *addition* to them."

2 cups sifted all-purpose flour	¾ teaspoon salt
2¼ teaspoons baking powder	1⅓ cups milk

1. Sift flour, baking powder and salt into a mixing bowl; pour in milk and mix briskly with a fork just until dry ingredients are moistened.

2. Drop dumplings by heaping tablespoonfuls into boiling kettle liquid (that of either Chicken Stew, page 20, or New England Boiled Dinner, below), cover kettle snugly and cook 12 minutes exactly (no peeking!).

3. To serve, spoon dumplings into large soup bowls, then ladle kettle mixture on top.

New England Boiled Dinner

Makes 8 to 10 servings

Mary Lourie likes to improvise with New England Boiled Dinner. Sometimes she makes it with a meaty hambone instead of with corned beef brisket, which traditional recipes call for. Sometimes she will add parsnips or turnips or rutabaga. "It just depends," she explains, "what I have on hand." She also makes a point of cooking the beets separately "so they don't color up the boiled dinner."

1 (6-pound) corned beef brisket, trimmed of excess fat
10 cups (2½ quarts) cold water
12 medium-sized carrots, peeled and cut in 2-inch chunks
16 new potatoes of uniform size, peeled
24 small white onions of uniform size, peeled
1 medium-sized cabbage, cut in 12 slim wedges (do not remove central core or cabbage wedges will fall apart)
Pepper to season
Salt to season (if needed; you may not need salt as corned beef is salty)
10 small- to medium-sized beets, scrubbed, boiled in their skins until fork-tender, then peeled

1.   Place corned beef in a very large heavy kettle, add water and bring to a simmer; skim off as much scum as possible, adjust heat so that water ripples gently, cover kettle and simmer brisket about 45 to 55 minutes per pound until fork-tender—4½ to 5½ hours in all.

2.   About 1½ hours before brisket is tender, skim as much fat from kettle liquid as possible. Add carrots, re-cover and continue simmering; after ½ hour, add potatoes, re-cover and simmer ½ hour. Add onions, pushing them down into kettle, re-cover and simmer 10 minutes. Add cabbage wedges, submerging them gently in kettle liquid, re-cover and simmer 15 to 20 minutes or until crisp-tender. Taste kettle liquid for seasoning, add pepper to taste and, if needed, salt.

3.   Remove brisket from kettle, slice thin across the grain and arrange on a heated large, deep platter. Wreathe with kettle vegetables, lifting them out with a slotted spoon. Add clusters of beets and serve.

Note:

The beets will take about 1 to 1½ hours to cook; time them carefully so that they are ready to serve at the same time as the boiled dinner.

Variation:

New England Boiled Dinner with Dumplings: Prepare New England Boiled Dinner as directed through Step 2. Remove brisket from kettle and keep warm. Prepare Old-Timey Dumplings (page 21), drop by heaping tablespoonfuls onto boiling kettle liquid, cover and boil 12 minutes. Meanwhile, slice the brisket thin. To serve, use large soup plates. Place a slice or two of brisket in each soup plate, then ladle dumplings, kettle vegetables, beets and liquid on top.

Vermont-Style Baked Beans

Makes 10 to 12 servings

Beans baked the Vermont way are somewhat sweeter than the more familiar Boston Baked Beans because they are made with maple syrup. For best results, bake the beans slowly in a heavy crockery pot so that the flavors mellow and marry. The following recipe makes a whopping amount, so halve it if you like.

2 pounds dried navy, pea or soldier beans, washed and sorted
11 cups cold water
½ pound salt pork, scored deeply criss-cross fashion
2 large yellow onions, peeled and scored deeply criss-cross fashion

4 teaspoons dry mustard
3½ teaspoons salt
¼ teaspoon pepper
1½ cups maple syrup (preferably *pure* maple syrup), or, if you prefer, 1 cup honey
¼ cup dark molasses

1. Soak beans overnight in the water in a large heavy kettle. Next day set kettle of beans and their soaking-water over moderate heat, bring to a boil, reduce heat so that beans bubble gently, then simmer, covered, for 40 minutes. Drain the beans, reserving the cooking water.

2. Place beans in a very large bean pot (about 3½- to 4-quart capacity). Push chunk of salt pork and onions well down into beans. Blend together mustard, salt, pepper, maple syrup and molasses. Pour over the beans and stir to mix. Now pour in enough reserved cooking water so that it is visible in the beans but does not cover them—about 3 cups. Reserve remaining cooking water to add later lest beans begin to boil dry.

3. Cover pot of beans and bake in a very slow oven (275°) for 3 hours, stirring every hour or so. Uncover beans and bake 1 to 1½ hours longer, stirring now and then, until they are touched with brown. If beans seem dry at any point, stir in just enough reserved cooking water to moisten them.

Scalloped Corn and Peppers

Makes 4 servings

In a strip of ground not much bigger than a bowling alley, Mary Lourie grows not only a profusion of flowers but also enough fruits and vegetables to last the year round. There are plenty of carrots and beets, tomatoes and cucumbers, radishes and lettuce, zucchini and butternut squash, and two particular favorites, sweet peppers and corn, which Mrs. Lourie likes to scallop.

1 medium-sized yellow onion, peeled and chopped
1 small sweet green pepper, cored, seeded and chopped
4 tablespoons butter or margarine
2 cups cooked, unseasoned fresh or frozen whole-kernel corn, well drained
2 tablespoons flour

1 cup milk
1 egg, beaten until frothy
¾ teaspoon salt
Pinch of pepper
Pinch of ground nutmeg
¾ cup soft breadcrumbs tossed with 1 tablespoon melted butter or margarine

1. Stir-fry onion and green pepper in 2 tablespoons of the butter in a large heavy skillet over moderately high heat 8 to 10 minutes until lightly browned. Mix in corn and set aside.

2. In a small saucepan, melt remaining 2 tablespoons butter and blend in flour. Mix in milk and heat, stirring, over moderate heat until thickened and smooth; turn heat to lowest point and let sauce mellow 3 to 4 minutes. Blend a little hot sauce into beaten egg, stir back into pan, then remove pan from heat. Season sauce with salt, pepper and nutmeg; combine sauce with corn mixture.

3. Spoon all into a well-buttered 1-quart casserole, top with buttered crumbs and bake uncovered in a moderate oven (350°) about 1 hour or until bubbly and browned. Serve oven-hot.

Bennington County Johnnycake

Makes one 9-inch round loaf

Every New England cook seems to have her own version of johnnycake. Some johnnycakes are thick, some are thin, some are fried on a griddle, some baked in the oven. The recipe here is a thick round baked corn bread and the way to serve it, according to Mrs. Lourie, is cut in wedges, split and drizzled with maple syrup.

1 cup yellow corn meal
1⅓ cups sifted all-purpose flour
¼ cup sugar
3 teaspoons baking powder
1 teaspoon baking soda

½ teaspoon salt
1 egg, lightly beaten
1 cup milk
¼ cup melted butter, margarine, or vegetable shortening

1. Combine corn meal, flour, sugar, baking powder, soda and salt in a mixing bowl. Combine egg, milk and melted butter in a large measuring cup. Make a well in the center of the dry ingredients, pour in the combined liquid ingredients and mix with a light touch just enough to moisten dry ingredients.

2. Pour batter into a well-greased 9-inch round layer-cake pan, then bake in a hot oven (400°) for about 30 minutes or until johnny-cake is nicely browned and springy to the touch. Serve hot with plenty of maple syrup.

Cranberry-Cheddar-Walnut Bread

Makes one 9½- × 5¾- × 3-inch loaf

If possible, use the ivory-hued, sharp Vermont Cheddar cheese for making this bread, but if this is unavailable, substitute any good sharp Cheddar. This recipe was given to Mrs. Lourie by one of her 4-H Club girls. It makes a large, flat-topped loaf.

3 cups sifted all-purpose flour
1⅓ cups sugar
2¼ teaspoons baking powder
1½ teaspoons baking soda
Finely grated rind of 1 orange
Finely grated rind of 1 lemon
⅓ cup vegetable shortening

Juice of 1 orange and juice of 1 lemon, plus enough water to total 1⅛ cups
1½ cups coarsely shredded sharp Cheddar cheese
2 eggs, lightly beaten
1½ cups fresh or frozen raw cranberries, very coarsely chopped
1 cup chopped walnuts

1. Place flour, sugar, baking powder, soda, orange and lemon rinds in a large mixing bowl. Stir to mix; then, using a pastry blender, cut in shortening until mixture is crumbly.

2. Mix in orange juice mixture, then cheese and eggs, stirring only enough to mix. Stir in cranberries and nuts.

3. Pour batter into a well-greased-and-floured 9½- × 5¾- × 3-inch loaf pan and bake in a moderate oven (350°) for about 1 hour and 10 minutes or until bread is nicely browned and springy to the touch. Remove bread from oven and cool upright in its pan on a wire rack 10 minutes. Turn bread out of pan and cool to room temperature before slicing. The bread is good spread with softened butter or cream cheese but is rich enough to enjoy with no spread at all.

Blueberry Muffins

Makes one dozen muffins

Because fresh blueberries have such a short season, we've worked out a way to make these splendid breakfast muffins of Mrs. Lourie's with frozen blueberries as well as with fresh ones.

2 cups sifted all-purpose flour
3 tablespoons sugar
3 teaspoons baking powder
1 teaspoon salt
⅞ cup milk
¼ cup vegetable oil

2 tablespoons maple syrup
1 egg, lightly beaten
1 cup fresh blueberries, washed and patted dry, *or* 1 10-ounce package frozen blueberries, thawed and drained very dry

1. Sift flour, sugar, baking powder and salt into a mixing bowl; combine milk with vegetable oil, maple syrup and egg. Make a well in the center of the dry ingredients, pour in combined liquid ingredients all at once and mix lightly just enough to dampen dry ingredients. Don't overmix or muffins will be tough—no matter if the batter is lumpy. Quickly fold in blueberries.
2. Spoon into well-greased muffin-pan cups, filling each about three-fourths full. Bake in a hot oven (400°) for 20 to 25 minutes or until muffins are nicely browned and have pulled from sides of muffin-pan cups. Serve hot with plenty of butter and, if you like, drizzlings of maple syrup.

Pumpkin Cupcakes

Makes about 20 cupcakes

These pumpkin cupcakes have somewhat the texture of fruit-nut bread. They are not particularly sweet, so frost them, if you like, using any favorite orange butter-cream or brown-sugar frosting.

½ cup butter, margarine or vegetable shortening
1⅓ cups sugar
2 eggs, beaten until frothy
1 cup mashed, cooked, unseasoned pumpkin or winter squash
2¼ cups sifted all-purpose flour
3 teaspoons baking powder

½ teaspoon baking soda
½ teaspoon salt
¾ teaspoon ground ginger
½ teaspoon ground cinnamon
½ teaspoon ground nutmeg
¾ cup milk
¾ cup coarsely chopped pecans or walnuts

1. Cream butter and sugar until light, beat in eggs, then mix in pumpkin.

2. Sift flour with baking powder, soda, salt and spices; add to creamed mixture alternately with milk, beginning and ending with dry ingredients. Mix in nuts.

3. Spoon into well-greased muffin-pan cups, filling each cup about three-fourths full. Bake in a moderate oven (375°) 25 to 30 minutes or until cakes begin to pull from sides of muffin-pan cups and tops are springy to the touch.

4. Cool cakes upright in their pans on wire racks for 5 minutes, then remove from pans and cool to room temperature before serving. Frost or not, as you wish.

Rolled Molasses Cookies

Makes 7½ to 8 dozen cookies

"I'm bound to keep my cookie jar full," says Mary Lourie, "because the children are always stopping by." She speaks not only of her grandchildren but also of the neighborhood children and the 4-H girls she teaches how to sew. Everyone's favorite seems to be these molasses cookies—crisp and spicy but not too sweet—which Mrs. Lourie bakes ahead and freezes.

4¼ cups sifted all-purpose flour
2½ teaspoons baking soda
1 teaspoon ground cinnamon
1½ teaspoons ground ginger
¼ teaspoon salt

½ cup sugar
1 cup molasses
½ cup melted vegetable shortening
½ cup buttermilk or sour milk

1. Sift together the flour, soda, cinnamon, ginger and salt; set aside.

2. In a large mixing bowl, combine sugar, molasses, shortening and buttermilk. Mix in sifted dry ingredients, about one-third at a time, beating after each addition.

3. Divide dough in 3 equal parts, wrap in foil or plastic food wrap and chill about 8 hours or until firm enough to roll.

4. Roll the dough, one-third at a time, very thin (about like pie-crust) on a lightly floured pastry cloth with a floured, stockinette-covered rolling pin. Cut with a 2½-inch biscuit cutter or in fancy shapes.

5. Space cookies about 1 inch apart on lightly greased baking sheets and bake in a moderate oven (375°) about 8 minutes or until browned around the edges. Remove from oven and let cookies firm up a minute or so on the baking sheets before transferring to wire racks to cool. Let cookies "crispen" about 30 minutes before serving.

Note:

Freeze the dough, if you prefer; then thaw the desired amount until soft enough to roll, cut, and bake the cookies as needed.

Mrs. Regina Correia-Branco
of
Essex County, Massachusetts

SHE grew up among the Portuguese Americans of New Bedford, Massachusetts, during the 1940s and 1950s and didn't, she says, "learn to speak English until I went to grammar school. Portuguese was my first language. I remember my first day at school—hearing strange new words, then running all the way home with these new words in my head."

An only child, Regina (then Regina Ventura) was "baby-sat" and brought up mostly by her maternal grandparents, neither of whom spoke English although they had immigrated to America around 1910. "My mother was born in this country; my father came over when he was about sixteen." Her parents did speak English—haltingly—but because both of them worked, Regina spent most of her young years steeped in the Old Country traditions that her grandparents passed along.

"Most of the Portuguese Americans in Massachusetts come from the islands—the Azores. So we were different. My father's people are from the north of Portugal around Oporto, my mother's people from Santarém near Lisbon."

Regina has the look of the northern Portuguese—fair skin lightly freckled, tawny brown hair that seems red in a strong light, hazel eyes. And she also has the slightly plumpish figure of a good cook although she confesses that she did not become interested in cooking until after she graduated from Wheaton College in 1956.

"My mother wasn't a very good cook—my grandmother was there to do it all and *she* was a terrific old-fashioned Portuguese country cook. She didn't do fancy or sophisticated things, just hearty everyday cooking."

But to Americans weaned on hotdogs and colas and canned soups, the foods of Regina's childhood sound exotic: *Caldo Verde* (green soup made out of potatoes and shredded kale), *Caldeirada* (fisherman's stew), *Bacalhau* (salt cod), husky home-baked breads and an array of the egg-rich puddings for which the Portuguese are famous.

Regina spent her junior year in Portugal and it was then that she "fell in love with the country" and almost everything Portuguese. She went straight back after graduation and spent three years working as an interpreter at the American Embassy in Lisbon.

There she took private cooking lessons from a man who had owned a restaurant in downtown Lisbon. "He came to my apartment once a week for about a year and a half and would prepare a complete meal —soup to nuts. That's when I began to get *seriously* interested in cooking.

"After I finished with him, I found a Brazilian woman who ran a catering service and she taught me a lot about the Portuguese Brazilian and Portuguese African cooking."

Regina pauses to bring out a huge, well-thumbed, loose-leaf notebook filled with handwritten Portuguese recipes which she has collected over the years. Some of the recipes date from her years of living in Portugal in the late 1950s, some from the 1960s when, as the wife of a Portuguese surgeon in Taunton and Cambridge (for whom she had worked as a bilingual secretary), she entertained on a lavish scale. "While I was married, I was preparing Portuguese dinners for anywhere from twenty to thirty persons at a time," she says. "Of course, I always served buffet—you have to with that many people."

Now that she is separated and living in Andover with her two children, she doesn't cook "Portuguese" as much as she would like.

"My kids love hotdogs and hamburgers, just like all other American kids. And frankly, I'm too busy to do much else these days." She is now teaching English and business courses at Andover Junior College— carrying a double load—but oddly, it is not Portuguese Americans with whom she is working, but Spanish-speaking students. She is fluent in Spanish as well as in Portuguese and says, with a touch of sadness, "I probably speak Spanish better today than I do Portuguese."

Fortunately, she will soon be speaking Portuguese again as a bilingual consultant with the Massachusetts Agricultural Extension Service, which is launching a new nutritional program to upgrade the diets of the Portuguese Americans of eastern Massachusetts.

Of her own cooking, Regina says somewhat wistfully, "Sure, I'd like to have the leisure to cook the Portuguese things, the kinds of things I remember my grandmother cooking, the kinds of things that were served at the saints' day festivals in New Bedford, the kinds of things I learned in Lisbon.

"Of course, if I'm doing a special dinner, I *will* cook Portuguese—Codfish Balls or *Bacalhau à Gomes de Sá* (salt cod with potatoes, onions, eggs, and olives), a lovely green salad made with fresh coriander. Or if it's a really fancy occasion, I'll roast a suckling pig or make stuffed squid.

"My daughter, who rebelled early against things Portuguese, is beginning to enjoy Portuguese food. And maybe one day my son will, too. But at the moment he couldn't care less."

What Regina Correia-Branco most looks forward to is the day when she will again have the time to put to good use that hefty notebook of handwritten recipes that she has spent years collecting.

Caldeirada (Portuguese Fish Stew)

Makes about 6 servings

During New England's whaling heyday, Portuguese fishermen (mostly Azorean) settled up and down the Massachusetts coast, bringing with them colorful customs and an equally colorful cuisine. One of their best recipes, according to Regina Correia-Branco, is *Caldeirada*, a robust fish stew. What goes into it depends upon what fish nets fetch up. The traditional *Caldeirada* contains shellfish (usually mussels) as well as fin fish. But Regina prefers to make it with fin fish only, using a combination of strong and delicately flavored local fish. She will sometimes add potatoes—an American innovation—to stretch the number of servings. "But," she cautions, "cook the potatoes on the side instead of in the stew so that they don't get funny-looking."

2 large onions, peeled and chopped
2 cloves garlic, peeled and minced
1 bay leaf, crumbled
¼ cup minced fresh parsley
5 tablespoons olive oil
6 fully ripe plum tomatoes, peeled and coarsely chopped (include juice), or 2 large vine-ripened tomatoes, peeled and coarsely chopped (include juice)

2½ pounds dressed, fresh fish (about equal parts haddock, eel, smelts and mackerel), cut in about 1½-inch chunks
1 cup good fish stock, or 1 cup water, or ½ cup each fish stock and dry white wine
2½ teaspoons salt (about)
¼ teaspoon freshly ground pepper (about)
3 potatoes, boiled until tender, peeled and sliced thin (optional)

1. In a large heavy kettle, sauté the onions, garlic, bay leaf and parsley in the oil about 5 minutes over moderate heat, just until limp and golden. Add tomatoes and their juice and simmer uncovered,

stirring now and then, about 20 minutes or just until flavors mingle and mixture has cooked down to a nice thickish sauce.

2.   Add the fish, pushing the chunks down into the sauce; then add the stock, salt and pepper. Cover and simmer slowly about 30 minutes or until flavors are well blended. If mixture seems soupy, boil uncovered a few minutes to reduce slightly. Add the potatoes, if you like, and heat 2 to 3 minutes longer. Taste for salt and pepper and add more, if needed. Ladle into large soup plates and serve, accompanied by chunks of crusty bread and a crisp green salad.

Caldo Verde (Green Soup)

Makes about 6 servings

"It's *so* simple," Regina Correia-Branco says of *Caldo Verde*, the green kale soup that is served almost daily in the areas of Massachusetts where Portuguese Americans live—New Bedford, Gloucester, Provincetown. "The main thing," she continues, "is to cut the kale as fine as you possibly can and to toss it into the soup just minutes before serving. The olive oil goes in at the end, too—just to add flavor."

3 large potatoes, peeled and cubed
2 quarts water
¼ pound *chorizo* or other garlic-flavored, smoked link sausage, sliced about ¼-inch thick
5 cups very finely sliced fresh kale (simply bundle several leaves together and slice into hair-thin filaments with a very sharp slicing knife)
⅓ cup olive oil
2 teaspoons salt (about)
¼ teaspoon freshly ground black pepper (about)

1.   Cook potatoes in the water in a large, heavy, covered kettle over moderate heat about 15 to 20 minutes or until you can mash them with a wooden spoon against the sides of the kettle.

2.   Meanwhile, sauté the *chorizo* slowly in a heavy skillet over moderately low heat, just enough to brown lightly on both sides. Reduce heat to low, cover skillet and let sausage continue cooking until you are ready to add it to the soup.

3.   When potatoes are tender, mash against the sides of the kettle (the potatoes are what thicken the soup), stir in the sausages, plus any juices they may have accumulated, and the kale. Cover and heat slowly 3 to 4 minutes. Stir in the olive oil, salt and pepper, taste and adjust seasonings, if needed.

4.   Ladle into large soup bowls and serve as a main course.

Portuguese Broiled Chicken

Makes 6 servings

One of Regina Correia-Branco's favorite ways to prepare chicken is to broil it after rubbing it with the classic Portuguese seasonings—garlic, bay leaf, salt and pepper. She pulverizes the garlic in a mortar with a pestle, using coarse (or kosher) salt as an abrasive.

2 cloves garlic, peeled and diced
1 tablespoon coarse or kosher salt
¼ teaspoon powdered or pulverized bay leaves
½ teaspoon freshly ground black pepper

1 tablespoon olive oil
2 tender young broiling chickens (about 1¾ pounds each), quartered

1. Using a mortar and pestle, grind together the garlic, salt and bay leaves to a thick paste. Blend in pepper and olive oil.
2. Rub each side of each piece of chicken well with the garlic mixture, place on broiler pan and let stand at room temperature for 30 minutes. Or, if you prefer, place chicken in refrigerator for about 30 minutes, then remove from refrigerator and let stand at room temperature 30 minutes before broiling.
3. Broil the chicken about 6 inches from the heat for 12 minutes. Turn chicken and broil 12 minutes longer or until nicely browned. Serve sizzling hot.

Wine-Marinated Roast Pork with Garlic and Bay Leaf

Makes about 6 servings

For a festive company dinner, Regina Correia-Branco likes to roast a suckling pig the Portuguese way, using only garlic, bay leaf, salt and pepper to season. She prepares more conventional pork roasts the same way but marinates them for two days in dry white wine before roasting.

2 cloves garlic, peeled and diced
1 tablespoon coarse or kosher salt
¼ teaspoon powdered or pulverized bay leaf
½ teaspoon freshly ground black pepper

1 center-cut, bone-in pork loin weighing about 4 pounds
3 cups dry white wine (such as a Portuguese *vinho verde*)

1.   Using a mortar and pestle, grind garlic, salt, bay leaf and pepper to a smooth paste. Rub well all over pork. Place pork in a large shallow bowl, pour in wine, cover and marinate 2 days in the refrigerator, turning pork in the marinade occasionally.

2.   When ready to roast the pork, place on a rack in a shallow roasting pan, pour marinade into pan and roast, uncovered, in a moderate oven (350°) for 2 to 2½ hours or until a meat thermometer, inserted in the center of the roast but not touching bone, registers 160°. Baste every 30 minutes or so with the combined pan drippings and marinade.

3.   Remove roast from oven and let stand at room temperature 20 minutes before carving.

Pork and Rice

Makes about 4 servings

Here is the way Regina Correia-Branco uses up leftover roast pork. "It's really a sort of pilaf," she explains.

1   medium-sized yellow onion, peeled and chopped
3   tablespoons roast pork drippings or butter
¾   cup minced leftover roast pork (Regina would use leftovers from her Wine-Marinated Roast Pork; recipe precedes)

1   cup converted rice
2   cups chicken broth
¼   teaspoon salt
⅛   teaspoon freshly ground black pepper

1.   Sauté the onion in the drippings in a heavy saucepan over moderate heat 3 to 5 minutes or until limp. Add pork and rice and sauté, stirring, 2 to 3 minutes, until rice is golden.

2.   Add broth, salt and pepper, bring to a boil, then adjust heat so that broth bubbles gently, cover pan snugly and cook about 30 minutes until rice is fluffy-tender. If rice seems too moist, cook uncovered 2 to 3 minutes to drive off excess moisture. Fork up and serve as either a main dish or a potato substitute.

Codfish Balls

Makes 6 to 8 servings

"When I lived in Cambridge, I was in charge of the Portuguese Table five years in a row at the National Food Festival," says Regina Correia-Branco. "I always made tons of Codfish Balls and Bacalhau à Gomes de Sá. And I once prepared thirty pounds of stuffed squid, which was a *bit* much." Regina makes Codfish Balls the Portuguese way—with plenty of garlic. If you're not fond of garlic, reduce the amount in the recipe to 1 clove.

1 pound boneless salt cod
Cold water (for soaking cod)
4 medium-sized potatoes, peeled and cut in ½-inch cubes
2 cups water (for cooking potatoes and cod)
1 large yellow onion, peeled and finely minced

2 cloves garlic, peeled and crushed
2 tablespoons minced fresh parsley
2 tablespoons olive oil
2 large eggs, separated
⅛ teaspoon pepper
Vegetable oil or shortening for deep-fat frying

1.   Soak the cod overnight in the refrigerator in just enough cold water to cover; change soaking water several times to remove excess salt.

2.   Next day, drain and rinse cod. Place potatoes in a large heavy saucepan, lay pieces of cod on top, pour in 2 cups water and bring to a boil. Reduce heat so that water boils gently, cover and cook about 20 minutes or until potatoes are very tender.

3.   Meanwhile, sauté onion, garlic and parsley in the olive oil in a heavy skillet over low heat about 10 minutes until onion is limp and golden; set aside.

4.   When potatoes are done, lift out pieces of cod with a slotted spoon and drain in a colander. Drain potatoes very dry, return pan to lowest heat and let warm 1 to 2 minutes to drive excess moisture from potatoes. Using a potato masher, mash potatoes well in pan.

5.   Pick over the cod carefully, removing any fragments of bone and skin; mince fine, then beat into potatoes. Mix in sautéed onion mixture, then the egg yolks and pepper. Beat the egg whites to soft peaks and mix in thoroughly.

6.   Into a deep-fat fryer pour enough oil (or melt enough vegetable shortening) to measure 2 inches deep. Insert a deep-fat thermometer and heat to 370°.

7.   Meanwhile, shape cod mixture into balls about 2 inches in diameter. Fry the balls, about 4 at a time, in the deep fat, keeping the

temperature as nearly at 370° to 375° as possible by raising and lowering burner heat. Fry the balls only to a rich golden brown—about 1 to 1½ minutes.

8. As the codfish balls brown, transfer them with a slotted spoon to a baking sheet lined with several thicknesses of paper toweling and set sheet uncovered in a very slow oven (250°) to keep warm while you fry the remainder of the balls. Serve piping hot.

Bacalhau (Salt Cod) à Gomes de Sá

Makes 4 to 6 servings

"The ideal proportions for this Portuguese main dish are about equal parts salt cod and potato," according to Regina Correia-Branco. She finds the recipe "perfect for big parties because it's easy to make, to hold and to serve. Some people brown the finished dish in the oven, but I just do it all together on top of the stove like a paella."

1 pound boneless salt cod
Cold water (for soaking cod)
1 quart boiling water
2 very large yellow onions, peeled and sliced thin
2 cloves garlic, peeled and minced
1 pound potatoes (preferably new potatoes), boiled, peeled and sliced thin
⅛ teaspoon powdered or pulverized bay leaf

2 tablespoons minced fresh parsley
5 to 6 tablespoons olive oil
Salt to taste (you may not need any, depending upon the saltiness of the cod)
¼ teaspoon freshly ground black pepper
1 hard-cooked egg, peeled and sliced thin
6 to 8 black olives (preferably Portuguese or Greek)

1. Soak the cod overnight in just enough cold water to cover, changing the water 2 to 3 times to get out all excess saltiness. Next day, drain and rinse the cod, then place in a saucepan, cover with boiling water and simmer uncovered about 15 minutes or just until tender. Drain, rinse and set aside.

2. In a paella pan or large, shallow flameproof casserole, sauté the onions, garlic, potatoes, bay leaf and parsley in 4 tablespoons of the oil 8 to 10 minutes over moderate heat until onions and potatoes are golden and touched with brown.

3. Cut the reserved salt cod in bite-sized chunks, add to paella pan and toss lightly to mix. Heat 3 to 5 minutes, just until cod is good and hot. Taste for salt and add, if needed, along with the pepper. Add an

additional tablespoon of olive oil, toss lightly, and if mixture seems somewhat dry, add the remaining tablespoon of oil and toss lightly once more.

4. Decorate the top of the dish with hard-cooked-egg slices and black olives and serve.

Boiled Potatoes with Coriander

Makes about 6 servings

Next to garlic, bay leaf and olive oil, the seasoning the Portuguese rely on most heavily is fresh coriander. The leaves are flat, rather like Italian parsley, to which coriander is related. "Coriander is wonderfully aromatic," says Regina Correia-Branco. "I like to roll boiled potatoes in chopped coriander, just as if I were making parsleyed potatoes. And I like to add it to my green salads as the Portuguese do." Fresh coriander is available at most Chinese and Latin American groceries (where it is known as *cilantro*).

5 tablespoons butter
1 tablespoon olive oil
3 tablespoons finely minced fresh coriander leaves

8 medium-sized potatoes, boiled in their skins until tender, then peeled
Salt and freshly ground pepper to season

1. In a large heavy skillet, melt the butter with the olive oil over moderately low heat. Add the coriander, then the potatoes, and warm 2 to 3 minutes, shaking the skillet, just until potatoes are nicely glazed and coated with coriander.
2. Sprinkle lightly with salt and pepper and serve.

Esparregado (Pureed Spinach)

Makes about 4 servings

"*Esparregado*," explains Regina Correia-Branco, "is always a puree of spinach or other greens flavored with onion and garlic. I usually use spinach, and when I have the time and am feeling ambitious, I will serve the *esparregado* in little baskets made out of fried shredded potatoes. The Portuguese always serve it in some kind of little container." You could, if you like, mound it in baked, hollowed-out tomatoes.

3 pounds tender young fresh loose-leaf spinach (loose-leaf meaning bunches of spinach rather than that sold in plastic bags), trimmed of wilted leaves and coarse stems
1 very large yellow onion, peeled and finely minced

1 large clove garlic, peeled and minced
4 tablespoons olive oil
½ teaspoon salt
⅛ teaspoon freshly ground pepper

1.   Wash the spinach several times by sloshing up and down in a sinkful of tepid water (be sure to rinse the sink out well before each successive washing). Lift out handfuls of spinach, shaking off excess moisture, and place in a very large kettle. Set over moderate heat, cover and steam about 15 minutes until very tender. You will not need to add any water to the kettle—the water clinging to the leaves is more than sufficient to steam the spinach. Drain the spinach in a colander, pressing out as much moisture as possible with a wooden spoon.

2.   While spinach steams, sauté onion and garlic in the oil in a heavy skillet over moderate heat, stirring frequently, 10 to 12 minutes until lightly browned.

3.   Place drained spinach, sautéed mixture, salt and pepper in an electric blender cup or, if you are lucky enough to have one, in the bowl of a Cuisinart food processor fitted with the chopping blade. Buzz in the blender or processor about 1 minute to puree. Taste for salt and pepper and add more if needed. Serve hot.

Green Salad with Coriander and Lemon

Makes about 6 servings

"The best salads, I think, are made with a combination of greens," says Regina. "I like to use Boston lettuce, Bibb, romaine and chicory in about equal parts. Then I toss in fresh chopped coriander and dress the salad with lemon juice instead of vinegar. And plenty of good olive oil, of course."

1 large garlic clove, peeled and quartered
⅓ cup fragrant olive oil (about)
8 cups mixed, crisp, prepared salad greens (Boston and Bibb lettuce, romaine and chicory in about equal proportions)

3 tablespoons minced fresh coriander leaves
Salt
Freshly ground black pepper
Juice of 1½ lemons (about)

1.   Drop the garlic into the olive oil and let stand at room temperature 3 to 4 hours so that the oil will absorb some of the garlic flavor.

2.   Place greens and coriander in a very large salad bowl, sprinkle lightly with salt and pepper, then drizzle with about half of the olive oil. Toss lightly—the leaves should just glisten. If they do not, add a little more oil, *slowly*. You don't want the leaves dripping with oil, merely lightly coated.

3.   Now drizzle in about two-thirds of the lemon juice, toss lightly, and taste. The salad should be nicely tart, but not puckeringly so. Be guided by your own sense of taste and add a bit more lemon juice, if needed.

4.   Serve as soon as the salad is dressed, so that the greens are nice and cool and crisp.

Portuguese Sweet Bread

Makes 2 tall round loaves

Among Regina Correia-Branco's fond childhood memories are the saints' day feasts held in New Bedford, Massachusetts. Most of the Portuguese Americans here came from the Azores, so an inevitable feast-day specialty was the egg-and-butter-rich Azorean Easter bread better known today as Portuguese Sweet Bread. Because of the dough's richness, it is too sticky to knead successfully without adding considerably more flour than the recipe specifies, so we suggest that you do the kneading in a heavy-duty mixer with a dough hook attachment. If you do knead by hand, flour the board liberally and use one hand only—at least in the beginning—until the dough is springy and malleable, not sticky.

2 packages active dry yeast
¼ cup very warm water
⅔ cup plus 1 tablespoon sugar
⅓ cup very warm milk

6½ cups sifted all-purpose flour (about)
1 teaspoon salt
8 eggs
¾ cup butter, at room temperature

1.   Sprinkle yeast over very warm water in a small bowl. (Very warm water should feel comfortably warm when dropped on wrist.) Stir until yeast dissolves; mix in the 1 tablespoon sugar. Set in a warm, draft-free spot and let stand 20 to 25 minutes until yeast begins to "work," forming a sponge that is about twice the volume of the original mixture. Stir down and mix in milk.

2.   Place 5 cups of the flour, the ⅔ cup sugar and the salt in a very large mixing bowl and make a deep well in the center. Scrape yeast mixture into the well, then break in the eggs—without stirring. Using a wooden spoon, gradually work the dry and moist ingredients together, slowly at first, then more quickly until mixture is smooth. If you are using a heavy-duty mixer, transfer dough at this point to largest mixer bowl.

3.   Beat the butter in, 1 tablespoon at a time. Continue beating hard until dough is smooth and elastic. With mixer set at slow speed, very gradually beat in the remaining 1½ cups flour. If dough still seems very soft and sticky (in humid weather, it may), add another ½ to ¾ cup flour. With the dough hook attachment, knead dough hard for 3 to 5 minutes, until very satiny and elastic. If you undertake hand kneading, expect 15 to 20 minutes of hard work. Keep flouring both your hands and the board well.

4.   Place the dough in a warm buttered bowl; turn over so greased side is up. Cover with a clean cloth and let rise in a warm, draft-free spot until doubled in bulk—about 1¼ to 1½ hours.

5.   Punch dough down, divide in half, then shape each half into a round loaf about 6 inches in diameter. Place each loaf in a well-buttered 1½-quart metal charlotte mold (it should measure about 7 inches across the top) or in a 1½-quart soufflé dish. Cover and again let rise in a warm spot until doubled in bulk—about ½ to ¾ hour.

6.   Bake loaves in a moderate oven (350°) for 40 to 45 minutes or until loaves are nicely browned and sound hollow when thumped with your fingers.

7.   Remove loaves from pans and let cool on wire racks before serving. Once the bread is cut, keep it tightly wrapped in plastic food wrap so that it will remain fresh and moist.

Torta de Laranja (Orange Torte)

Makes about 6 servings

This remarkable dessert made of eggs, sugar, orange, and a pinch of cinnamon—nothing more—is an egg crêpe baked in a jelly-roll pan, then rolled up in a towel lavishly sprinkled with sugar. Regina, who learned to make it when she was living in Lisbon, says it is "one of the few Portuguese egg sweets that isn't too cloying for Americans. The tartness of the orange helps."

¾ cup sugar
3 large eggs
Juice and finely grated rind of 1
    navel orange

Pinch of ground cinnamon
½ cup sugar (for coating towel in
    which torte will be rolled)

1. With the mixer set at high speed, beat the ¾ cup sugar and the eggs very hard for about 5 minutes or until no sugar grains are discernible on the tongue. Stir in orange juice, rind and cinnamon and beat slowly, just to combine.

2. Pour into a generously buttered-and-floured 15½- × 10½- × 1-inch jelly-roll pan (don't neglect to butter and flour the sides of the pan) and bake uncovered in a hot oven (425°) for 12 to 15 minutes or until mixture bubbles into "hills and valleys" and is dappled with brown.

3. While torte bakes, spread a clean tea towel or dish towel out on a counter top; heavily sugar an area of the towel that is slightly larger than the jelly-roll pan (you'll need ½ cup sugar at least).

4. When torte is done, remove from oven and loosen from pan by running a knife around the edges. Quickly invert onto the sugared area of the towel, then lifting the towel at one end, let the torte roll up on itself, gathering sugar as it goes (for best results, roll beginning at short end). Lop towel over roll and let stand about 3 hours before slicing and serving. You can top with whipped cream if you like, although the Portuguese wouldn't dream of such a thing.

Mrs. Mary Rohrer
of
Lancaster County, Pennsylvania

SHE is not at all sure she wants to be interviewed. She is modest, a Pennsylvania Dutch Mennonite who has devoted all seventy-eight years of her life to serving others—and to serving God.

Talking about herself is a new experience for Mrs. Mary Rohrer of Manheim, Pennsylvania, Route 6. She is uncomfortable doing it, but she agrees, "If you will put in, 'The Glory to be to God, not to me.'"

Such an attitude in this day of press agentry and ego trips may seem phony. But there is nothing phony about Mary Rohrer. She is one of those rare persons who put self last. She wears plain dress—simply cut cotton frocks in muted colors which she makes herself, black shoes and stockings, a net prayer cap. It is the Mennonite way, the way she has followed since she was a little girl, growing up with nine brothers and sisters on a farm just a few miles away from the community where she lives today.

Mary Rohrer's ancestors began farming in Lancaster County in the middle 1700s. Like the other Pennsylvania Dutch families who settled into the hill-and-dell land of Lancaster, Lebanon and Berks counties, they weren't Dutch at all. Her mother's people, the Reists, emigrated from Switzerland, her father's people, the Mummaus, from Germany. Dutch, as in Pennsylvania Dutch, is in fact a corruption of *Deutsch*, meaning German.

Today Pennsylvania Dutch country is an area where, despite the homogenization of the rest of America, Old World ways (speech, dress, hefty German food) persist, especially among the "horse-and-buggy" Amish sect.

In her lifetime, however, Mary Rohrer has seen significant changes, changes that have touched her own life. She now drives a car instead of a horse and buggy, she has a telephone (but no television), her kitchen is modern (with an electric range, refrigerator, and freezer). But the recipes she uses are the old Pennsylvania Dutch ones—Red Beet Eggs, *Schnitz und Kneppe*, Rivvel Soup with Green Peas, Potpie—many of them learned by watching her mother in the old farm kitchen. She knows them all by heart, but she keeps, in addition, a notebook of old family favorites, tucking in, now and then, a particularly good recipe from a daughter, friend, or neighbor.

Cooking comes naturally to Mary Rohrer, and has ever since she was a child.

"I remember," she says, "we would be out in the garden and Mother would say to me, 'Mary, you go in and cook supper, make mushy milk [cornmeal mush] or something.'"

At a young age, she also learned how to *schnitz* (dry) apples, how to roll "potpie" (egg noodles), how to make cheese.

"Experience is already the best lesson," she says.

And experience undoubedly did more than school to prepare Mrs. Rohrer for the life she would one day lead as a farmer's wife.

"I stopped the country school when I was fourteen," she admits, "then became a farmer girl, helping put up tobacco and pick strawberries."

In her early twenties, she spent three summers as a waitress in Asbury Park, New Jersey. "The girls from college there thought they had hard work, but we country girls thought it easy."

Mary Rohrer (née Mummau) did not marry until she was "near twenty-five." She met her husband, J. Norman Rohrer, at a gathering at his own house, then saw him again about two weeks later at a Mennonite Love Feast (Communion). They began dating "pretty regular," but then Norman left to hike his way west to California, picking up work along the way.

"He left in April," Mrs. Rohrer recalls, "came back right after Christmas and we were married February 6, 1923—before planting time." When they first went to housekeeping on the old 118-acre Rohrer Homestead, neither of them knew how to make ends meet.

"I said, 'Let's farm for market,' and so we began going to market heavy. Sometimes we'd dress a hundred chickens, then load up the little truck with chickens and eggs and vegetables.

"After a while, we grew strawberries by the acre. We were the first to let people come in and pick their own berries and our strawberry patch was a picture one year—sometimes we'd have a hundred pickers in the patch in a day."

For twenty years, the Rohrers were in the strawberry business, always selling berries by the pound instead of by the box. It was hard work, but the children pitched in when they were old enough.

Of Mary Rohrer's five children, three are alive today: Mary Elizabeth, who with her daughter, Lois, and foster-daughter, Shirley, now lives with Mrs. Rohrer; Dorothy, whose home is about thirty-five miles away; and Arlene, who farms the old homestead with her husband.

In 1956, Norman and Mary Rohrer left the farm, but not the country. They built Whispering Leaves, a red brick house on Colebrook Road nearby, moved in in July and began taking tourists who wanted a quiet week or weekend in the country with plenty of good food. But in December of that year, Norman died, leaving his widow to go it alone with the help of their oldest daughter, Kathryn Jane. Then, in 1972, Kathryn Jane died. Mary Rohrer did not close Whispering Leaves (she doesn't know the meaning of the word quit) but continued to operate it with the help of her second daughter.

"We get a lot of people from New York," Mrs. Rohrer says. "And we get a lot of repeaters. We can sleep nineteen."

"Sleep," it might be added, also means "eat," for Mary Rohrer cooks hearty Pennsylvania Dutch pancake-and-sausage breakfasts for her guests, then at 4 P.M. sharp covers the big, square kitchen table with a whopping Pennsylvania Dutch supper, along with such traditional "sweets and sours" as pickled beets and chowchow, Buttermilk Coffee Crumb Cake and Shoo-Fly Pie or Lemon Sponge Pie.

One would think that at seventy-eight Mary Rohrer would be slowing down. Not at all. She is perpetual motion. She now does allow herself an afternoon catnap, but within half an hour or so she is up and about again, hoeing her vegetable garden (which she calls "going to the doctor," because gardening, she believes, is good medicine for both body and soul); simmering giant kettles of Chicken-Corn Soup or Chicken Potpie; helping a neighbor "put up" peas; baking berry pies for a Mennonite fund-raising sale; refinishing a set of chairs she has picked up at a country auction; adding another coil or two to a huge braided rug she is making to order.

She is active, moreover, in volunteer work for the Mennonite Central Committee, which aids the needy in forty-five countries around the world as well as in America, and as if all these weren't enough, she is the one in her neighborhood to whom others turn for help, support and advice.

But gardening and cooking are what she seems particularly to enjoy.

"I *like* to cook," she says simply. In fact, if she doesn't have tourists coming for a weekend, she will often invite friends or family over for Sunday dinner just to have "helpers to eat."

"I tell people to come hungry and fill up."

And lucky the person who does.

Chicken-Corn Soup

Makes about 1 gallon, enough for 14 to 16 servings

There are as many versions of Chicken-Corn Soup as there are Pennsylvania Dutch cooks. At its best, it's a stew-thick mixture made with chicken and hard-cooked eggs and fortified further with either egg noodles or rivvels (small egg-and-flour dumplings). Mrs. Rohrer prefers noodles. What she adds to her soup depends upon what she has in her garden. Sometimes she will add green beans or limas, sometimes even tomatoes, but then she calls the soup Chicken Broth Soup with Vegetables instead of Chicken-Corn Soup. The version that follows is the classic Lancaster County Chicken-Corn Soup, made golden with saffron.

1 stewing fowl (about 5 pounds)
4 quarts water
2 cups chopped onion
1 large garlic clove, crushed (an optional that Mrs. Rohrer likes to add)
2 cups diced celery
4 cups fresh whole-kernel sweet corn, cut off the cob, or 2 10-ounce packages frozen whole-kernel corn

5 teaspoons salt
¼ teaspoon pepper
¼ teaspoon saffron strands, crushed
1 cup chopped parsley
2 cups uncooked wide egg noodles
2 hard-cooked eggs, shelled and chopped

1. Remove giblets from fowl. Place liver and heart in a small bowl; cover and refrigerate to use in Step 4.

2. Place fowl, neck and gizzard in a very large heavy kettle; add water and bring to a simmer over moderate heat. Adjust heat so that mixture bubbles gently; cover and simmer 2 to 2½ hours or until fowl is tender enough to pierce easily with a fork. Remove fowl and gizzard from broth and cool until easy to handle; discard neck. Strain broth and skim off as much chicken fat as possible.

3. Return broth to kettle, add onion, garlic (if used) and celery; cover and simmer 45 minutes; add corn, salt, pepper and saffron. Cover and simmer 45 minutes longer.

4. Meanwhile, skin chicken; discard skin. Strip meat from bones and cut in bite-sized pieces. Remove liver and heart from refrigerator and chop; also chop gizzard. Return chicken meat and chopped giblets to kettle; add parsley and simmer uncovered 15 to 20 minutes.

5. Add noodles and boil, covered, stirring now and then, 12 to 15 minutes—just until noodles are tender and no raw taste remains. Stir in chopped hard-cooked eggs and simmer about 5 minutes longer.

6. Transfer to a large tureen, garnish with a little additional chopped parsley and, if you like, wedges of hard-cooked egg.
   Note:
The soup freezes well, but it's best to freeze the mixture at the end of Step 4—that is, before the noodles and hard-cooked eggs are added. If you freeze the soup in quart containers, allow about ½ cup wide egg noodles and 1 small chopped hard-cooked egg per quart of frozen soup. Simply bring soup to the boil, add noodles and chopped egg and proceed as directed in Steps 5 and 6.

Rivvel Soup with Green Peas

Makes 6 servings

Rivvel (dumpling) soups have a lumpy look and, in fact, rivvel means "lump." Mrs. Rohrer makes plain Rivvel Soup (nothing more than rivvels cooked in salted milk), but she prefers Rivvel Soup with fresh home-grown sweet peas. "You might make it with corn once," she adds. "And if you've chicken broth, you might use half that and half milk for the soup."

1 quart milk, or 2 cups chicken broth and 2 cups milk
3 cups freshly shelled or frozen green peas
1½ teaspoons salt
⅛ teaspoon pepper
Pinch of ground nutmeg or mace (optional)

2 tablespoons butter

Rivvels:
1 cup sifted all-purpose flour
¼ teaspoon salt
1 egg, slightly beaten
¼ cup milk

1. Heat milk to simmering in a large saucepan over moderate heat. Add peas, salt, pepper and nutmeg or mace, if you like. Cover and simmer—do not boil—about 10 minutes or until peas are tender.
2. *To make rivvels:* Combine flour and salt in a medium-sized mixing bowl, add egg and milk and stir briskly and lightly just to make a soft dough.
3. Adjust heat under soup so that mixture bubbles gently, then using the quarter-teaspoon of a measuring spoon set, drop rivvel dough into soup, scattering it over surface. Cover and simmer 5 minutes. Add butter and as soon as it melts, serve the soup.

Variation:

Rivvel Soup with Corn: Prepare exactly like Rivvel Soup with Green Peas, but for the peas substitute 3 cups whole-kernel sweet corn cut from the cob or 3 cups frozen whole-kernel corn.

How to "Schnitz" Apples

When the Pennsylvania Dutch talk about "schnitzing" apples, they mean peeling, coring, slicing, and drying them. "Schnitz" are simply dried apples. Mrs. Rohrer's way is to spread the apple slices out on brown paper on top of her furnace in the basement. "I just forget about them, and in two or three days they are nice." According to her, the best drying apples are sweet ones—Red or Golden Delicious, Stayman. Once the apples are schnitzed, she bundles them into medium-sized plastic bags and stores them in her freezer to use in making *Schnitz und Kneppe* (Dried Apples with Dumplings and Bacon or Ham). It is possible to dry apples in the oven, provided you have one that will maintain a very low keep-warm temperature, about 175°. Simply line baking sheets with brown paper, spread the apple slices out one layer deep and place in oven to dry—it will take 15 to 16 hours in a 175° oven. The best way to prepare the apples, Mrs. Rohrer says, is to peel, core and quarter them, then slice each quarter crosswise about ⅛-inch thick. One large Delicious apple, schnitzed, will yield about ¾ cup.

Schnitz und Kneppe
(Dried Apples with Dumplings)
Makes 6 servings

Mrs. Rohrer's version of *Schnitz und Kneppe* differs from the traditional recipe in that she cooks the apples with cubes of lean, smoky bacon instead of with ham. The dish is then served as an accompaniment to the meat—pork or ham—instead of as the meat dish itself. If you are using commercially dried apples, prepare them this way: Measure out 2 cups of dried apples, then add just enough cold water to cover—about 3 cups. Let stand 8 to 10 hours, or overnight. Drain and reserve the soaking water, then, when preparing the recipe, add enough tap water to the soaking water to total 2 quarts (8 cups) and proceed as directed.

¼ pound lean, smoked slab bacon, cut in about ½-inch cubes	*Kneppe* (*Dumplings*):
8 cups water	2 cups sifted all-purpose flour
2 cups sliced dried apples (*schnitz*), soaked overnight	2 teaspoons baking powder
2 tablespoons light brown sugar	1 teaspoon salt
½ teaspoon salt	2 eggs
	1 cup milk
	¼ cup butter or margarine, melted

1. Place bacon and water in a large heavy kettle and bring to boiling; add dried apples, adjust heat so mixture bubbles gently, cover and cook 40 to 45 minutes until apples are tender. Stir in brown sugar and salt.

2. *To prepare kneppe:* In a medium-sized mixing bowl, combine flour, baking powder and salt. Beat eggs lightly in a small bowl; add milk and butter. Make a well in center of dry ingredients, pour in egg mixture, and stir briskly just to make a soft dough.

3. Bring apple mixture to boiling, then drop in heaping tablespoons of *kneppe*, making, as Mrs. Rohrer says, "about six nests on top of the apples." Cover tight and cook 12 minutes. "You dasn't peek," cautions Mrs. Rohrer, "or the *kneppe* won't be fluffy."

4. To serve, spoon *kneppe* into soup bowls, then ladle apples, bacon and liquid on top.

Lancaster County Chicken Potpie

Makes 8 to 10 servings

"Potpie" in Pennsylvania Dutch country means big squares of home-made egg noodles used to plump up chicken stew (Chicken Potpie). There are all kinds of potpie—fluffy ones leavened with baking powder, tender ones shortened with lard and "slippery" ones, which are plain egg noodles. Mrs. Rohrer favors the "slippery" kind and uses them not only in the traditional Chicken Potpie, but also to fortify beef or chicken broth, which she brews out of bones and trimmings. Like most of the Lancaster and Lebanon County Pennsylvania Dutch, Mrs. Rohrer uses saffron to color and flavor her Chicken Potpie. In the past, the Pennsylvania Dutch grew their own autumn-blooming crocuses, from which they plucked the deep golden stamens to dry into saffron.

1 broiler-fryer (3 to 3½ pounds)
10 cups water
1 celery stalk
½ teaspoon saffron strands, crushed
2 teaspoons salt (about)
⅛ teaspoon pepper (about)
2 medium-sized yellow onions,
  peeled and cut in thin wedges
2 medium-sized Irish potatoes,
  peeled and cut in 1-inch cubes,
  or 1 medium-sized Irish potato
  and 1 sweet potato, each peeled
  and cut in 1-inch cubes
½ cup thinly sliced celery

¼ cup minced parsley
3 tablespoons all-purpose flour
  blended with ¼ cup cold water
  (optional thickening)

Potpie:
2 eggs
2 tablespoons water
½ teaspoon salt
1¾ to 2 cups sifted all-purpose flour

Garnish (optional):
Chopped parsley
Wedges of hard-cooked egg

1.   Remove giblets from chicken. Place chicken, neck, gizzard, water, celery stalk, saffron and water in a large heavy kettle. Dice the liver and heart, then cover and refrigerate to use in Step 5. Set kettle over moderate heat, bring to a boil, adjust heat so that water ripples gently, then cover and simmer about 1 hour or until chicken is very tender.

2.   Remove chicken from broth, cool until easy to handle, then remove and discard skin. Strip meat from bones and cut in bite-sized pieces; chop gizzard; set aside for Step 5. Discard neck.

3.   Strain broth, skim off as much fat as possible and return broth to kettle. Add salt, pepper, onions, potatoes and sliced celery; bring to a simmer, cover and cook 25 minutes.

4.   *Meanwhile, make potpie:* Place eggs, water and salt in a medium-sized mixing bowl and beat lightly to mix; stir in 1 cup of the flour. Then, with your hands, work in enough of the remaining ¾ to 1 cup flour to make a very stiff dough. Divide in half. Roll dough, half at a time, on a lightly floured pastry cloth or board into as thin a sheet as possible, about a 15-inch square. Using a fluted or plain pastry wheel, cut dough into 1-inch squares.

5.   Add reserved chicken meat, gizzard, heart and liver to kettle. Bring to a rolling boil, then slide in squares of potpie, a few at a time, pushing well down into broth. When all potpie have been added, cover kettle and simmer 20 minutes—*without peeking.*

6.   Stir in parsley, re-cover and simmer about 5 minutes longer, just until noodles are tender and no longer taste raw or floury. Taste broth for salt and pepper and add more, if needed, to suit your taste. If you would like a thicker broth, briskly stir a little hot broth into

flour-water paste, stir mixture into kettle and heat and stir until mixture thickens and has bubbled 3 minutes.

7. Ladle all into a large tureen and garnish, if you like, with chopped parsley and wedges of hard-cooked egg. Or, if you prefer, simply spoon into large soup plates directly from the kettle, which is Mrs. Rohrer's way.

Raw-Fried Potatoes

Makes 4 to 6 servings

Whenever she wants something "good and filling," Mrs. Rohrer will stir up a batch of Raw-Fried Potatoes. They are similar to hashed browns, except that raw instead of cooked potatoes are fried, which gives them a crisper texture.

6 medium-sized Irish potatoes	¾ teaspoon salt (about)
2 to 3 tablespoons lard	Pinch of pepper

1. Peel the potatoes, quarter lengthwise, then slice each quarter about ⅛-inch thick.

2. Heat 2 tablespoons of the lard in a large iron skillet over moderate heat until good and hot, add potatoes and fry, scraping browned ones up from the bottom with a pancake turner, about 25 minutes or until tender and nicely browned. Add the additional 1 tablespoon of lard, if needed, to keep potatoes from sticking to skillet. Add salt and pepper, tossing to mix in, then taste and add a little more if necessary. Serve piping hot.

Red Beet Eggs

Makes 6 servings

Mrs. Rohrer, in making Red Beet Eggs, would use her home-grown, home-pickled beets, but, she says, you can make a good quick version using commercially canned beets. Red Beet Eggs are better if allowed to marinate in the refrigerator 2 to 3 days before serving, because the beet juice seeps all the way through the hard-cooked egg whites, adding color and flavor.

1 can (1 pound) small whole beets (do not drain)	¾ teaspoon salt
1 cup cider vinegar	¼ cup water (about)
⅓ cup sugar	8 hard-cooked eggs, shelled

1. Empty beets and their liquid into a small saucepan; add vinegar, sugar and salt and heat just until sugar dissolves; cool to room temperature.

2. Place eggs in a medium-sized bowl (or in a half-gallon preserving jar, which is the way Mrs. Rohrer does it), pour in beet mixture and add just enough water so that liquid covers eggs. Cover and marinate in the refrigerator 2 to 3 days, stirring now and then, or inverting the jar of eggs and beets gently a few times, so that all eggs redden evenly.

3. Spoon beets, eggs and some of the liquid into a serving bowl and serve.

Note:

Red Beet Eggs make excellent picnic fare.

Buttermilk Coffee Crumb Cake

Makes one 13- × 9- × 2-inch loaf

The Pennsylvania Dutch have an insatiable sweet tooth. Mrs. Rohrer will often set out for noonday dinner or for supper (served at 4 o'clock sharp) not one, but two or three or *four* sweets—pudding, pie, cake, cookies. Among her recipe file of sweets is this rich and dark coffee crumb cake with a crunchy, sugary crust.

2½ cups sifted all-purpose flour	1 large egg
1 teaspoon cinnamon	1½ cups buttermilk
1 teaspoon baking soda	
1 teaspoon salt	*Crumb Topping:*
½ cup (1 stick) butter or margarine, or ½ cup vegetable shortening	½ cup sifted all-purpose flour
	½ cup firmly packed light brown sugar
2 cups firmly packed light brown sugar	¼ cup (½ stick) butter or margarine

1. Sift together flour, cinnamon, soda and salt onto a piece of wax paper; set aside.

2. Cream butter, margarine, or shortening in a large mixing bowl until light, then add sugar gradually, continuing to cream until light; beat in egg. Set aside.

3. *To prepare crumb topping:* Mix flour and sugar in a medium-sized mixing bowl, then cut in butter, margarine or shortening with a pastry blender until the mixture has the texture of coarse crumbs.

4. Finish making cake batter by adding sifted dry ingredients to creamed mixture alternately with buttermilk, beginning and ending with dry ingredients.

5. Pour batter into a well-greased 13- × 9- × 2-inch baking pan; scatter crumbs evenly on top.

6. Bake in a moderate oven (350°) 45 minutes or until cake begins to pull from sides of pan and top springs back slowly when pressed with a finger. Cool cake upright in its pan on a wire rack 15 to 20 minutes before cutting. Cut in large squares and serve.

Shoo-Fly Pie

Makes one 9-inch pie

"I don't often anymore make Shoo-Fly pies," admits Mrs. Rohrer, "because I have to have helpers to eat." But she has in her files half a dozen different recipes for shoo-fly pies and this is the one she likes best. It is what is known as a "wet-bottomed" pie (many are very dry, almost cake-like). Molasses, by the way, integral to all shoo-fly pies, is sometimes a misnomer—most Pennsylvania Dutch cooks use what they call "light molasses" or "king syrup," which is not molasses but corn syrup. This recipe uses both molasses and dark corn syrup, which accounts for its rich but not over-molassesy flavor.

Bottom Part:
¾ cup dark corn syrup
¼ cup molasses
1 cup boiling water
1 teaspoon baking soda
1 egg, lightly beaten

Top Part:
1 cup sifted all-purpose flour
2 tablespoons shortening or lard
⅔ cup firmly packed dark brown sugar
1 unbaked 9-inch pie shell

1. *To prepare bottom part:* In a medium-sized mixing bowl, combine corn syrup, molasses and water; stir in soda. Beat a little molasses mixture into the egg, then stir back into mixing bowl.

2. *To prepare top part:* With a pastry blender, mix together flour, shortening or lard and sugar until mixture has the texture of coarse crumbs. Mix 1 cup of the crumbs into the molasses mixture and pour into unbaked pie shell. Scatter remaining crumbs on top.

3. Bake in a hot oven (400°) for 25 minutes or until crust is lightly browned and filling puffy. Remove from oven and let cool to room temperature before cutting.

Lemon Sponge Pie

Makes one 9-inch pie

"My family would eat it better than lemon meringue pie," Mrs. Rohrer says of Lemon Sponge Pie, a Pennsylvania Dutch classic. It is cake-like on top with a layer of tart lemon custard underneath.

1 cup sugar	2 tablespoons melted butter
3 tablespoons all-purpose flour	1 cup milk
Juice of 1 lemon	Pinch of salt
Finely grated rind of 1 lemon	1 unbaked 9-inch pie shell
1 large egg, separated	

1. Combine sugar and flour in a medium-sized mixing bowl. Stir in lemon juice and rind; beat in egg yolk, then melted butter. Stir in milk.

2. Beat egg white with salt until fairly stiff peaks form, then fold into lemon mixture until no streaks of white show. Pour mixture into unbaked pie shell.

3. Bake in moderate oven (350°) 35 to 40 minutes or until crust is lightly browned and filling puffy and touched with brown. Cool about 15 minutes before cutting. Good warm or cold.

Mary Rohrer's Homemade Tomato Juice

Makes about 3 quarts (or 6 pints)

Last year Mary Rohrer filled up her freezer and, in addition, canned some 200 quarts of fruit and vegetables—all from her own garden. Whenever she has a good crop of tomatoes, she will make tomato juice as well as can whole tomatoes.

12 very large, ripe, strongly acid tomatoes, washed, cored and cut in thin wedges (no need to peel)
1 cup diced sweet green pepper
1½ cups chopped onion
1 celery stalk, diced
⅓ cup sugar
1 tablespoon salt

1.   Place all ingredients in a large heavy enamel kettle, bring to a simmer over moderate heat, cover and simmer 35 to 40 minutes, stirring now and then, until tomatoes have cooked down to juice.

2.   Put mixture through a food mill or press through a fine sieve.

3.   Return strained juice to kettle and bring to a full rolling broil. Pour into 3 hot, sterilized quart-sized preserving jars, leaving ¼-inch headroom at the top. Screw caps on tight, then process 30 minutes in a boiling water bath. Store on a cool, dark, dry shelf.

Note:

If you prefer to use pint-size jars, process for 20 minutes. This recipe will make 6 pints.

Mrs. Charles Seymour
of
Talbot County, Maryland

"WHEN it comes to cooking," Mary Seymour begins, "I'm a great one for just puttin' in, you know, a dab of this, a pinch of that."

That's the way she has always cooked. And that's the way her mother cooked back in the early 1900s when Mary Seymour (then Mary Harrison) was growing up with six brothers and a sister at Bar Neck on Tilghman Island on Maryland's Eastern Shore.

"Mother was a good cook," she continues. "At least *we* thought so. But she was a plain cook. I mean, she didn't go in so much for fancy things. In those days you didn't have a lot of the fancy foods we have now. Why, I remember the first time we bought a loaf of bread at the store. We thought we really *had* something because we'd always made our own bread. And frostings—in those days, you boiled the frosting to make it thick because there was no such thing as 10X sugar."

It was from her mother that Mary Harrison learned her knack for and love of cooking. "I always helped in the kitchen; being the oldest girl in such a big family, I had to.

"I remember at Christmas we made a lot of cakes that we stored in lard cans. No, not fruit cakes. We'd make one-two-three-four cakes—that's the only kind of cake most people made around here in those days. And we baked a rich black-walnut cake, a black-walnut *pound-cake* I guess you'd call it. I have that recipe still." (It is included among the recipes that follow.)

But what Mary Seymour remembers best from her childhood is seafood. Living as her family did less than a hundred yards from Chesapeake Bay, they had, almost at their front door, all the blue crabs and oysters and fin fish they could eat. "My father," she continues, "was a commercial waterman; that is, he fished and he oystered. By trade he was a ship's carpenter, but he earned his living on the water except for a few years when he turned his hand to farming. Even when he wasn't farming, we always kept about three hogs and a flock of chickens. We had a vegetable garden, too. So there was always plenty to eat."

The "plenty," wrested from land and sea, was turned into old-time, sustaining Eastern Shore fare: soft-crusted (rather than crispy) fried chicken served with a nut-brown gravy, scalloped oysters layered into a pan with crushed soda crackers, batter-fried oysters, steamed blue crabs (something of a misnomer in that the crabs are plenty spicy), fried soft-shell crabs, moist and chunky crab cakes the size of hamburgers, Rock Stew or Pie made with a fish that Marylanders call "rock" but others know as striped bass and, of course, mountains of fried fish. "I expect my husband likes fried fish as much as any seafood," says Mrs. Seymour.

Mrs. Seymour's husband, Charles, was born and brought up on a farm near the little town of Trappe, the community where they now live.

"I met him," Mary Seymour says, "in 1930 at a dance over on Tilghman Island. I was through high school by then and working at a general store in Tilghman. From then on we saw a right good bit of one another and we got married in 1933. I wasn't quite thirty."

She and Charles settled down in the historic Eastern Shore town of Easton (which today has been proudly and impressively restored), lived there for about a year and a half, then moved into the country community where they now live and, as Mrs. Seymour says, "went to farming." They didn't own the land, but, though those were Depression times, within a few years they had saved up enough to buy a farm of their own. For a while they raised broilers for market (the Delmarva Peninsula where the Seymours live is one of the largest poultry producers in America).

The weathered old poultry house still stands behind the Seymour's gray-shingled, two-story farmhouse shaded by black-walnut trees but it is no longer in use now that Mr. Seymour has retired. And most of the old farm has been sold off. "We only have about six acres now," says Mrs. Seymour.

While she and her husband farmed, they grew corn, wheat, and soybeans and raised chickens, of course. "We did right well with chickens," she says, her tone not in the least boastful. "We'd take them as baby chicks, then in nine weeks time raise them up to three and a half or four pounds." The Seymours did all the work themselves. Their only child, a son, was killed at the age of twenty in a "drowning accident over on the Choptank River."

Now that they are more or less retired, the Seymours no longer have heavy farm chores to fill their days. But they are scarcely idle. Mary Seymour, a handsome, erect woman in her seventies, is blessed with the energy of a forty-year-old. Her hair is snow-white now, but her brown eyes sparkle with enthusiasm and curiosity. She is active in church (the Trappe United Methodist Church) and in the White Marsh Homemakers Club (a farm women's educational club affiliated with the Maryland Agricultural Extension Service). Moreover, she pitches in to help neighbors at hog-killing or beef-slaughtering time.

"What I like best," she continues, "is working in the ground." Flowerbeds encircle the house and yard, and the windows lining three sides of her huge apple-green kitchen are filled with potted plants.

Her husband traps muskrat in winter, fishes and goes crabbing in summer. Mary Seymour is kept busy in the kitchen, cleaning and cooking the catch. Not that she minds. "There's just nothing better," she says, "than fresh-caught fish or soft crabs or big fat blue crabs." She also cooks the muskrat.

And whenever Charles Seymour finds his crab pot filled, as he often does in summer, they invite friends and neighbors over for an old-time crab feast on the lawn.

Rock Stew

Makes 4 hearty servings

The rock used to make Rock Stew is a fish, not a stone. You may know it as striped bass. This recipe is one Mrs. Seymour remembers her mother making. "Sometimes she'd put the stew in a casserole, cover it with a crust and bake it. Then we'd call it Rock Pie."

3 tablespoons butter	⅛ teaspoon pepper
2 medium-sized yellow onions, peeled and coarsely chopped	2½ pounds cleaned and dressed fresh striped bass, cut crosswise in 1½-inch slices (the fish should
4 medium-sized potatoes, peeled and cut in ½-inch cubes	not be boned)
2½ cups water	2 tablespoons minced parsley
1½ teaspoons salt	

1. Melt the butter in a large heavy kettle, add the onion and sauté lightly over moderate heat 8 to 10 minutes or until golden. Add the potatoes, toss in the butter, let cook about 2 minutes, then add the

water, salt and pepper. Let the liquid come to a simmer, cover and simmer slowly about 30 to 40 minutes or until potatoes are firm-tender.

2.   Lay the slices of fish in the stew, pushing them down gently, re-cover and simmer about 10 minutes. Carefully turn the fish over, sprinkle parsley over surface of stew, re-cover and simmer about 10 minutes longer or until fish will flake at the touch of a fork.

3.   To serve, lift a slice of fish into a soup bowl, then smother with potatoes, onions and kettle broth.

Fried Soft-Shell Crabs

Makes 4 servings

"We always used to say, 'when the locusts bloom, it's soft crab time,' " explains Mary Seymour. On the Eastern Shore of Maryland, locusts bloom along about May, and that's when everyone looks forward to feasting on soft-shell crabs. Mr. Seymour keeps a crab pot out on the Choptank River nearby and traps enough soft- and hard-shell crabs to enjoy all season long. When it comes to cooking "soft crabs," as she calls them, she handles them gently. "I don't flour them," she says. "Some people do. But I don't want anything more than salt and pepper. Any richness the crabs get, they get from the frying." She starts frying them top-side down and cooks them covered from start to finish so that they cook through without drying out.

How does she clean soft-shell crabs? "Well," she begins, "you cut back far enough on the front of the crab to take the mouth and eyes out. Then you lift up one point of the top shell and take out the dead men's fingers—the spongy-looking parts. It's actually the crab's lungs, I suppose. Then you lift up the opposite point of the shell and take out the dead men's fingers on that side. You wash out each side real good where you've removed the dead men's fingers, then you turn the crab over and cut off the apron at the back. Wash the crab in cool water and it's ready to fix."

8 to 12 soft-shell crabs, cleaned (if crabs are unusually small, allow 3 per serving)
Salt and pepper

Vegetable oil (for frying; you need about "a quarter inch of oil in the bottom of the skillet," says Mrs. Seymour)

1.   Sprinkle both sides of each crab lightly with salt and pepper.

2.   In a very large heavy skillet, which has a lid, heat the vegetable oil over moderately high heat until ripples appear on the surface.

Place 3 to 4 of the crabs top-side down in the oil, reduce heat if needed so that crabs don't sputter too vigorously, place the lid on the skillet and fry about 3 to 5 minutes or until the top sides are a pretty brown. Turn the crabs over, re-cover and fry another 3 to 5 minutes until they are nicely browned on the flip side. Drain on paper toweling, then keep hot in a very slow oven (250°) until all the crabs have been fried.

Maryland Steamed Blue Crabs

Makes 6 to 8 servings

Mrs. Seymour's favorite way to cook hard-shell blue crabs is to steam them over a mixture of cider vinegar and water. To season, she uses a locally manufactured powdered seafood seasoning called Old Bay, which is compounded of celery salt, cayenne, dry mustard and assorted herbs and spices. (If you use the ingredients listed in the recipe, you'll come up with a blend that approximates, if not duplicates, Old Bay.) Of course, if you live in an area where Old Bay Seasoning is sold, by all means use it as Mrs. Seymour does, sprinkling it over the crabs as you layer them into the kettle. Here's a tip she offers for handling live crabs: "Put them in the icebox for several hours before you cook them. That way they'll be numb and easier to handle. Some people turn them on their back and pierce them with an ice pick to stun them. But we don't like to do that."

1 tablespoon celery salt
¼ teaspoon cayenne pepper
½ teaspoon powdered mustard
1 teaspoon paprika
¼ teaspoon ground ginger
1 bay leaf, very finely crumbled (if you have a mortar and pestle, pulverize the bay leaf)
⅛ teaspoon ground mace
⅛ teaspoon ground cinnamon
Pinch of ground cloves
Pinch of ground cardamom
12 live hard-shell blue crabs (alive and lively)
2 cups cider vinegar
1 cup water

1. Blend together the celery salt, cayenne, mustard, paprika, ginger, pulverized bay leaf, mace, cinnamon, cloves and cardamom; set aside.
2. Chill the crabs for several hours in the refrigerator to numb them so that they will be easier to layer into the kettle. Crabs that are thrashing about are very difficult to handle—their claws are not pegged as lobsters' claws are so it's easy to get nipped.

3. Stir together the vinegar and water and pour into a large, deep enamel kettle (a 3- to 4-gallon size is about right). Fit a rack into the bottom of the kettle. Place a layer of crabs in the kettle and sprinkle liberally with the seasoning mix (or with Old Bay Seasoning, if available). Continue layering crabs into the kettle, sprinkling with the seasoning mix, then cover with a close-fitting lid.

4. Set the kettle of crabs over moderately high heat and bring to a boil. Reduce heat so that liquid bubbles gently. After about 3 minutes, check the kettle—the crabs should have turned red. The minute the crabs turn red, re-cover the kettle and steam for 20 minutes exactly. "Crabs don't take too much cooking," Mrs. Seymour cautions.

5. Pile the crabs on a hot platter and serve. To eat, pull off the claws, crack them and pick out the meat. As for the body of the crab, pull off the hard top shell, then break off the legs. Scrape off and discard the gills or "dead men's fingers," then remove the digestive organs located in the center part of the body. The rest is all edible—the snowy "lump" or backfin meat, the smaller nuggets found in other pockets in the bottom shell. "As a matter of fact," says Mrs. Seymour, "if the crab is *cooked,* I don't think there's anything in it that will hurt you. People used to say that if you ate the 'dead men's fingers,' you'd die. But it's not so—you should see what people eat at crab feasts!"

Tilghman Island Crab Cakes

Makes 4 servings

"Most people use eggs in their crab cakes," says Mary Seymour, "but I don't like to. It's another meat to me, plus if you don't use a lot of mayonnaise or something in the mixture to loosen it up, the eggs dry the crab out and make it tough. The mixture should be juicy and soft but still thick enough to hold together. You should shape it just enough to stick the cakes together, but try not to handle it too much or the crab will pack down too tight. Now I remember when I was a girl, my mother didn't even bother to pat out the crab cakes—with eight children, she didn't want to take the time. She just dumped the crab mixture in a great big skillet and stirred it over the heat—sort of like crab hash. You could do it that way, if you like. But I do take time to shape the crab cakes. I make right good-sized ones—about 2½ inches across and I guess 'bout an inch thick. Of course, I never was accused of making my crab cakes all the same size."

1 pound lump or backfin crab meat, picked over for bits of shell and cartilage, then flaked with a fork
1 tablespoon minced parsley
1 tablespoon grated onion
1 tablespoon prepared spicy brown mustard

1½ slices white bread, broken into small pieces and soaked in ⅓ cup milk (do not squeeze the milk out of the bread after soaking)
½ teaspoon Worcestershire sauce
½ teaspoon salt
Pinch of pepper
3 to 4 tablespoons butter (for browning the crab cakes)

1.   Mix together all ingredients except the butter, shape into 8 cakes about 1 inch thick, then cover loosely and chill in the refrigerator 1 hour.

2.   Melt 3 tablespoons of the butter in a very large heavy skillet and when it begins to sizzle gently, add crab cakes and brown about 4 to 5 minutes on a side. Handle the crab cakes gently, turning with a pancake turner—they're soft and fragile and may fall apart if treated with a heavy hand. If needed, add the additional tablespoon of butter to keep crab cakes from sticking. Serve skillet-hot.

Crab Imperial

Makes 4 servings

Mrs. Seymour's recipe for Crab Imperial is simpler than many. She does not add egg ("it dries the crab meat"), or green pepper ("we don't like it much"). And she doesn't use much mustard either ("we'd rather taste the *crab* than the *hot*").

1 pound lump or backfin crab meat
½ cup mayonnaise
½ teaspoon salt
½ teaspoon dry mustard
2 teaspoons minced parsley

Pinch of cayenne pepper
Pinch of black pepper
1 cup fine soft breadcrumbs mixed with 2 tablespoons melted butter (topping)

1.   Pick over crab meat carefully, removing any bits of shell or cartilage but trying to keep the lumps of meat as nearly intact as possible.

2.   Add mayonnaise, salt, mustard, parsley, cayenne and black pepper and fork lightly to mix.

3.   Pile into scrubbed crab shells or scallop shells, or individual ramekins or into a 6-cup shallow casserole or *au gratin* dish. Scatter buttered crumbs on top.

4.   Bake in a hot oven (400°) for 12 to 15 minutes or until browned and bubbly.

Scalloped Oysters

Makes 4 to 6 servings

Here's how Mrs. Seymour scallops oysters: "Put a layer of saltine crumbs in a buttered casserole, add a layer of oysters and sprinkle with salt and pepper. Top with more crumbs. Build up as many layers as you like. Put crumbs on top, dot with butter, then pour in milk just until you can see it. Bake in a fairly hot oven till good and brown." That's all there is to it. But for those who would like more specific proportions, we've worked out the following recipe.

3 cups moderately coarse soda-cracker crumbs	Salt
	Pepper
4 dozen small shucked oysters, drained	3 tablespoons butter
	¾ cup milk (about)

1.   Arrange a layer of cracker crumbs over the bottom of a well-buttered, shallow, 2-quart casserole. Top with a layer of oysters and sprinkle with salt and pepper. Repeat until all oysters and crumbs have been used—the top layer should be of crumbs.

2.   Dot top well with chips of butter, then pour in milk. The milk should just be visible from the top, so add a bit more if the ¾ cup is insufficient.

3.   Bake in a hot oven (400°) for 15 to 20 minutes or just until liquid bubbles and cracker topping is dappled with brown.

Batter-Fried Oysters

Makes 4 servings

"How do we like oysters best? Well, my husband likes them batter-fried," says Mrs. Seymour. "I put some of the oyster liquor in the batter for extra flavor. But I don't use any baking powder. My husband claims that makes the batter puff up too much."

2 dozen fairly large shucked oysters, drained	⅔ cup sifted all-purpose flour (about)
Salt and pepper to season	1 cup vegetable shortening (for frying the oysters)
½ cup oyster liquor	
6 tablespoons milk	

1. Pat the oysters dry on paper toweling, then sprinkle both sides with salt and pepper.

2. For the batter, combine the oyster liquor and milk in a small bowl, then whisk in just enough sifted flour to make a batter about the consistency of pancake batter (the ⅔ cup of flour should be just about the right amount). "You don't want the batter too thick," says Mrs. Seymour. "But you don't want it too thin either, or it won't stick on the oysters. When you take a little bit up on a spoon, it should mound instead of running off the spoon."

3. Heat the shortening in a heavy, medium-sized skillet until a bread cube dropped in will bubble fairly vigorously. Dip oysters in batter, then fry, 6 to 8 at a time, about 3 to 4 minutes on a side, or until batter is a rich golden brown. Drain on paper toweling and serve.

Eastern Shore Fried Chicken

Makes 4 servings

This isn't quite the classic Maryland Fried Chicken, but almost. The principal difference lies in the gravy. Traditionally, Maryland Fried Chicken is served with a pale milk gravy. Mrs. Seymour follows her mother's method of boiling the giblets into stock, then using it to make a brown gravy. The skillet to use for frying the chicken is, according to Mary Seymour, "a great big iron one. Nothing fries chicken better."

1 3½- to 4-pound broiler-fryer, disjointed (reserve all the giblets except the liver for making giblet stock, which will be used in making Brown Gravy)
Salt
Pepper
⅔ cup flour (for dredging chicken)
½ cup vegetable shortening (for frying chicken)
1 recipe Brown Gravy (recipe follows)

1. Sprinkle both sides of each piece of chicken, including the liver, well with salt and pepper; roll chicken in flour to dredge, shaking off the excess. Or, if you prefer, put the flour in a brown-paper bag and shake the chicken in the flour to coat evenly.

2. In a very large heavy iron skillet, which has a lid, heat the shortening over moderately high heat until good and hot—to test, add a piece of chicken. It should sizzle. Add all pieces of chicken and as soon as they begin to brown, "put the top on the skillet," as Mrs. Sey-

mour says. Check often and turn the chicken as needed so that it turns a rich topaz brown all over. Reduce the heat, if necessary, the chicken shouldn't fry too fast. "It should take about 35 to 40 minutes in all," says Mrs. Seymour. Keep the lid on the skillet for about the first 25 minutes of cooking, then remove for the final 10 to 15 minutes if you want the chicken to crispen.

3.   Drain chicken on brown paper or paper toweling and serve hot with Brown Gravy. In Maryland, the gravy may be ladled over biscuits or potatoes. And some people even ladle it over their chicken, which is never done in the states farther south.

Brown Gravy

Makes about 2 cups

Serve with Eastern Shore Fried Chicken (recipe precedes).

Gizzard, heart and neck of a broiler-
    fryer
1 quart water
5 tablespoons pan drippings from
    frying chicken

6 tablespoons flour
1 teaspoon salt
⅛ teaspoon pepper

1.   Simmer gizzard, heart and neck in the water, uncovered, over low heat for about 1 hour or until stock has reduced by about one-half and taken on a rich giblet flavor. Reserve giblets to use in soup; strain the stock, measure out 2 cups and reserve (any remaining stock may also be used in soup).

2.   After you have prepared Eastern Shore Fried Chicken, pour off all but 5 tablespoons drippings from the skillet. Blend in the flour, raise heat slightly, then scrape and stir, getting up all the browned bits in the skillet (these are what give the gravy its brown color).

3.   Lower heat under skillet, pour in the 2 cups reserved giblet stock and heat and stir until thickened and smooth. Add salt and pepper, turn heat to lowest point and let gravy mellow 3 to 5 minutes or until no raw floury taste remains. Pour into a heated gravy boat and serve with Eastern Shore Fried Chicken.

Fricasseed Muskrat

Makes about 2 servings

"It used to be we thought only poor folks ate muskrat," says Mrs. Seymour. "But nowadays it seems like people around here just can't get enough of it. The meat is dark but not at all oily like 'possum. My husband traps muskrats out on the marsh in the wintertime—he's been doing it since he was a boy. A good black muskrat skin will bring about five dollars these days, a good brown one somewhat less. My husband says muskrat is the most easily digested meat there is." Here, just as she dictated it, is the way Mrs. Seymour prepares muskrat.

"You take a muskrat that's been skinned and cleaned and wash it thoroughly to get most of the blood out; you'll need two or three waters 'cause, you know, muskrat is very bloody. Put it in salt water for about 30 minutes—*cold* salt water. Then take it out and parboil it for 20 to 25 minutes, something like that. Of course, if it's a big muskrat and you think it's going to be tough, you parboil it a little longer. Now I disjoint it—just cut it up in small pieces like I would a chicken—*after* I parboil it, because it's easier to handle the meat—muskrat meat is *so* slippery. Then I put oil or shortening in a pan—a skillet or a casserole—flour the muskrat, put it in the pan and brown it. You always want to brown it a little bit at first. Then cover it all over with onions, I mean slice onions all over the muskrat. Add salt and pepper, of course. Put a little water in with it, put a top on, then put the pan in the oven and leave it till it gets real tender. I'd cook it at about 400° —you've already parboiled and browned the muskrat. And if it cooks too fast, you can cut the heat back a bit. Then if you want to crispen the muskrat a little, you take the top off toward the end. How long do I cook it? Well, that would depend on the 'rat, but I 'spose you ought to cook it three-quarters of an hour at least. You want it *real* tender. And, of course, give it time to make its own gravy."

Talbot County Potato Salad

Makes 8 to 10 servings

"The potato salad I make is a simple one," admits Mary Seymour. "I don't add eggs—there are already eggs in the dressing." The dressing she uses is an old-fashioned homemade one (recipe follows). "A lot of folks," she continues, "boil the potatoes in their jackets. I peel them first because it's the only way they will absorb the salt flavor from the cooking water." Does she dress the salad hot or cold? "Well, I remember that when my mother made this salad, she used a hot dressing if the potatoes were cold and a cold dressing if the potatoes were hot. And I do it pretty much her way."

10 medium-sized potatoes, peeled	3 celery ribs, diced
6 cups cold water mixed with 2 teaspoons salt	1¾ to 2 cups Homemade Salad Dressing (recipe follows)
1 medium-sized yellow onion, peeled and chopped	⅛ teaspoon pepper
	½ teaspoon salt (if needed to taste)

1.   Boil the potatoes, covered, in the salt water 20 to 25 minutes until firm-tender. Drain and cool until easy to handle. Cut into ½-inch cubes.

2.   Place potatoes in a large mixing bowl, add onion and celery, 1¾ cups of the dressing and the pepper. Toss to mix and, if mixture seems dry, add the remaining ¼ cup dressing. Taste for salt, add the ½ teaspoon if needed and toss again. Serve as soon as the salad cools to room temperature or, if you prefer, cover and chill well before serving.

Homemade Salad Dressing

Makes 1 quart

Mrs. Seymour pitches in and helps cook for church, club and community suppers, so the original version of her Homemade Salad Dressing is a quantity recipe—it makes a gallon. "Whenever I make the dressing at home," she says, "I use just three eggs and cut everything else back accordingly." She uses the dressing for both potato salad and coleslaw. It's a fairly sweet dressing, so if you prefer a less sweet flavor, reduce the amount of sugar to about ⅔ cup.

1 cup sugar	1 tablespoon prepared spicy brown mustard
2 tablespoons flour	
1½ teaspoons salt	1¼ cups cider vinegar
3 eggs	1 cup water
	2 tablespoons butter or margarine

1.   In the top of a double boiler, blend the sugar with the flour and the salt. Add the eggs and mustard and beat at high speed with a mixer until very thick. Stir in the vinegar and water.

2. Set the double boiler top over simmering water and heat, stirring constantly, about 5 minutes or until thickened and smooth—the dressing should be about the consistency of stirred custard. Remove from heat, add butter and when it melts, blend in. Pour into a 1-quart jar with a close-fitting cover and store in the refrigerator. Mrs. Seymour says that the dressing keeps well for several weeks.

Corn-Meal Muffins

Makes about 1½ dozen

"The Lions Club at Trappe used to ask me to come down and make the corn-meal muffins for their dinners," says Mrs. Seymour. "I finally got around to setting down the recipe."

1½ cups *stone-ground* yellow corn meal
½ cup sifted all-purpose flour
1 tablespoon baking powder
3 tablespoons sugar
½ teaspoon salt
1 egg, lightly beaten
1 cup milk
3 tablespoons melted vegetable shortening or vegetable oil

1. In a large mixing bowl, combine the corn meal, flour, baking powder, sugar and salt. Combine egg, milk and shortening in a large measuring cup.
2. Make a well in the center of the dry ingredients, pour in combined liquid ingredients and stir briskly just enough to mix—batter should be lumpy.
3. Spoon into greased muffin-pan cups and bake in a hot oven (400°) about 20 to 25 minutes or until lightly browned. Serve hot with plenty of butter.

Black-Walnut Bran Bread

Makes two 9- × 5- × 3-inch loaves

"Do we have black-walnut trees here?" Mrs. Seymour repeats the question. "My, yes, I should say so! They're the only kind of shade trees we have," she adds, pointing to two giant trees just outside the living-room window. She likes the flavor of black walnuts for both cakes and breads, especially this rich and dark quick-bread recipe and the smooth, golden Black-Walnut Poundcake that follows. You can substitute California walnuts if black walnuts are unavailable, but don't expect the bread or the cake to have quite the same flavor.

4 cups bran flakes
½ cup sugar
3 cups sifted all-purpose flour
½ teaspoon salt
1 cup coarsely chopped black walnuts

1 cup seedless raisins
2 eggs, well beaten
⅓ cup vegetable oil
2 cups milk
1 cup molasses with 2 teaspoons baking soda stirred in

1. In a large mixing bowl, stir bran flakes with sugar, flour, salt, walnuts and raisins until bran flakes, nuts and fruit are well dredged with the dry ingredients.

2. In a smaller bowl, beat the eggs with the oil and milk just enough to blend. Make a well in the dry ingredients, pour in the molasses-soda mixture, then the egg mixture, and stir with a wooden spoon just enough to mix. Batter will be quite thin.

3. Pour batter into two well-greased-and-floured 9- × 5- × 3-inch loaf pans (batter will no more than half fill each pan). Bake in a moderately slow oven (325°) for about 1 hour or until breads have pulled from sides of pans and are springy to the touch. The loaves will not entirely fill the pans. Remove from oven, cool loaves upright in their pans on wire racks for 10 minutes, then remove from pans and cool thoroughly before slicing. The bread is good spread with butter or cream cheese.

Black-Walnut Poundcake

Makes one 9-inch bundt or tube cake

You won't need any frosting for this cake—it's rich enough without it —but you might like to add a dusting of confectioners (10X) sugar.

3 cups sifted all-purpose flour
2 teaspoons baking powder
1 teaspoon salt
1 cup butter, at room temperature
2 cups sugar

4 eggs, at room temperature
1 cup milk, at room temperature
1 teaspoon vanilla
1 cup very finely chopped black walnuts

1. Sift the flour with the baking powder and salt and set aside.

2. Cream the butter and sugar very hard until silvery and light. Add the eggs, one at a time, beating well after each addition.

3. Combine the milk and the vanilla, then add to the creamed mixture alternately with the sifted dry ingredients, making sure that you begin and end with the dry ingredients. Beat only enough to blend. Fold in the walnuts.

4. Spoon batter into a well-greased-and-floured 9-inch (12-cup) bundt pan or into a greased-and-floured 9-inch tube pan.

5. Bake in a moderate oven (350°) for 50 to 60 minutes or until cake is springy to the touch and has pulled from sides of pan. Remove cake from oven, cool upright in its pan on a wire rack for 15 minutes, then loosen edges with a thin-bladed spatula and turn cake out of pan. Cool completely before cutting.

The South

Mrs. Flournoy P. Pool
of
Halifax County, Virginia

SHE has been cooking for nearly seventy-five years and, according to her four children, sixteen grandchildren, five great grandchildren (to say nothing of dozens of in-laws and other relatives), she is the source of all the wonderful old Virginia recipes they relish and remember today.

Mrs. Flournoy Pool lives today on the old Woltz farmstead near Virgilina, Virginia, where she was born eighty-odd years ago. Annie Woltz Pool was a beauty in her day. You can see that yet—in the slim, straight figure, the steel-gray hair pulled back from a brow almost as fair and unfurrowed as a baby's, in the eyes the color of cornflowers that don't "miss a trick." As for energy, Annie Pool would put many women half her age to shame. She isn't one to fritter the days away in front of a television set, although she does admit that she and her husband can't handle the heavy farm chores they once did.

Still, she tends her vegetable garden, "a great big one" beside the two-story white frame farmhouse that stands high on a hill of hardwoods overlooking the John H. Kerr Reservoir. Last year alone Annie Pool put up 150 quarts of fruits and vegetables and filled a 100-pound freezer to "overflowing." She dried apples (from trees on the 127-acre farm), she made grape juice, jam and jelly from what the old Scuppernong and James vine had borne, and she helped her husband and their son Heath (who lives with his family not far away) at hog-butchering time.

"We haven't been killing so many hogs lately," Annie Pool explains. "Four this year. But this is more meat than we can eat."

To step into Annie Pool's cool cellar is to see at first hand what conservation is all about. Jars of home-canned fruits and vegetables, pickles and preserves line one long wall, punctuated now and again by a great crock of snowy home-rendered lard. Hams, hunks of side meat and loops of sausage swing from the rafters, bushels and pecks of potatoes (both the Irish and the sweet) checkerboard the floor.

Out in the smokehouse there are new hams laid down in salt, while last year's hams hang from the ceiling in the half light. They have been given waftings of hickory smoke ("about six days' worth") and are now being left to age into the mahogany-hued, firm-fleshed country hams that have made Virginia famous.

Annie Pool's kitchen is big and bright, lined on two sides by windows, and it's here that the whole family gathers each Thanksgiving for a whopping feast of ham and turkey with all the trimmings (there were forty-two this year, ranging in age from "young uns in arms" to octogenarians). Annie Pool doesn't prepare the dinner single-handed—everyone who comes contributes something to the spread. But Annie does a good share of the cooking and almost invariably cooks the ham and roasts the turkey. There are pies, of course, and cakes (maybe one of her ambrosial fresh-coconut cakes) and an assortment of cookies.

"I like to cook anything that comes up," Annie Pool says. And she has been doing it as long as she can remember. She doesn't remember exactly when she began to cook in earnest. But she does remember playing house with her cousins down the yellow-dirt road, preparing "doll tea parties and doll dinners. We used to roast one of the partridges my Uncle George had hunted," she reminisces, "stuffing and all. That would be our turkey. We would cut our doll biscuits out with a thimble. And we'd make miniature pies—mostly Lemon Chess pies—in muffin pans. We thought it all powerful good."

It wasn't all child's play on the Woltz farm, however. Even though young Annie Woltz grew up with a half-sister, two sisters and three brothers (not to mention a half-brother and two other half-sisters who lived close enough "to come over near 'bout every day"), there were more than enough chores to go around. Annie Woltz knew plenty about cooking—and about running a farm—by the time she had finished the community school and married Flournoy Pool in her late teens. She knew Flournoy Pool well, too. His folks' farm was just down the road and the two of them had gone to church and Sunday school together (they were married in December of 1909).

At first, before allotments restricted the amount of tobacco that could be grown and before a large chunk of their farm (the fertile low ground) had to be sold to accommodate the huge Kerr Reservoir and recreation area that today straddles the border county of central Virginia and North Carolina, the Pools concentrated on tobacco. Today they have leased out their tobacco acreage ("too much work for old folks"), but, together with their son Heath, they do raise beef cattle and hogs and most of the hay and corn needed to feed them.

The Pools are alone on the farm now, although they can expect company almost every day. Their daughter Louise and their son Heath, both of whom live in South Boston just ten miles away, try to look in several times a week. The Pools can also look forward to frequent visits from their older son Tom, who lives in Clarksville, Virginia, and their youngest child Ella, who now makes her home in Greensboro, North Carolina.

The big family get-togethers, however, are at Thanksgiving and in late summer about the time that the corn and tomatoes and butterbeans are "coming in." That's when the men bring out the great black iron pot, set it up in the yard and lay a fire under it, while the women get busy shelling butterbeans and cutting corn for the whopping batch of Brunswick Stew that will bubble lazily most of the day.

Once the pot is on, the adults retreat to the shade of the oaks or the veranda lining the front of the house. They sit and visit, reminiscing about "the good ole days," while the children play. As the day wears on, the giant cauldron of stew scents the summer air and hones the appetites, and pretty soon the tables are set up in the yard, piled high with slaw and ham and potato salad, biscuits and cakes and cookies.

Everyone grabs a plate, then tucks into what the Pool family all consider the very best food to be found in Virginia.

Farm-Style Vegetable Soup

Makes 8 to 10 servings

The best soups in the world are those made out of absolutely fresh vegetables. That's why Annie Pool's vegetable soups taste so special. We say soups, plural, because whenever she and her husband "have a hankering for soup," she goes out into the garden and picks or pulls up whatever it is she needs.

1 slice of side meat ("and a good hefty one," says Annie Pool. "Hefty" can be interpreted to mean about ½ pound. Side meat is simply smoked and cured meat from the side of a hog. If you don't have it, substitute ¼ pound *lean* salt pork and score it deeply, criss-cross fashion, with a sharp knife)

6 cups cold water or chicken, beef or vegetable stock

8 medium-sized potatoes, peeled and cut in small cubes

6 medium-sized carrots, peeled and sliced thin

1 very large yellow onion, peeled and coarsely chopped

1 quart canned tomatoes (preferably home-canned)

2 cups shelled fresh baby limas (you can use the frozen)

2 cups fresh (or frozen) whole-kernel corn

3 tablespoons butter

1½ teaspoons salt (about)

¼ teaspoon pepper (about)

½ cup thin spaghetti, broken in about 1-inch lengths (Optional: Annie Pool tosses a handful of spaghetti into her soup toward the end if it needs thickening)

1. Place side meat, water or stock, potatoes, carrots, onion, tomatoes and limas in a very large heavy kettle. Set over moderate heat and bring to a boil. Reduce heat so that mixture bubbles gently, cover, then simmer for about 2 hours or until vegetables are very tender.

2. Add corn, butter, salt and pepper, and simmer uncovered for about ¾ hour or until flavors seem well blended. Taste for salt and pepper and add more, if needed. If you like, toss in the spaghetti, stir well, then cook, stirring occasionally, 8 to 10 minutes, or until spaghetti is tender.

3. Ladle into large soup plates and serve. To accompany, Annie Pool would put out a fresh-baked batter bread or batch of buttermilk biscuits.

Note:

This soup keeps well in the refrigerator for several days and, indeed, seems to improve with age.

Brunswick Stew

Makes about 20 to 25 servings

Brunswick Stew is popular throughout Virginia, the Carolinas and Georgia, and, as might be expected, recipes for it vary from state to state, indeed, from community to community. The Pools' Brunswick Stew differs from the traditional versions in that it contains beef as well as chicken. The secret of a good Brunswick Stew, according to Annie Pool, is "to put the corn in last" so as not to lose its "just-picked" flavor. "Put the salt in last, too," she cautions. "Butterbeans [limas] and most other vegetables, too, will be a heap more tender if you don't put the salt in in the beginning."

1 stewing hen, about 6 to 7 pounds
6 pounds beef chuck or rump, in one piece
12 cups water
6 large yellow onions, peeled and coarsely chopped
18 medium-sized potatoes, peeled and cubed
6 cups shelled fresh baby lima beans

3 pints canned tomatoes (Mrs. Pool would use home-canned tomatoes)
6 cups fresh whole-kernel sweet corn (you'll need about 10 to 12 ears)
¼ cup sugar
⅓ cup butter
Salt and pepper to taste

1. Put the hen, neck and giblets, and the beef on to cook in the water in a very large heavy kettle, or if you prefer, in two separate kettles, using 6 cups of water for each. Cover and simmer about 1½ hours or until hen and beef are both tender. Lift hen from broth, remove and discard skin and separate meat from bones. Cut meat into fairly good-sized chunks, mince the giblets and set both aside. Remove beef from broth, cut meat from bones, cube and reserve. Skim and discard as much fat as possible from the broth.

2. If you have cooked the hen and beef separately, combine the broths in one very large heavy kettle for making the Brunswick Stew. Add the onions, potatoes and lima beans, cover and simmer very slowly about 30 minutes, until almost, but not quite, tender.

3. Return the chicken, giblets and beef to the kettle, add the tomatoes and simmer uncovered about 20 minutes. Add the corn, sugar and butter and simmer uncovered, stirring occasionally, about 20 minutes longer. Season to taste with salt and pepper, turn heat to lowest point and let flavors mingle about 10 to 20 minutes. The Pools, knowing instinctively when the stew is done, don't bother with precise simmering times. If the heat is low enough, the stew can simmer lazily most of the morning or afternoon, gathering strength and flavor. To serve, ladle into large soup bowls and accompany with corn bread.

Note:

Brunswick Stew freezes well. Simply cool to room temperature, ladle into freezer containers, leaving about ½-inch head space, snap on lids, label and quick-freeze at 0°.

Sweet Corn Pudding

Makes 6 servings

Sweet corn is the corn to use for this baked pudding. And the fresher
the better. Annie Pool grows her own and thus can get the sweet,
milky kernels from cob to casserole in less than an hour's time, before
the corn's natural sugars begin to turn to starch. The kernels must be
cut from the cob cream-style, which is pesky to do but not difficult.
Here's the easiest way: With a sharp knife, score each row of kernels,
cutting right down the center. Then, with the blade of the knife held
at right angles to the cob, scrape all pulp and milk from the cob, using a brisk back-and-forth motion. The finished pudding, filled with
corn and thickened with eggs, is as soft and quivery as a custard.
"Milk," explains Annie Pool, "dries the pudding out so I add a little
water to keep it soft." She bakes the pudding "slow" just until "it
doesn't shake" when you nudge the dish.

4 cups fresh cream-style corn (you'll
   need about 8 medium-sized ears)
⅓ cup sugar blended with 2 tablespoons flour
1 teaspoon salt

¼ teaspoon pepper
1¾ cups milk
¼ cup water
4 eggs, lightly beaten
1 tablespoon melted butter

1.   Place the corn in a large mixing bowl, stir in the sugar-flour mixture, salt and pepper.
2.   Combine milk, water and eggs and mix into corn. Blend in the
melted butter.
3.   Pour into a buttered 2½-quart casserole and set in a large baking pan. Place pan on middle oven shelf, then pour in about 1½ inches
of water. Bake uncovered in a moderately slow oven (325°) for about
1 hour and 20 minutes or until pudding is set in the center. Serve at
once as a vegetable.

Old Virginia Batter Bread

Makes one 8-inch round loaf

"The one thing I'd always request when I went to Aunt Annie's to
visit," says her niece Anne Lewis Anderson, "was batter bread. Hers
was the best I ever ate." How does Annie Pool make it? "I just guess

at the recipe," she says, "but I cook it quick." Her batter bread is a corn bread baked in a heavy iron skillet. It must be made with old-fashioned stone-ground corn meal (Annie Pool prefers the white meal) because the regular commercial meal is too granular to make good batter bread. Stone-ground meal has a texture much like that of flour. The lard used is hog lard (it flavors the bread as well as shortens it), but you can, if you prefer, substitute vegetable shortening.

2 cups stone-ground corn meal
1 tablespoon sugar
½ teaspoon salt
¼ teaspoon baking soda
⅓ cup lard or vegetable shortening
2 eggs, lightly beaten

1½ to 2 cups buttermilk (you will need enough to make a batter about the thickness of pancake batter; the amount of buttermilk needed will vary according to the fineness of the corn meal used, the thickness of the buttermilk and the size of the eggs)

1.   Combine the corn meal, sugar, salt and baking soda in a large mixing bowl.

2.   Place the lard in an 8-inch heavy iron skillet, set in a hot (425°) oven and let melt. Meanwhile, mix the eggs lightly into the combined dry ingredients, then stir in just enough buttermilk to make a batter about the consistency of pancake batter.

3.   Remove skillet from the oven, tilt so that lard greases both the sides and the bottom, then pour the hot lard into the batter. Stir briskly just to mix.

4.   Pour batter into the hot skillet and bake in a hot oven (425°) until firm and lightly browned, about 25 minutes. Serve oven-hot, directly from the skillet. The way to eat batter bread is to cut it into wedges as you would a cake, then to split each wedge horizontally and tuck in a lump or two of sweet butter while the bread is still hot enough to melt it.

Buttermilk Biscuits

Makes about 16 biscuits (including re-rolls)

Hardly a day goes by that Annie Pool doesn't make up a batch of Buttermilk Biscuits. "They're no bother," she says. Besides, a meal just wouldn't be "fittin' " without fresh-baked bread of some sort.

2½ cups sifted self-rising cake flour
½ teaspoon baking soda
⅓ cup lard (hog lard is what Annie
   Pool uses, but you can substitute
   vegetable shortening)

1 cup buttermilk (or just enough
   to make a dough stiff enough to
   roll)

1. Combine flour and soda in a large mixing bowl. Cut in the lard with a pastry blender until mixture is the texture of coarse meal. Add buttermilk all at once and fork briskly just until dough holds together.

2. Turn dough out on a lightly floured board or pastry cloth and knead lightly about 8 times. Roll out to a thickness of ½ inch, then cut into rounds with a biscuit cutter.

3. Space biscuits 1 inch apart on ungreased baking sheets and bake in a hot oven (425°) for 10 to 12 minutes or until lightly browned. Serve straight away with plenty of butter.

Lemon Chess Pie

Makes one 9-inch pie

You can look long and hard but you won't find a better lemon pie than this one. It is not a meringue-topped pie, but the type known in the South as a "chess pie"—a thick, sweet, butter-smooth mixture not unlike the English Lemon Curd or Lemon Cheese. One explanation of the derivation of the word "chess" is, in fact, that it is a corruption of "cheese." Another is that "chess" derives from "chest," where "keeping" or "chest" pies such as this one were stored in the days before refrigeration.

1½ cups sugar
½ cup butter, at room temperature
3 eggs, lightly beaten
Finely grated rind of 1 large lemon

Juice of 1 large lemon
1 tablespoon milk
1 9-inch unbaked pie shell (use your
   favorite recipe)

1. Cream the sugar and butter until fluffy and light, then beat in the eggs. Mix in lemon rind and juice and lastly the milk. The mixture at this point will have a "curdled" look, but don't be alarmed. It will smooth out beautifully in the baking.

2. Pour mixture into pie shell and bake in a moderately slow oven (325°) for about 40 minutes or until pie is golden brown and puffy and mixture no longer "shakes" when pan is nudged.

3. Cool pie to room temperature before serving. The filling will "fall" as the pie cools, but this is perfectly proper for a chess pie. When serving, cut the slices small—this pie is uncommonly rich.

Fresh Coconut Custard Pie

Makes two 8-inch pies

Another superlative old Virginia pie. You can use packaged or canned coconut instead of the freshly grated, but don't expect the pie to have the same delicate flavor or moist texture. For best results, use fresh coconut and grate it moderately fine.

2 cups sugar
4 tablespoons flour
½ teaspoon salt
4 eggs, separated
½ cup melted butter
1½ cups milk, at room temperature

2 cups moderately finely grated fresh coconut (you'll need about ½ coconut)
2 8-inch unbaked pie shells (use your favorite recipe)

1. Mix together the sugar, flour and salt. Whisk the egg yolks lightly, then mix in, along with the melted butter and the milk.
2. Beat the egg whites to soft peaks and fold in gently but thoroughly, until no streaks of white or yellow remain. Fold in the grated coconut.
3. Divide the mixture evenly between the two pie shells and bake in a slow oven (300°) for about 45 minutes or until, as Annie Pool says, "pies do not shake" when the pans are nudged.
4. Cool pies to room temperature before serving.

Shirttail Pies

Makes 6 pies (including re-rolls)

Shirttail Pies are nothing more than half-moon pies filled with apples, then fried in deep fat so that the crimped edges ripple like shirttails. For the filling, Annie Pool uses dried apples. There are apple trees aplenty on the Pool farm and what apples the family cannot eat fresh, Mrs. Pool cans or dries. You will find directions for drying apples elsewhere in this book (see page 47).

Filling:
2 cups dried apples
2 cups water
⅓ cup sugar
⅛ teaspoon ground cinnamon

Pastry:
2¼ cups sifted all-purpose flour
¼ teaspoon salt

⅓ cup lard or vegetable shortening
½ cup cold water (about)

2 quarts (about) vegetable oil or melted vegetable shortening for deep fat frying (you will need 1½ to 2 inches of fat in the deep-fat fryer)

1. *To prepare the filling:* Do this first so that filling has a chance to cool while you prepare the pastry. Place apples and water in a very heavy saucepan, cover and simmer slowly about 1 hour, until apples are very soft. Uncover, turn heat very low and let cook until all moisture has evaporated. Mix in sugar and cinnamon and cool to room temperature.

2. *For the pastry:* Mix flour and salt in a large mixing bowl, then cut in lard with a pastry blender until mixture is the texture of coarse meal. Add water slowly, tossing mixture quickly with a fork, until pastry holds together.

3. Roll pastry very thin (slightly thinner than for piecrust) on a lightly floured board or pastry cloth. Using a 6-inch saucer as a pattern, cut pastry into rounds (from this amount of pastry, you should be able to cut 6 rounds if you include the re-rolls).

4. Place about ⅓ cup of the cooled apple filling in the center of each round, moisten the edges of each lightly with water, fold over into a half-circle, then crimp edges firmly with the tines of a fork to seal. Prick the tops of each pie several times with a fork to allow steam to escape as the pies fry.

5. Fry the pies, one at a time, in hot fat (375° is the best temperature to use because it allows the pastry to cook through before it browns). Turn the pies in the deep fat as needed so that they brown evenly on both sides. It will take 4 to 5 minutes for each pie to cook properly.

6. Drain the pies well on paper toweling and serve hot or cold. "Either way they're good," says Annie Pool.

Annie Pool's Applesauce Cake

Makes one 9-inch tube cake

Because this cake calls for more applesauce, nuts and raisins than do most applesauce cake recipes, it is unusually moist and dark. Mrs. Pool doesn't frost the cake because, as she says, "it's powerful rich."

3½ cups sifted all-pupose flour	2 teaspoons ground cinnamon
2 cups seedless raisins	1 teaspoon ground cloves
2 cups coarsely chopped walnuts or	1 cup butter, at room temperature
pecans or a mixture of the two	2 cups sugar
2 teaspoons baking soda	2 eggs
½ teaspoon salt	2 cups thick, sweetened applesauce

1.   Measure out ¼ cup of the flour, sprinkle over the raisins and nuts and toss well to dredge; set aside. Sift the remaining 3¼ cups flour with the soda, salt, cinnamon and cloves, and set aside also.

2.   Cream the butter until very light and fluffy, then gradually add the sugar, creaming all the while. Beat in the eggs one at a time.

3.   Add the sifted dry ingredients alternately with the applesauce, beginning and ending with the dry ingredients and beating after each addition just enough to mix. Fold in the dredged raisins and nuts.

4.   Spoon batter into a well-greased-and-floured 9-inch tube pan and bake in a moderate oven (350°) for about 1 hour and 20 minutes or until cake pulls from sides of pan and is springy to the touch. Cool cake upright in its pan on a wire rack for 20 minutes, then loosen around edges with a spatula, turn out on rack and cool thoroughly before cutting.

Fresh Coconut Cake

Makes one three-layer 9-inch cake

The nearest thing to ambrosia, Annie Pool's relatives all declare, is her Fresh Coconut Cake. "It simply melts in your mouth," says one niece. "Pshaw!" Annie Pool dismisses the compliments. "It's just a yellow cake with coconut icing." Well, not quite. She has a couple of secrets up her sleeve, which she divulges in telling how to make the cake. First, she uses only fresh coconuts—"I 'spect two or three for one cake." And instead of grating them she grinds them in a meat grinder fitted with a fine blade. Finally, she saves the water drained from the coconuts and sprinkles each cake layer liberally with it before she smooths on the icing. "Keeps the cake moist," she says.

Cake:
3 cups sifted all-purpose flour
2 teaspoons baking powder
Pinch of salt
1 cup butter, at room temperature
2 cups sugar
4 eggs, separated
1 cup milk

1 teaspoon pure lemon extract
½ teaspoon vanilla

Coconut Icing:
2 to 3 coconuts (you will need 11 cups of ground coconut in all)
4 cups sugar
1⅓ cups water
3 tablespoons butter

1.   *For the cake:* Sift the flour with the baking powder and salt and set aside.

2.   Cream the butter until very light and silvery, then gradually add the sugar, creaming all the while. Continue to beat until very light. Mix in the egg yolks, again beating until fluffy.

3.   Combine the milk with the lemon extract and vanilla. Add the sifted dry ingredients alternately with the milk, beginning and ending with the dry and beating after each addition only enough to blend. Beat the egg whites to soft peaks and fold in gently but thoroughly.

4.   Divide the batter among 3 well-greased and well-floured 9-inch layer-cake pans, then bake in a moderate oven (350°) for 35 to 40 minutes or until layers pull from sides of pans and are springy to the touch. Cool layers upright in their pans on wire racks for 10 minutes, then loosen around edges with a spatula and invert layers on wire racks. Cool several hours before icing.

5.   *For the coconut icing:* To loosen the coconut meat inside the shell, rap each coconut all over with a hammer before cracking it. With an ice pick or nail, pierce two of the "eyes" in each coconut and drain the liquid into a measuring cup; reserve the liquid. Now with a hammer, crack the coconuts into manageable pieces. Separate the shell from the meat, then using a vegetable peeler, pare away the brown skin adhering to the meat. Rinse the coconut meat in cool water and pat dry. Grind the coconut by putting through a meat grinder fitted with a fine blade. When all the coconut is ground, measure it. You will need 8 cups ground coconut to mix into the icing and another 3 cups to sprinkle between the layers and on top of the cake.

6.   Place sugar and water in a medium-sized heavy saucepan, insert a candy thermometer and set over moderate heat. Cook and stir just until sugar has dissolved, then cook uncovered and *without stirring* until candy thermometer registers 232° F. To prevent sugar from crystallizing out, brush down the sides of the pan where crystals have

collected with a pastry brush moistened in hot water. When syrup has reached 232° F., turn heat off, drop in butter and let mixture cool for 20 minutes. Beat hard for about 1 minute, then pour syrup over the 8 cups of coconut and toss well to mix.

7.   To frost the cake, first brush any loose crumbs from individual cake layers, then trim away any uneven portions so that layers will stack evenly. Center the first layer on a circle of cardboard cut to fit on a large cake plate. Sprinkle 4 to 6 tablespoons of the reserved coconut liquid evenly over layer to moisten it. Spread—not too thickly—with icing, then sprinkle lightly with reserved ground coconut. Top with second layer; again sprinkle liberally with reserved coconut liquid, spread with icing and sprinkle with coconut. Set top layer in place, then gently but firmly press layers together, anchoring them in the icing. Sprinkle top layer with reserved coconut liquid. Spread coconut icing over top, then pat firmly around the sides of the cake. This icing is fairly crumbly because of the quantity of fresh coconut used, but it *will* stick to the cake if you press it on firmly and persist. Rinse your hands occasionally with warm water as they become sticky. After all the icing is on the cake, sprinkle the reserved ground coconut over the top. Let cake stand about 2 to 3 hours before cutting. For serving, use an extra-sharp knife with a serrated blade and cut with a gentle sawing motion so that you do not break the cake apart. It's delicate and tender, which is of course why "it melts in your mouth."

Edna's Tea Cakes

Makes about 6 dozen cookies

"These don't dry out or stale so fast 'cause there's no milk in them," Annie Pool says of these old Virginia sugar cookies. The recipe comes from her older half-sister, Edna Woltz, and has been a family favorite for nearly a hundred years. Small wonder, because the flavor is pure butter, sugar and eggs. Add a teaspoon of vanilla, if you like, but Annie Pool never does.

1 cup butter
2 cups sugar
4 eggs
1 teaspoon baking soda

¼ teaspoon salt
6 to 6½ cups sifted all-purpose flour (amount needed will vary according to the size of the eggs)

1.   Cream the butter and sugar until light and fluffy, then beat in the eggs, one at a time, creaming all the while.

2.   Stir in the soda and salt; add the flour, about 1 cup at a time, mixing well after each addition. You will want only enough flour to make the dough stiff enough to roll; it should still be soft, about the consistency of biscuit dough.

3.   Roll the dough out, about one-fourth of it at a time, on a lightly floured board or pastry cloth to a thickness about like piecrust. Cut into rounds with a floured 2½-inch cooky cutter.

4.   Space cookies about 1½ inches apart on ungreased baking sheets and bake in a moderate oven (375°) 10 to 12 minutes, until very pale tan. Remove cookies at once to wire racks to cool. Let cookies "crispen" about half an hour before eating. Store in airtight canisters.

Mrs. Jesse R. Watkins
of
Trigg County, Kentucky

"I don't cook anything that isn't from scratch," says Lois Watkins of Cadiz, Kentucky. Certainly, she is cooking from scratch at the moment —pickling peppers (a peck, at least) that her husband has brought in from the farm. She bustles about her newly remodeled kitchen— a cheerful combination of pumpkin, gold the hue of ripe corn and olive—which lies along the front of the trim white frame house she and her husband built on Main Street in the mid-1930s.

Although she now lives in town, Mrs. Watkins was born and brought up on a farm in the southernmost part of Trigg County, Kentucky.

"The Kentucky-Tennessee state line ran right through the middle of my Granddaddy's farm," she says. "He died when my Daddy, George Madison Scott, was a little boy and to divide up the land, they drew lots. My Daddy pulled his share out of a hat when he was only eight years old. He got the Kentucky part of the farm and there wasn't a building on it."

So Lois Scott was a Kentucky farm girl, instead of a Tennessee farm girl, although there was plenty of visiting back and forth across the state line among the members of the big Scott family.

"No," she admits, "I didn't do much cooking when I was little. It was too much fun being outdoors—feeding the chickens or gathering the eggs. Besides, my mother was a splendid cook. A wonderful seamstress, too, so she did most of the housework."

In fact, Mrs. Watkins came to cooking late. After high school she went to Austin Peay State College in Clarksville, Tennessee, and studied to be a grammar school teacher. She married for the first time soon after graduation, settled down to housekeeping in Clarksville, but was widowed early. She came home to Kentucky and began teaching the seventh and eighth grades in the little town of Cadiz. That was in the early 1930s.

At a carnival one weekend, she met a young banker named Jesse Watkins. Like her, he had been brought up on a farm in Trigg County. The couple hit it off at once, began seeing a good bit of one another and were married in 1935.

"I still didn't know much about cooking," says Lois Watkins. "But Jesse's mother was a wonderful cook. I ate at their house a lot and most of what I now know about cooking I learned from her. In fact, most of my favorite recipes today are ones that Jesse's mother gave me.

"Fortunately, Jesse will eat almost anything, although he is partial to sweets. I remember the first thing I tried to make for him was a meringue pie. The meringue didn't work out somehow, so when I served the pie to Jesse, I said, 'I guess the meringue fell.' He said, 'I didn't know there was any meringue *on* the pie!'

"It's a funny thing. I *still* can't make a good meringue. After all these years. I've tried about every recipe I know, but it seems like my meringues are either too tough or too runny. Now *you* wouldn't have a good meringue recipe, would you? My family loves meringue pie."

Her family consists of a daughter, Rosemary, who is married to an attorney in Lexington, Kentucky (they have a son and a daughter), and a son, Jesse, an engineer, who lives with his wife and two little girls in Charlotte, North Carolina.

Her husband, who was president of the Trigg County Farmer's Bank is semiretired now but still serves as a bank director and also runs the family farm, 400 acres in the Mount Zion Community of Trigg County. "We raise beef cattle," says Mrs. Watkins, "Herefords and Angus."

Lois Watkins, a tiny, sprightly woman with close-cropped salt-and-pepper hair and blue, laughing eyes, doesn't do all the cooking today; indeed she never did. She was too busy—at first teaching, then clerking in the ready-to-wear department of the store that her husband owned. "I have a marvelous cook, Edna Acrey, who came to us when the children were small and has been with us ever since. Edna taught me a lot about cooking. She's one of those natural-born cooks who never use a recipe and who just know how to put things together."

This is not to suggest that Lois Watkins doesn't cook much these days. She does. Now that she and her husband have more time, they entertain a lot, both at home and at the community center where they meet regularly with other senior citizens of the community. And she will be sure to cook "up a storm" whenever the children and grandchildren are coming to visit, making certain that they won't go hungry for any of their particular favorites: Buttermilk Jam Cake with Chocolate Icing (everyone's choice), Corn Light Bread, Pecan Pie, Brown Sugar Pie and Chess Pie.

"It's not really fancy cooking that I do," says Lois Watkins. "But at least I don't cook the way most young folks do today, *including* my daughter. They just run up to the supermarket and buy a box of this or a box of that."

Kentucky Burgoo

Makes about 12 servings

"This is the best Burgoo in the world," says Mrs. Watkins of this classic Kentucky meat-and-vegetable stew. "It's the way it was made by a Mrs. Jordan who owned the Pete Light Springs Restaurant here in Cadiz a few years back." Mrs. Jordan made Burgoo in restaurant quantities, so we've quartered her whopping recipe. Burgoo is as traditional to Kentucky as the Mint Julep, and, like the Julep, it is served at Kentucky Derby festivities. Oddly, the originator of the recipe was a French chef named Gus Jaubert, who served Confederate General John Hunt Morgan and his cavalrymen during the War Between the States (as the Civil War is known south of the Mason-Dixon line). The original recipe, it is said, was made with blackbirds, and Jaubert, his French-accented English further hampered by a hairlip, pronounced "blackbird stew" in such a way that it came out "Burgoo." Almost every Kentucky cook has her favorite recipe for Burgoo, but all agree that it should be made with at least two different kinds of meat (some cooks use four), and should contain "as many vegetables as you can lay your hands on." A good Burgoo simmers for four or five hours, and chefs preparing it in thousand-gallon quantities for Derby Day have been known to cook it as long as twenty hours. "It should be thick," Burgoo specialists insist, "yet still thin enough to eat with a spoon."

1 chicken breast
1 chicken thigh
1 chicken liver
1½ pounds boneless pork shoulder
6 cups cold water
½ pound dried great northern beans, washed and sorted and soaked overnight in 2 cups cold water
1 quart canned tomatoes (preferably home-canned)
2 cups finely chopped onions
1 quart canned whole-kernel corn (preferably home-canned)
1 quart canned green peas (preferably home-canned)
1½ teaspoons salt (about)
¼ teaspoon freshly ground black pepper (about)
¼ cup butter or margarine

1.   Place the chicken breast, thigh and liver, the pork and the 6 cups cold water in a large heavy kettle (a 4-gallon size is about right), bring to a simmer, cover and simmer 30 minutes. Remove chicken pieces and reserve. Re-cover and continue simmering the pork about 1½ hours longer or until very tender. Skin and bone the chicken and put through a meat grinder fitted with a coarse blade. Grind the pork when tender.

2.   Return chicken and pork to stock in kettle, add the beans and their soaking water, the tomatoes (do not drain), the onions, the corn and green peas (both well drained). Cover and simmer very slowly for 1 hour.

3.   Uncover the kettle, add the salt, pepper and butter, and continue simmering for 3½ to 4 hours, stirring now and then, until flavors are well balanced and consistency is quite thick. Taste for salt and pepper and add more, if needed. Ladle into soup bowls and serve with hot biscuits or soda crackers.

Chicken Croquettes with Mushroom Sauce

Makes 6 servings

These croquettes are a luncheon favorite of Mrs. Watkins'. They can be made with leftover turkey or pork roast as well as with chicken and, unlike many croquettes, are unusually light considering the quantity of meat in them.

4 cups finely ground cooked chicken (for this amount you will need about a 3½- to 4-pound roasting chicken, simmered until tender, cooled, skinned and boned, and put through a meat grinder fitted with a medium-fine blade)
1 cup finely minced celery
1 tablespoon finely grated onion
1 teaspoon sage
4 tablespoons butter
4 tablespoons flour

1 cup milk
1¼ teaspoons salt
⅛ teaspoon freshly ground black pepper
1 egg, lightly beaten with 1 tablespoon milk
1 cup cracker meal
Vegetable oil or shortening for deep-fat frying
1 recipe Mushroom Sauce (recipe follows)

1.   Mix chicken and celery in a large bowl and reserve.

2.   Sauté onion and sage in the butter in a small heavy saucepan over moderate heat 3 to 4 minutes, just until onion is golden. Blend

in flour. Add milk and heat, stirring constantly, until thickened and smooth. Mix in salt and pepper and let sauce mellow over low heat 3 to 4 minutes or until no raw floury taste remains. Combine sauce with chicken mixture, then chill several hours, until firm enough to shape.

3. Using your hands, shape the chicken mixture into small "logs" about 3 inches long and 1½ inches wide. Dip logs in beaten egg, then roll in cracker meal to coat evenly. Arrange croquettes on a wax-paper-lined baking sheet and set uncovered in the refrigerator; chill for about 3 hours so that the coating will stick.

4. Pour vegetable oil into a deep-fat fryer to a depth of about 2 inches (or melt enough vegetable shortening in the fryer to equal a depth of 2 inches). Insert a deep-fat thermometer and heat fat to 365°. Fry the croquettes, about four at a time, turning as needed so that they are a nice golden brown all over. Try to keep the temperature of the deep fat as nearly at 365° as possible by raising or lowering the burner heat (if the fat is too cool, the croquettes will become greasy; if it is too hot, they will brown outside before they have a chance to heat through to the centers). Drain the browned croquettes on paper toweling. When all have been fried, set uncovered in a very slow oven (250°) for about 20 minutes. Serve with Mushroom Sauce.

Mushroom Sauce

Makes about 2½ cups

4 tablespoons butter	4 tablespoons flour
1 tablespoon finely grated onion	1 cup milk
½ pound fresh mushrooms, wiped clean and sliced thin	1 cup light cream
Pinch of ground nutmeg	½ teaspoon salt
	Pinch of pepper

1. Melt butter in a heavy saucepan over moderate heat, add onion, mushrooms and nutmeg and stir-fry about 5 minutes or until mushrooms release their juices. Blend in flour.

2. Add milk and cream and heat, stirring constantly, until sauce is thickened and smooth. Reduce heat to low and let sauce mellow 3 to 5 minutes or until no raw floury taste remains. Season with salt and pepper and serve as a topping for Chicken Croquettes (recipe precedes).

Creamed Corn

Makes 4 servings

"I guess you could say that corn is our favorite vegetable," says Mrs. Watkins. "We grow it on the farm and have it most every day in season, on the cob or creamed."

4 cups fresh sweet corn, cut off the cob cream-style (see index); you will need 12 to 14 medium-sized ears of corn)
½ cup water
4 teaspoons sugar

¾ teaspoon salt
⅛ teaspoon freshly ground black pepper
2 tablespoons bacon drippings
3 tablespoons light cream

1. Simmer the corn in the water, covered, ½ hour over low heat; uncover and simmer 15 to 20 minutes to drive off excess moisture.
2. Stir in remaining ingredients and let corn mellow over lowest heat about 10 minutes, until flavors are well blended.

Corn Light Bread

Makes about 8 servings

"This is the best corn bread I ever put in my mouth," says Mrs. Watkins. "It's an old family recipe that comes from my mother-in-law." The bread is unusual in that it is first steamed, then baked. The texture is dense—rather like pound cake. Serve the bread piping hot so that spreadings of butter will melt and seep in.

2½ cups stone-ground white or yellow corn meal
⅔ cup sifted all-purpose flour
½ cup sugar

1 teaspoon baking soda
1 teaspoon salt
2 cups buttermilk
¼ cup melted lard or butter

1. Mix together in a large bowl the corn meal, flour, sugar, soda, and salt. Add buttermilk and melted lard or butter, then beat vigorously for about 1 minute.
2. Pour batter into a 2-quart (8-cup) steamed-pudding mold that has been well greased and dusted with corn meal, or lacking that, into an 8-inch tube pan, greased and dusted with meal. Snap the lid on

the pudding mold or cover tube pan snugly with aluminum foil. Put container on a rack over boiling water in a covered kettle and steam 35 minutes.

3.   Lift bread container from kettle, uncover and bake in a moderately hot oven (375°) for 35 minutes or until bread pulls from sides of pan or mold and is lightly browned. Loosen bread from container with a thin-bladed spatula, turn it out, cut into wedges and serve at once with plenty of butter.

Blue Grass Chess Pie

Makes one single-crust 9-inch pie

Chess pies are great favorites throughout the South, but the recipes vary significantly. What is called a chess pie in North Carolina is known elsewhere as a brown-sugar pie (see recipe that follows this one); in Kentucky, a chess pie is a thick, sweet egg-custard pie flavored with vanilla.

1½ cups sugar
½ cup butter, softened to room temperature
3 large eggs
2 tablespoons flour
¾ cup light cream

¼ teaspoon salt
1½ teaspoons vanilla
1 9-inch unbaked pie shell (use your favorite recipe or one of the pastry recipes in this book; see index)

1.   Cream the sugar and butter until smooth; beat in the eggs, one at a time, using a wooden spoon. Beat in the flour, then blend in the cream, salt and vanilla.

2.   Pour filling into pie shell and bake in a moderately slow oven (325°) for about 45 minutes or until filling is puffy and the color of amber. The pastry should be lightly browned.

3.   Remove pie from oven and cool to room temperature before cutting.

Brown-Sugar Pie

Makes one 9-inch single-crust pie

An easy pie to make and a sinfully rich one.

2 cups firmly packed light brown sugar
4 large eggs
¼ cup light cream
Pinch of salt
⅓ cup melted butter

1 teaspoon vanilla
1 9-inch unbaked pie shell (use your favorite recipe or try one of the pastry recipes in this book; see index)

1. Using a wooden spoon, blend together the sugar, eggs, cream and salt. Add the butter gradually, beating hard to incorporate. Stir in the vanilla.

2. Pour filling into pie shell and bake in a moderately slow oven (325°) for 50 to 60 minutes or until pie is puffy and browned (pastry should be lightly browned, too).

3. Remove pie from oven and cool to room temperature before serving. (The filling will fall slightly and take on an almost jelly-like consistency, but this is as it should be.) Cut the slices small.

Trigg County Pecan Pie

Makes one 9-inch single-crust pie

"Now this is truly a pecan pie," explains Mrs. Watkins, "because you don't have to hunt around for the nuts." They are here in abundance, baked in a smooth, egg-thickened brown-sugar filling. When serving the pie, cut the pieces small because the pie is unusually rich.

1¼ cups firmly packed light brown sugar
⅓ cup melted butter
¼ cup light corn syrup
3 large eggs
½ cup light cream

1 teaspoon vanilla
¼ teaspoon salt
2 cups pecan halves
1 9-inch unbaked pie shell (use your favorite recipe or one of the pastry recipes in this book; see index)

1. Blend together the brown sugar and butter, pressing out all lumps of sugar. Mix in the corn syrup, then beat in the eggs, one at a time, using a wooden spoon. Stir in the cream, vanilla and salt, then mix in the pecans.

2. Pour into pie shell and bake in a moderately slow oven (325°) about 40 minutes, or until filling is puffy and pastry lightly browned.

3. Remove pie from oven and cool to room temperature before cutting.

Buttermilk Jam Cake

Makes a two-layer, 9-inch cake

This is another of Mrs. Watkins's mother-in-law's recipes. The cake is a dark and spicy one, made moist by the hefty amount of jam stirred into the batter. The filling is a thick spreading of tart jelly. The Chocolate Icing Mrs. Watkins uses is a dark and silky fudge icing. This is an unusual combination of flavors, and not, perhaps, one that everyone will like, especially purists who prefer their chocolate "straight"; you might, if you like, substitute Browned Butter Frosting for the Chocolate Icing.

1½ cups sugar
¾ teaspoon salt
¾ teaspoon ground nutmeg
¾ teaspoon ground cloves
1½ teaspoons ground cinnamon
6 tablespoons vegetable shortening
2 medium-sized eggs
¾ cup sieved blackberry or raspberry jam

2⅔ cups sifted all-purpose flour
1½ cups buttermilk in which 1½ teaspoons baking soda have been dissolved
1 cup currant or blackberry jelly (for filling)
1 recipe Chocolate Icing, or 1 recipe Browned Butter Frosting (both recipes follow)

1. In a large mixing bowl, combine sugar, salt and spices. Add shortening and cream mixture until fluffy; beat in eggs, one at a time, then mix in jam.

2. Add the flour alternately with the buttermilk-soda mixture, beginning and ending with the flour.

3. Divide batter between two well-greased 9-inch round layer-cake pans that have been lined with wax paper (grease the paper also), then bake in a moderate oven (350°) for about 45 minutes or until cakes pull away from sides of pans and are springy to the touch. Remove cake layers from oven and cool upright in their pans on wire racks for 5 minutes, then remove from pans, peel off wax paper, and cool to room temperature before filling and frosting.

4. Spread one cake layer with jelly, sandwich the second layer on top, then spread sides and top of cake with frosting, swirling it into peaks and valleys.

Chocolate Icing

Makes enough to frost one 9-inch, two-layer cake

3 tablespoons butter
3 1-ounce squares unsweetened chocolate
1 pound sifted confectioners (10X) sugar

¼ teaspoon salt
1 egg
1 teaspoon vanilla
2 to 3 tablespoons light cream

1.   Melt butter and chocolate in a small heavy saucepan over lowest heat.
2.   Combine sugar and salt in a large mixing bowl. Pour in chocolate mixture and stir to mix; work in the egg and vanilla and 2 tablespoons of the cream.
3.   Beat hard until mixture reaches a good spreading consistency, adding the additional tablespoon of cream if necessary.

Browned Butter Frosting

Makes enough to frost one 9-inch, two-layer cake

⅓ cup unsalted butter
1 pound sifted confectioners (10X) sugar

⅛ teaspoon salt
⅓ cup light cream (about)
1 teaspoon vanilla

1.   Melt the butter in a small saucepan over moderate heat, then let butter bubble and brown (it should be a rich topaz color).
2.   Combine the sugar and salt in a mixing bowl, mix in the browned butter, then beat in just enough cream to make the frosting a good spreading consistency. Stir in the vanilla and continue beating until frosting is fluffy and smooth.

Bourbon-Spiked Eggnog

Makes about 12 punch-cup servings

"It may seem like this isn't enough bourbon to flavor the eggnog," says Mrs. Watkins. "But it is. We don't like eggnog really strong."

8 eggs
½ cup sugar
2 quarts milk, heated to simmering
1 pint vanilla ice cream, softened
  until mushy

⅔ cup bourbon
1 cup heavy cream, whipped to soft
  peaks
Ground nutmeg

1. Beat the eggs with the sugar until very smooth and thick. Pour the milk into a large heatproof punch bowl, add the ice cream, then slowly blend in the beaten egg mixture. Gradually add the bourbon.

2. Fold in the whipped cream, then dust the bowl of eggnog lightly with nutmeg.

Angie's Pickles Cut Crossways

This old-fashioned pickle recipe is set down exactly as it was copied from Mrs. Watkins's notebook of handwritten receipts. The pickles, she says, are "good and crisp and sweet."

For each gallon of sliced cucumbers, allow ¾ cup salt. Place cucumbers and salt in a crock, add water to cover and let stand 7 days. Drain. Put a rounded tablespoon of alum in the crock, add fresh water to cover and let stand 2 days. Drain. Place the cucumbers in a large kettle, cover with water, add ½ tablespoon ginger and boil ½ hour. Drain and reserve. Bring to a boil 1 quart vinegar, 5 cups sugar, 1 tablespoon whole allspice, 1 stick cinnamon and 1 teaspoon celery seed. Add the drained cucumbers. When the mixture comes to a boil, pack cucumbers in hot jars and pour in syrup to cover.

Note:

It goes without saying that the jars should then be sealed and, to play it safe, processed for 10 minutes in a boiling water bath (212°).

Mrs. Oscar McCollum
of
Rockingham County, North Carolina

"ALL I ever wanted as a little girl was to grow up, get married, and have a lot of children so I could cook for them," says Mrs. Oscar Mc-Collum of Route 5, Reidsville, North Carolina, as she zips off another spiral of peel from the apples she is paring for pie and applesauce.

That, as it turns out, is exactly what happened. Mrs. McCollum (née Garnet Walker) grew up on a farm in Caswell County (just next door to Rockingham where she now lives), met Oscar McCollum at her high school's senior class party, courted for two years, married him at nineteen, moved over the county line, and settled into her life as a farmer's wife.

She was well prepared. "We always raised our vegetables at home and had our own chickens, hogs and cows. And I'd been cooking since I was little 'cause my mother said she'd rather do the housework."

Mrs. McCollum's first efforts at cooking proved disastrous. "When I was eight," she says, "I made my first cake. It was a coconut cake and, boy, was it a mess! My mother wasn't home, so I just went in the kitchen and tried to copy what I'd seen her do. I knew the cake needed liquid, but I didn't know *what* or how much so I didn't put in any and the cake just fell apart. But my two brothers ate it anyway. Later my mother told me I should have added a half a cup of milk. That's how much I knew!"

Despite her false start, Mrs. McCollum never was discouraged "out of cooking." By the time she had reached high school, after years of cooking for her mother, father, sister, and two brothers, she could, single handedly, put three whopping meals on the table every day. She was so good in home economics, in fact, that her high school principal let her keep taking that course instead of continuing with French. "If the teacher had to be away," she remembers, "I'd take over the class and teach the others. I really enjoyed that."

So Mrs. McCollum never felt any qualms about marrying a farmer, or about having to feed a hard-working husband and, at harvest time, the hired help as well.

"I didn't do a whole lot of cooking when we first married," she says, "because we lived the first six months with Oscar's folks. But then we moved into our own house—Oscar had bought himself a farm next to his daddy's two years before we were married. And we've lived in that house ever since—for thirty-nine years. Every time another baby would come along, we'd put up another room. Folks used to joke about it, say, 'Well, I reckon Garnet's expecting again because Oscar's putting another room on the house.'"

The McCollum's have six children—five sons and one daughter, the baby of the family. Four of the sons have left the farm, but John, the second-oldest, farms with his father and lives with his wife and family just across the red dirt road in a mobile home. The McCollums' daughter Susan now attends the University of North Carolina at nearby Greensboro.

The McCollums are a close-knit family and gather once or twice a year for big family reunions. "If we didn't do that," says Mrs. McCollum, "we just wouldn't know each other."

The biggest reunion—with so many family members attending that it has to be held at the Lawsonville Community Clubhouse—is the Thanksgiving Reunion. "We divide up the cooking," says Mrs. McCollum, "but I usually do the roast turkey and dressing."

Turkey is about the only item Mrs. McCollum has to buy for that feast—or any other. "We have a gobbler and a hen on the farm," she says, "but we don't kill them. I have them around just because I love to hear them holler and because they look so pretty out in the yard."

Though the McCollums' principal crop is tobacco, they also grow on their 300 acres all the fruits, nuts, and vegetables they need. They raise their own chickens (for eggs and for eating), ducks, hogs, dairy cows, and beef cattle. They cure their own country hams, render their own lard, even make their own sausage.

"About the only things I have to go to the store for," says Mrs. McCollum, "are sugar and salt and flour."

Have her children favorites among all the things she cooks? "Well, Susan loves my fried chicken. John and Hal like my pies—my husband, too; he says my sweet-potato pie is his favorite. And then Alvin likes my poundcake.

"Cakes are what I like best, especially fancy decorated cakes. I'm right pan-poor, I make so many different cakes. People will call me up and ask me to bake a wedding cake—sometimes I make as many as fifteen wedding cakes a year. And they'll call up and ask me to make a children's birthday cake. I took a course over at Rockingham Community College on cake decorating. And I now give right many cake-decorating demonstrations—at my Home Demonstration Club, the Lawsonville Club, and at other clubs around the county, too.

"When the children were little, I used to carry cakes over to the County Fair—they were in the 4-H Club and always showing something, a calf or some chickens. So I took my cakes. And it seemed like we did take a lot of ribbons." Mrs. McCollum's cakes, although she'd be the last to tell you, have won many a blue ribbon.

Now that her children are grown, she doesn't enter cakes at the fair anymore, but she still bakes a cake once or twice a week for the family. And she dishes up, in her sprawling country kitchen, three hefty meals a day complete with fresh-baked biscuits or corn bread. She has not one but two stoves—a giant old wood range that she has had ever since she married ("I use it when the weather's cold") and a modern electric range ("It doesn't heat up the house so much so I cook on it in the summer").

"I do my best cooking," she says, "when everybody's out working in the fields, because I know they're wondering what I'm going to serve.

"The only day I don't cook is Sunday. That's my day to rest. I'll go to church, then just come home and put my feet up and watch the TV."

Not that anyone in the family complains. There's always plenty left over from Saturday—fried chicken perhaps or country ham or spareribs, coleslaw, and probably half a feathery poundcake, too, baked just the day before.

Pork-Sausage-and-Tomato Pies

Makes 6 individual-size pies

"These are really good," says Mrs. McCollum, "because the juice from the tomatoes kind of drips down into the sausage meat." Mrs. McCollum makes saucer-sized pies, but you can also make smaller ones to serve as hot appetizers.

1 recipe Short and Tender Piecrust   2 small juicy-ripe tomatoes, sliced
   (see page 107)   ½-inch thick
¾ pound bulk sausage meat

1. Prepare piecrust as directed and divide in half; set aside while you brown the sausage.

2. Shape sausage into cakes about 2½ inches across and ½-inch thick. If you have a roll of sausage meat, simply slice ½-inch thick. Fry sausage in a heavy skillet over moderate heat 10 to 12 minutes, turning cakes or slices after 5 or 6 minutes so that both sides are lightly browned. Lift with a slotted spoon to paper toweling and drain well.

3. Roll out piecrust, half at a time, on a lightly floured cloth, to a thickness of about ⅛-inch, then cut into circles, using about a 6-inch saucer as a pattern. Transfer pastry circles to a baking sheet and moisten the rim of each with a little water. Place a sausage cake in the middle of each circle, then gather edges of pastry up over sausage and pinch together, leaving a small hole in the center so that the sausage shows through.

4. Bake in a very hot oven (450°) about 15 minutes until just beginning to brown. Place a tomato slice in the center of each pie and bake about 15 minutes longer, or until nicely browned and bubbling. Serve hot.

Variation:

Pork-Sausage-and-Tomato Pielets: Prepare piecrust as directed and set aside. Place sausage meat in a large heavy skillet, break up with a fork and fry over moderately low heat, continuing to break up, about 10 minutes or just until the pink color has disappeared; drain on paper toweling. Roll out the piecrust, half at a time, cut into 12-inch squares, then divide into 4-inch squares. Transfer pastry squares to two baking sheets and moisten each corner of each pastry square with a little cold water. Spoon about 1 tablespoon of sausage meat into the center of each 4-inch square, bring opposite corners up on top and pinch to seal so that you have little "bandana-like" bundles. Bake in a very hot oven (450°) for 12 to 15 minutes until squares begin to brown. Place half a cherry tomato, cut-side down, in the center of each pie, then bake 10 to 12 minutes longer until bubbly and browned. Serve hot as appetizers. Makes about 20 to 24 small pies.

Southern Fried Chicken

Makes 4 servings

"Whenever we want chicken," says Mrs. McCollum, "I just go out in the yard and catch one. It doesn't seem to me like I do anything special about frying chicken, but my children like the way I do it, especially Susan—it's her favorite. It's real crispy and brown outside and juicy all the way to the bone. I always make chicken gravy, too, so we can spoon it over hot biscuits."

1 frying chicken (about 3 pounds), cut up
2 teaspoons salt (about)
¼ teaspoon pepper (about)
½ cup unsifted all-purpose flour
Lard for frying (or, if you prefer, vegetable oil or shortening)

1 tablespoon water

Chicken Gravy:
4 tablespoons drippings
⅓ cup unsifted flour
2 cups water
½ teaspoon salt
⅛ teaspoon pepper

1. Lay chicken pieces in a shallow baking dish or pan, sprinkle all over with salt, cover and refrigerate overnight. Next day, pour off all accumulated juices and pat chicken dry on paper toweling. Sprinkle chicken well with pepper, then roll in flour to coat, shaking off excess.

2. In a large iron skillet over moderate heat melt enough lard to measure about 1 inch deep. Continue to heat—"when it's frying temperature," says Mrs. McCollum, "you'll begin to see a little steam rising up." Lay in pieces of chicken (it doesn't matter which side first) and adjust heat so chicken doesn't brown too fast (heat should be moderate or moderately low). Cook chicken 30 minutes on one side, then turn and cook 30 minutes longer. Add water, clap on a skillet lid, and let stand until the fat stops sputtering. Lay chicken pieces out on paper toweling to drain, also laying paper toweling on top, while you make the gravy. "If the chicken's to be good and crispy, you don't want it to sweat," explains Mrs. McCollum. Serve the fried chicken hot or cold.

3. *For the chicken gravy:* Pour all drippings from skillet, measure out 4 tablespoons and return to skillet. Add flour and heat and stir until the flour turns a pretty brown. Add water, salt, and pepper; heat and stir slowly until gravy thickens and "you don't get a raw flour taste"—about 5 minutes. Pour into a gravy boat and serve with fresh-baked biscuits. The McCollums don't put gravy over the chicken but take oven-hot biscuits, split them in half, and spoon the gravy over them. Makes about 2 cups gravy.

Carolina-Style Barbecued Spareribs

Makes 6 servings

In North Carolina, old-fashioned barbecue sauce isn't something thick and red made with ketchup, tomatoes, or tomato paste. It contains no tomatoes at all—only vinegar, salt, pepper, butter, and a little bit of sugar. Here is Mrs. McCollum's recipe for barbecued spareribs. "The sauce isn't a real hot one," she says, "I use it for barbecuing rabbit and chicken, too."

6 pounds spareribs
3 quarts water

Barbecue Sauce:
1 cup cider vinegar

⅓ cup butter
3 tablespoons light brown sugar
1 teaspoon black pepper
⅛ teaspoon cayenne pepper
¼ teaspoon salt

1. Cut spareribs into sections 3 ribs wide; place in a deep, heavy kettle, add water, cover and simmer over low heat 1 hour and 15 minutes.

2. *Meanwhile, prepare barbecue sauce:* Combine all ingredients in a small saucepan, bring to a simmer, then turn off heat and keep warm.

3. Remove spareribs from cooking liquid, arrange one layer deep in a very large shallow roasting pan and baste well with Barbecue Sauce. Broil 10 to 12 minutes about 5 inches from heat until crusty and brown, basting once after 5 minutes. Turn ribs over, baste again and broil 10 to 12 minutes longer, again basting after 5 minutes. Serve topped with any Barbecue Sauce left in the roasting pan.

Note:
The liquid in which the spareribs simmered can be skimmed of fat and used to cook vegetables or to make soups or stews.

Country Ham and Red-Eye Gravy

Makes 4 to 6 servings

If you live in an area where you can buy country ham, use it for this recipe. If not, use very thin center-cut ham steak. The flavor won't be the same, but the ham steak will be good. The Red-Eye Gravy isn't ladled over the ham but over hot biscuits, split in half, or over boiled rice or hominy grits.

¼ pound fat back, cut in small   ham or ham steak (about 1½
  cubes   pounds total)
6 serving-sized (about 3 × 5 inches   1 tablespoon water
  and ⅛-inch thick) slices country   1 cup weak coffee

1.   In a large iron skillet which has a lid, render fat back over moderate heat until most of the fat comes out; discard crispy brown cubes.

2.   Fry ham slices on both sides in the drippings, and when slices are good and brown add the water. Clap on the lid and let cook just until drippings stop sizzling.

3.   Put the ham slices on a warm platter, pour the drippings into a small heatproof bowl and add the coffee to the skillet. Bring quickly to a simmer, scraping up from the bottom all browned bits (these are the "red eyes"), then pour into the bowl of drippings. Dip the fat off the top until there is only a thin layer left. Pour gravy into a gravy boat and serve with the ham, along with fluffy biscuits, rice or hominy grits.

Tar Heel Scalloped Tomatoes

Makes 4 to 6 servings

"This is a real old recipe," says Mrs. McCollum. "One I grew up on. I put up my own tomatoes, so I use them. But you could use store-bought canned tomatoes."

3 cups   home-canned   (or   store-   3 tablespoons sugar
  bought canned) tomatoes   1 teaspoon salt
¼ cup butter   ⅛ teaspoon pepper
3 cups medium-coarse stale (but   Ground allspice
  not dry) breadcrumbs

1.   Heat tomatoes and butter in a saucepan over moderate heat just until butter melts. Mix in crumbs, sugar, salt and pepper.

2.   Spoon into a buttered 9- × 9- × 2-inch baking dish, sprinkle ground allspice lightly over the top, then bake uncovered in a hot oven (400°) for 40 to 45 minutes or just until mixture seems set in the middle and is lightly browned. Let stand at room temperature about 5 minutes before serving.

Old South Cabbage

Makes 4 servings

"I boil cabbage, turnip greens or collards with a hunk of fat back," says Mrs. McCollum. "Or sometimes with a piece of salt pork or a ham bone. It gives them a nice meaty flavor."

1 square (about 4 inches) fat back or salt pork
2 cups water

1 small cabbage (about 2 pounds), trimmed, cored and cut in bite-sized chunks
½ teaspoon salt (about)
⅛ teaspoon pepper (about)

1. Make deep crisscross cuts over surface of the fat back or salt pork, then boil it in the water in a covered, large saucepan for 30 minutes.

2. Add cabbage, re-cover and simmer 8 to 10 minutes, just until tender but still crisp, tossing now and then in the "pot likker." Season to taste with salt and pepper. With a slotted spoon, lift cabbage to a heated serving bowl.

Carolina Coleslaw

Makes 6 to 8 servings

"This isn't a fancy recipe," says Mrs. McCollum. "But we like it. And it gets better and better the longer it sits in the refrigerator."

1 large cabbage (about 3 pounds), trimmed, quartered and cored
1 medium-sized sweet green pepper, cored, seeded and minced (for color, use ½ green pepper and ½ sweet red pepper)
1 medium-sized sweet onion (Bermuda or Spanish), peeled and chopped fine

Dressing:
1 cup sugar
1 teaspoon salt
1 teaspoon dry mustard
1 teaspoon celery seed
1 cup cider vinegar
⅔ cup vegetable oil

1. With a sharp knife, slice each cabbage-quarter very fine; combine with green pepper and onion in a large bowl and toss to mix.

2. *For the dressing:* Mix sugar, salt, mustard and celery seed in a

small saucepan, add vinegar and oil and let come to a boil over moderate heat, stirring until sugar dissolves. Pour over cabbage and toss well to mix. Cool to room temperature, then cover and refrigerate until ready to serve.

Self-Rising Biscuits

Makes about 1½ dozen

"I bake up a batch of biscuits most every day. If I really want them pretty, I'll take a little rendered chicken fat and go over the top of each biscuit just as soon as they come out of the oven."

4 cups sifted self-rising flour   1⅓ cups milk
½ cup lard

1.   Place flour in a large mixing bowl, then cut in lard with a pastry blender until mixture is crumbly and about the texture of uncooked oatmeal.
2.   Pour in milk all at once and mix briskly and lightly with a fork just until dough clings together in a soft ball.
3.   Turn out on a lightly floured pastry cloth; turn over (knead) about 5 times—lightly—then roll ½-inch thick. Cut with a 2¾-inch biscuit cutter, place biscuits about 1 inch apart on ungreased baking sheets and bake in a very hot oven (450°) about 15 minutes, until lightly browned. To give biscuits a satiny finish, brush the tops with a little melted butter or rendered chicken fat the minute they come from the oven. Serve piping hot.

Wild-Blackberry Cobbler

Makes 8 servings

"You can do most any berries this way—cherries, too. I use blackberries mostly because they grow wild all 'round the farm. Usually I serve my cobbler plain, but if I want to get a little fancy, I make Nutmeg Sauce to spoon over it."

4 cups juicy-ripe blackberries,
  washed
2½ cups sugar
½ cup butter

2 cups sifted self-rising flour
2 cups milk
2 eggs, beaten until frothy

1. Heat berries, ½ cup of the sugar and the butter in a saucepan over moderate heat just until sugar dissolves and butter melts.

2. Mix remaining 2 cups of sugar with the flour in a mixing bowl, stir in milk, then eggs, and beat just until blended. Pour batter into a buttered 13- × 9- × 2-inch baking pan, then spoon blackberries on top, covering batter as evenly as possible.

3. Bake uncovered in a moderate oven (350°) for about 40 minutes, just until set. Let cool about 5 minutes before spooning into serving dishes. Serve plain or with Nutmeg Sauce (recipe follows).

Nutmeg Sauce

Makes about 1¼ cups

1 cup sugar
2 tablespoons flour
½ teaspoon ground nutmeg

1 cup water
1 tablespoon cider vinegar
½ teaspoon lemon juice

1. Mix sugar, flour and nutmeg in a small saucepan; stir in water, vinegar and lemon juice.

2. Set over moderate heat and cook, stirring constantly, until thickened and no raw flour taste remains—about 5 minutes. Serve hot over fruit cobblers or plain cake.

Short and Tender Piecrust

Makes enough for one 9- or 10-inch double-crust pie, or
two 9- or 10-inch pie shells

"I roll my piecrust thicker than some folks," says Mrs. McCollum, "because I like a little crust to my pie—'specially if it's short."

2 cups sifted all-purpose flour
¼ teaspoon salt

½ cup lard
⅓ to ½ cup cold water

1. Place flour and salt in a large shallow mixing bowl, add lard and cut in with a pastry blender until crumbly—about the texture of uncooked oatmeal.

2. Add water, a few drops at a time, tossing briskly with a fork; as soon as the mixture holds together, stop adding water.

3. Roll out pastry, one-half at a time, on a lightly floured pastry cloth to desired size and shape.

Sweet-Potato Pie

Makes one 9-inch single-crust pie

"This is my husband Oscar's favorite pie."

½ recipe Short and Tender Piecrust (recipe precedes)
2 medium-sized sweet potatoes, boiled in their skins until fork-tender
¼ cup butter
1 cup sugar
½ cup milk
1 egg
1 teaspoon vanilla
⅛ teaspoon ground nutmeg
Pinch of salt

1. Prepare piecrust as recipe directs, roll out and fit into a 9-inch pie pan, making a fluted edge. Set aside.

2. Peel sweet potatoes, then mash with butter until smooth and creamy. Mix in sugar and milk, add egg and beat briskly with a fork to blend. Stir in vanilla, nutmeg and salt. Pour into pie shell.

3. Bake in a hot oven (400°) for 30 to 35 minutes, until pastry is nicely browned and filling seems set around the edges. Cool to room temperature before cutting.

Raisin Cake with Almond Icing

Makes one 9-inch bundt cake

"Now this is a good cake, I'm tellin' you. I make it right often and at Christmastime when I have to bake fruit cakes, I just make up my Raisin Cake batter and add whatever I want to that batter—chipped candied cherries and citron, chopped nuts."

Cake:
2 cups sugar
2 cups hot water
1 cup butter or, if you'd rather, margarine
3 cups seedless raisins
2 teaspoons ground cinnamon
1 teaspoon ground cloves
1 teaspoon salt
2 teaspoons baking soda

3½ cups sifted all-purpose flour

Almond Icing:
2¼ cups sifted confectioners (10X) sugar
⅓ cup butter or margarine, at room temperature (or, if you want a snow-white icing, vegetable shortening)
¼ teaspoon almond extract
¼ cup milk (about)

1. *To prepare cake:* Place sugar, water, butter, raisins, cinnamon, cloves and salt in a very large heavy saucepan, set over moderate heat, bring to a boil, then let boil, uncovered, for 1 minute. Remove from heat and stir in soda (mixture will froth and bubble up which is why you need a big pan). Cool to room temperature.

2. Stir in flour, about one-third at a time. Pour into a well-greased-and-floured 9-inch bundt pan and bake in a moderate oven (350°) 1 to 1¼ hours or until cake begins to pull from sides of pan and top springs back slowly when pressed with a finger.

3. Cool cake upright in its pan on a wire rack 10 minutes, then turn out on the rack and cool to room temperature.

4. *To make almond icing:* Cream together the confectioners sugar, butter and almond extract, then add just enough milk to make about the consistency of a medium cream sauce. The icing should be thin enough to pour slowly, but not syrupy. With the cake still on the rack (put a piece of wax paper underneath to catch the drips), drizzle icing over top so that it runs down the sides sort of like icicles. Let icing harden before cutting the cake—about 1 to 2 hours.

Blue Ribbon Poundcake

Makes one 10-inch tube cake, or one 9-inch bundt cake and one small loaf cake (7⅜ × 3⅝ × 2¼ inches)

"It seemed like I just couldn't find a poundcake recipe that suited me," says Mrs. McCollum, "so I just kept experimentin' and experimentin' until I got one that was real moist inside and had a little sugary crust on top. If my ducks are laying, I'll use duck eggs in my poundcake. They make the best cakes in the world because they're so rich. But hen eggs work real well, too. I flavor my poundcake with lemon or sometimes with both lemon and vanilla, but I reckon some folks would rather use pure vanilla. This makes a right big cake—I bake it in a ten-inch tube pan when it's just family, but if I want a fancy-looking cake, I'll use a nine-inch bundt pan and then bake what's left of the batter in one of those little bitty loaf pans for my grandchildren." Mrs. McCollum's poundcake, by the way, won her a blue ribbon at the Rockingham County Fair.

4 cups sifted all-purpose flour
1 teaspoon baking powder
½ teaspoon salt, if you like ("I don't like much salt in a pound-cake," says Mrs. McCollum, "and sometimes I don't use any.")
Pinch of ground nutmeg
2 cups unsalted butter, at room temperature

3 cups sugar
6 large eggs, at room temperature
1 cup milk, at room temperature
2 teaspoons lemon extract or vanilla, or 1 teaspoon each lemon extract and vanilla

Optional Garnishes:
Confectioners (10X) sugar
Fresh whole strawberries

1.   Sift together the flour, baking powder, salt and nutmeg and set aside.

2.   Cream butter until very light and fluffy, then add sugar gradually, creaming all the while. "You don't want any of those little sugar grains to show," says Mrs. McCollum, "so you have to add the sugar real slow and beat real hard."

3.   Add the eggs, one at a time, beating after each addition just enough to mix.

4.   Combine the milk and the flavoring (lemon, vanilla or lemon and vanilla). Add the sifted dry ingredients alternately with the milk, beginning and ending with the dry ingredients. "I usually do this in four or five different additions," says Mrs. McCollum, "with the mixer at real low speed."

5.   Pour into a well-buttered-and-floured 10-inch tube pan (filling to within about 2 inches of the top). (Or use a 9-inch bundt pan and spoon the remaining batter into a 7⅜- × 3⅝- × 2¼-inch loaf pan.) Bake in a slow oven (300°) for about 1 hour and 20 minutes, or until cake just begins to pull from the sides of the pan and a finger pressed gently on the top of the cake leaves a print that vanishes slowly. ("I don't like a cake to bounce back on me when I press it," says Mrs. McCollum. "It won't be moist.") The bundt cake, she says, won't take quite as long to bake as the tube cake—about 1 hour or 1 hour and 10 minutes, and the little loaf should be done in about 45 minutes.

6.   Cool cake (or cakes) upright in the pan on a wire rack for 10 minutes, then turn out on the rack and cool to room temperature before cutting. Serve as is or garnish, if you like, with a dusting of 10X sugar and a few red, ripe strawberries.

Variation:

Strawberry Shortcake: Slice the poundcake about 1½ inches thick and top each slice with about ⅔ cup crushed fresh strawberries sweetened to taste and, if you like, a gob or two of whipped cream.

Yeast-Raised Chocolate Cake with Bittersweet Frosting

Makes two 9-inch layers

"This is one of the best chocolate cakes I know," says Mrs. McCollum. "It doesn't seem like the yeast will make it rise—you have to let the batter sit in a cool place overnight—but it does."

Cake:
¾ cup butter, at room temperature
2 cups sugar
3 eggs, well beaten
1 teaspoon vanilla
⅔ cup sifted cocoa (not a mix)
3 cups sifted cake flour
1 cup milk
1½ teaspoons active dry yeast, softened in ¼ cup lukewarm water

1 teaspoon baking soda
¼ cup warm water

Bittersweet Frosting:
1 cup butter
4 squares (1 ounce each) unsweetened chocolate
4¼ cups sifted confectioners (10X) sugar
2 eggs, well beaten
1½ teaspoons vanilla

1. *To prepare cake:* Cream together the butter and sugar until fluffy and light. Add eggs, vanilla and cocoa and mix well. Add flour alternately with the milk, beginning and ending with the flour and beating after each addition. Stir in softened yeast mixture.

2. Cover mixing bowl with a clean dry cloth and let batter stand overnight in a cool spot.

3. Next morning, dissolve soda in the warm water and mix quickly into batter. Divide batter between two greased-and-floured 9-inch layer-cake pans and bake in a moderate oven (350°) 40 to 45 minutes or until cakes begin to draw from sides of pans and tops spring back slowly when pressed with a finger.

4. Cool layers upright in pans on wire racks 10 minutes, then turn out on racks and cool completely.

5. *To make bittersweet frosting:* Melt butter and chocolate together in a small saucepan over low heat. Mix into sugar along with eggs and vanilla. Beat until smooth and of a good spreading consistency.

6. Frost one layer, place second layer on top, then frost top and sides of cake, swirling frosting into hills and valleys.

Jerusalem Artichoke Pickle Relish

Makes about 6 half-pints

Jerusalem artichokes (related to the sunflower and not to the French globe artichoke) grow wild all over the South and, indeed, over much of the eastern United States. Southern cooks learned long ago to dig up their crunchy, potato-like tubers and turn them into pickles and relishes. Jerusalem artichokes are so popular today that many farm cooks, like Mrs. McCollum, plant beds of them so that they won't run short "come picklin' time." If you live in the South, you won't have much difficulty finding Jerusalem artichokes; if not, ask for them in specialty produce markets or health-food shops.

Because of their knobbiness and irregular shapes, Jerusalem artichokes are virtually impossible to peel. The best technique is simply to scrape away the skin with a paring knife, then to rinse the tubers well in cool water. This is a slow job, so have patience. But the relish is crisp and tart—delicious with almost any meat.

1 quart scraped and moderately coarsely ground Jerusalem artichokes (about 2 to 2½ pounds artichokes)
1 pint moderately coarsely ground sweet red peppers
1 pint moderately coarsely ground yellow onions

1 gallon cold water mixed with 1 cup pickling salt (brine)
1¼ cups sugar
2½ cups cider vinegar
4 teaspoons white mustard seeds
1 tablespoon ground turmeric

1. Soak the artichokes, peppers and onions in the brine for 3 hours in a covered enamel or stainless steel kettle. Drain in a colander lined with a clean dish towel, then bundle up the mixture in the towel and twist and squeeze out all liquid possible. (Because of the quantity, you will probably have to drain the mixture in two batches.) When mixture is squeezed as dry as possible, place in a large bowl.

2. Wash and rinse 6 half-pint preserving jars and their closures, then keep each jar immersed in a separate pan of simmering water until needed.

3. Mix sugar, vinegar, mustard seeds and turmeric in a large stain-

less steel or enamel saucepan, bring to a boil and boil, uncovered, for 1 minute. Pour over artichoke mixture and stir well to mix. Pack relish into hot jars, leaving ¼-inch head space at the top of each jar. Wipe jar rims and seal. Process jars 10 minutes in a boiling water bath (212° F.). Lift jars from water bath, complete seals if necessary, and cool to room temperature; check seals, label, and store on a cool, dark, dry shelf.

Mrs. Mary Sheppard
of Middleton Place
Dorchester County, South Carolina

THE Low Country is the tidewater swatch of South Carolina that begins along about Charleston and sweeps south toward Savannah,
Georgia, lapped by the Atlantic all the way. It is a land where Spanish moss drapes itself upon a calligraphy of live oaks, where the air
is pure essence of gardenia and tea olive and where once-proud rice
plantations, all but wiped out by the Civil War, nonetheless offer
nostalgic glimpses of the antebellum South.

It is also a land of unique cuisine, as African and West Indian as it
is English, a land of superlative cooks who work miracles with chicken
and seafood, okra and hot peppers, sesame seeds and rice.

One such cook is Mary Sheppard of Middleton Place, who has
cooked for five generations of Middleton descendants, beginning in
1923 in Charleston, then moving, two years later, a dozen or so miles
up the Ashley River to cook for the J. J. Pringle Smiths at their vast
country estate. Mary, then Mary Lees Washington, was all of eighteen
when she went to Middleton.

Explaining her move to Middleton Place, Mary says, "Miz Smith
needed a younger cook up here. She had an old lady who had been
here since slavery times, but she couldn't do fancy cooking. So Miz
Smith brought me up here to do parties." Mary has lived at Middleton
ever since, in a trim red-brick bungalow at the edge of a shady grove,
cooking for succeeding generations, including the present one, the
Charles H. P. Duells (Mr. Duell is Mrs. Smith's grandson).

"Miz Smith taught me 'most everything I know," Mary continues. "I
stopped school in the fourth grade. But Miz Smith—and her daughter
and Mr. Smith—were very nice to me. I could go to them and ask them
anything and they would teach me."

Of course Mary had already learned a good bit about cooking—the basics, at least—from her mother, who was an excellent cook. "I was an only child," Mary says, "and I mostly followed after my mother every time she cooked." By the time she was nine or ten, Mary could batter-fry chicken with the best of them and cook vegetables, grits, and rice. "My mother taught me how to cook rice the *right* way," she says. "To steam it so it would keep soft."

But the fancier dishes Mary learned from Mrs. Pringle Smith. "Miz Smith would go to parties and get receipts and come back and tell me how something looked and tasted. Then she would say, 'Mary, let us try it.' Of course, we'd try it out on the dogs first. Not real dogs. What Miz Smith meant was that we'd try it out at home first and see how it came out. If it was good, then we would serve it at parties."

There were plenty of parties at Middleton Place in the old days. "I sometimes cooked for as many as thirty-four," Mary remembers. She remembers, in particular, the day the old coal stove went out "up at the big house," the day she had to "tote" everything over to her own small kitchen, cook it, then "tote" it back.

"I like to had a heart attack," Mary says. But she managed so gracefully that none of the dinner guests was any the wiser.

Although Mary thinks of the Smiths and Duells as "family," she does have a family of her own. Within a year of coming to Middleton Place, she met and married Thomas Sheppard, who worked at the plantation as a truck driver. When he died in 1946, Mary stayed on at Middleton. It was home to her and to her son, who lives today just ten miles down the river road at Pierpont. Mary has, in addition, three grandchildren ("all growed up") and four great-grandchildren, whose photographs parade across the bureaus and tabletops of Mary's living room.

Life is easier for Mary today than it was when Middleton was a "working farm" with a big vegetable garden, strawberry beds, fig bushes and pear, peach, and pecan trees. "We grew sugar cane and made our own syrup," Mary says. "We raised mushrooms in the basement of the springhouse, and we had our own pork." She helped with the churning, canning, and pickling, in addition to cooking. "Ain't nothin' around here now 'cept flowers," Mary continues. A *slight* understatement—Middleton, with its acres of azaleas, camellias and formal gardens laid out in 1741, ranks as one of the most magnificent gardens of the Western world.

Today, as a National Historic Landmark, Middleton Place is open year-round to the public. No one now lives in "the big house," which has been turned into a museum. The plantation stableyards have been given over to craft demonstrations—spinning, weaving, potting, candle dipping, forging—to show visitors what life was like during the eighteenth and nineteenth centuries.

Mary is more or less retired now. Certainly she no longer cooks on the grand scale that she once did. Still, she is very much a part of Middleton Place, taking tickets at "the big house," answering visitors' questions, manning the telephone when the plantation office is closed, trouble-shooting.

"Mary knows more about Middleton than any of us," said one of the staff recently. And she is beloved by them all. On the occasion of her fiftieth anniversary at Middleton, they surprised her with a big party. There was plenty of good Low Country food, which Mary, as guest of honor, was able to sit back and enjoy.

"I done so much cooking," she says, "that I'm through with it now."

Don't you believe it! Mary still cooks for herself, her friends, and her family. And clearly she loves it.

Okra Gumbo

Makes 10 to 12 servings

Rare is the Southerner who doesn't like okra, and equally rare the non-Southerner who does. To both we recommend Mary Sheppard's Okra Gumbo, which has already won many converts.

1 meaty ham hock (about 2 to 2½ pounds), skinned and trimmed of excess fat
2 pounds beef shank, trimmed of excess fat
3 quarts water
2 large yellow onions, peeled and coarsely chopped
2 cups canned tomatoes (preferably home-canned)
3 tablespoons tomato paste
¾-pound fresh young okra, washed, trimmed and sliced ¼-inch thick, or 1 10-ounce package frozen sliced okra
4 teaspoons sugar
1 teaspoon salt (or to taste)
¼ teaspoon black pepper
Pinch of cayenne pepper
¼ teaspoon crumbled leaf thyme
2 cups fresh whole-kernel corn, or 1 10-ounce package frozen whole-kernel corn
2 cups fresh, shelled baby limas, or 1 10-ounce package frozen baby limas

1. Place ham hock, beef shank, water, and onions in a very large heavy kettle and bring to a boil over moderate heat. Lower heat so that liquid bubbles gently, cover and simmer about 4 hours or until meat falls from the bones. Uncover and simmer 2 hours longer or until broth has reduced by about one-third. Remove and discard bones, then skim as much fat from broth as possible. Cut any large pieces of meat into bite sizes and return to kettle.

2. Add tomatoes, tomato paste, okra, sugar, salt, black pepper, cayenne, and thyme, cover and simmer 30 minutes.

3. Add corn and limas, re-cover and simmer 45 minutes. Uncover and simmer 10 to 15 minutes longer. Taste for salt and add more, if needed. Ladle into large soup bowls and serve. Delicious with Bacon-Flavored Corn Sticks (page 124).

Batter-Fried Chicken

Makes 6 servings

Of batter-frying chicken, which Mary Sheppard learned as a little girl, the trick, she points out, is getting the batter the right consistency. "You want it *just* thick enough to hold on the chicken. And your fat got to be real hot. Then the chicken comes out nice and brown and crisp."

2 young broiler-fryers (2½ to 3 pounds), disjointed
2 teaspoons salt
¼ teaspoon pepper

Batter:
1 egg, lightly beaten
½ cup milk

2 tablespoons flour
1½ cups flour (about), for dredging the chicken
3 pounds vegetable shortening for deep frying (this can be strained after the chicken is fried, then saved and used again)

1. Sprinkle each piece of chicken on all sides with salt and pepper; spread pieces out on a baking sheet and let stand at room temperature about 1 hour.

2. *For the batter:* Combine the egg and milk in a shallow bowl, then beat in the flour until smooth. Dip each piece of chicken in batter, then roll in dredging flour until lightly coated on all sides.

3. Deep-fry the chicken, about 3 or 4 pieces at a time, in hot fat (350° to 360° is the best temperature), turning with tongs until chicken is a rich golden brown on all sides. This will take 12 to 15 minutes. Keep raising and lowering the burner heat as needed to maintain temperature of fat as nearly at 350° to 360° as possible.

4. As each batch of chicken browns, lift it from deep fat onto a baking sheet lined with several thicknesses of paper toweling and set uncovered in a very low oven (about 250° F.) to keep warm while you fry the remaining chicken.

Chicken Purloo

Makes about 6 servings

Here's one of Mary's favorite ways to use up leftover roast chicken (the recipe works equally well with leftover roast turkey). "Purloo," by the way, is how "pilau" is pronounced in the South Carolina Low Country. This isn't a true pilau—the chicken mixture is ladled over the rice instead of being mixed with it. But it's delicious nonetheless.

½ pound small mushrooms, wiped clean with a damp cloth and quartered
2 tablespoons grated onion (optional)
3 tablespoons butter
6 tablespoons roast chicken (or turkey) drippings or 6 tablespoons bacon drippings
7 tablespoons flour
2 cups water

3 cups cubed leftover roast chicken or turkey (make the chunks of meat fairly large, especially the white meat; Mary often slices the white meat)
2 hard-cooked eggs, peeled and diced
1¼ teaspoons salt (or to taste)
⅛ teaspoon pepper
4 cups hot cooked rice

1.   Sauté the mushrooms (and, if you like, the onion) in the butter over moderate heat about 5 minutes until lightly browned; set aside.

2.   Place drippings and flour in a large heavy saucepan, set over moderately low heat and heat, stirring constantly, until the sauce is a rich rust-brown—about 5 minutes. Add water and heat, stirring, until thickened, about 3 minutes. Turn heat very low and let sauce simmer uncovered about 10 minutes to mellow the flavors.

3.   Mix in the mushrooms, chicken, eggs, salt and pepper and simmer, uncovered, over low heat for 15 minutes. Taste for salt and add more if needed.

4.   Make a bed of rice on a medium-sized platter and pour the chicken mixture on top. To garnish, Mary uses quartered hard-cooked eggs and crisp celery leaves.

Deviled Crab

Makes 4 servings

"I like all seafood," Mary Sheppard says. And she likes to catch it, too. Whenever she has time, she will carry her bamboo pole down to the Ashley River marshes or maybe just drop a line in one of the famous Butterfly Lakes at Middleton Place. "I pull up a lot of catfish," she says. "Crabs, too. They just catch a hold of the line." Her two favorite ways to cook crabs are to boil them, with just a little vinegar added to the cooking water, and to devil them. Mary's recipe for Deviled Crab is different from many in that she adds no mustard at all. What gives it "bite" is red pepper.

⅓ cup minced onion
⅓ cup minced green pepper
2 tablespoons butter or margarine
1 pound lump or backfin crabmeat, picked over for bits of shell and cartilage, then flaked
¾ cup soft, fine breadcrumbs
1 egg, beaten until frothy
½ cup mayonnaise

½ teaspoon salt
¼ to ½ teaspoon cayenne pepper, depending upon how "hot" you like things

Topping:
¾ cup fine, soft breadcrumbs tossed with 1 tablespoon melted butter or margarine

1. Sauté the onion and green pepper in the butter or margarine over moderate heat about 5 minutes, until limp; cool, then mix with all remaining ingredients (except topping).

2. Spoon crab mixture into 4 large, well-scrubbed crab or scallop shells or spoon into a 1-quart *au gratin* dish. Scatter topping over all.

3. Bake, uncovered, in a moderate oven (350°) about 25 minutes or until bubbling and browned. Serve at once.

Mary Sheppard's Spinach-and-Egg Casserole

Makes 4 to 6 servings

"I made this recipe up one night," Mary says. "And from *then on* I had trouble on my hands. Miz Smith liked it so well that I was making it for guests and parties and all."

1 pound washed and trimmed tender young spinach leaves (weigh the spinach after trimming it; for 1 pound trimmed spinach you'll need 1¼ to 1½ pounds untrimmed spinach), *or* use 2 10-ounce packages frozen chopped spinach, cooked by package directions, drained well but not seasoned
4 tablespoons butter or margarine

4 tablespoons flour
⅛ teaspoon cayenne pepper
1½ teaspoons salt
1½ cups milk
1 cup soft fine breadcrumbs or coarse cracker meal
2 hard-cooked eggs, peeled and sliced thin
1 cup finely shredded sharp Cheddar cheese
1 bacon strip, cut in 1-inch lengths

1.   If using fresh spinach, place rinsed spinach in a large kettle, set over moderate heat, cover and steam about 10 minutes or until tender. Do not add water—the rinse water clinging to the leaves is moisture enough to steam the spinach. Drain spinach in a fine sieve, pressing very dry. Chop coarsely and set aside.

2.   Melt butter in a small saucepan over moderate heat; blend in flour, cayenne and salt. Add milk and heat, stirring constantly, until thickened and smooth—about 3 minutes.

3.   To assemble the casserole, butter a 6-cup baking dish well, then layer the ingredients in this way: half the breadcrumbs, half the spinach, slices of 1 hard-cooked egg, one-third of the sauce and half the cheese; next, the remaining spinach, slices of the remaining egg, one-third of the sauce and the remaining cheese; then the remaining one-third of the sauce; and finally, top with remaining crumbs. Arrange bacon pieces on top.

4.   Bake uncovered in a moderate oven (350°) for about 40 to 45 minutes or until bubbling and browned.

Steamed Rice

Makes 4 servings

"One thing my Mama taught me to cook right when I was a little girl was rice," says Mary. "Right" means "steam." According to Mary, the only way to be sure that the rice will neither scorch nor stick, and to be sure that it will be light and fluffy with every grain distinct, is to steam it. Mary uses a stack-steamer, steaming vegetables on the bottom and the rice in the top compartment. "The rice got to be on the top," she says. "Otherwise it gets gummy." We've found that you don't need a proper steamer to steam rice, that you can use a double boiler almost as successfully.

1 cup converted (not quick-cook-   2 cups water
  ing) rice

1.   Place rice and water in the top of a double boiler, set over gently boiling water, cover snugly and steam 40 minutes.

2.   After about 25 to 30 minutes, lift the cover and begin forking the rice. "You got to fork it up often to keep it fluffy," Mary cautions. Be sure to re-cover the rice after you have forked it up.

Hoppin' John

Makes about 6 servings

Hoppin' John is the traditional New Year's dish in and around Charleston. "It's 'sposed to be good luck," Mary explains. "You eat it with greens [turnip salad or collards]. They're 'sposed to be good luck, too." Mary makes Hoppin' John with dried cowpeas (field peas) as do most Low Country cooks. But if you have difficulty obtaining them, use dried black-eyed peas instead; in many parts of the South, Hoppin' John *is* made with black-eyed peas.

1 cup dried cowpeas or black-eyed peas, washed and sorted
¼ pound lean slab bacon, cut in ½-inch cubes
2½ cups water

⅛ teaspoon cayenne pepper
⅛ teaspoon black pepper
1¼ teaspoons salt (or to taste)
3 cups hot cooked rice

1. Place dried peas, bacon and water in a medium-sized, heavy kettle and bring to a boil over moderate heat. Reduce heat so that liquid ripples gently, cover kettle snugly and simmer just until peas are firm-tender—cowpeas won't need much more than 20 minutes' cooking, black-eyed peas 40 to 45. Drain liquid from peas (save to add to soups).
2. Add cayenne and black pepper and salt and toss lightly to mix. Add rice and toss lightly again. Taste for salt and add more if needed. Serve hot as a potato substitute. Especially good with roast pork or pork chops.

Cheese Biscuits with Ham

Makes 1 dozen

If you visit Middleton Place, be sure to have lunch in the tearoom there and be sure, too, to have the cheese biscuits sandwiched together with thick slices of ham. Delicious! Cheese biscuits are an old Southern specialty and the best ham to use is Virginia or country ham. Any leftover baked ham sliced cold and fairly thick works well, however. Mary Sheppard's recipe for Cheese Biscuits, given here, is a little different, because she adds just enough cayenne pepper for nip and uses ice water instead of milk in the dough.

2 cups sifted all-purpose flour
2 teaspoons baking powder
1 teaspoon salt
¼ teaspoon cayenne pepper
⅓ cup vegetable shortening

1 cup fairly coarsely shredded
   sharp Cheddar cheese
¾ cup ice water
12 slices baked ham, about ¼-inch
   thick and 2¾ inches square

1. In a mixing bowl, stir together flour, baking powder, salt and cayenne pepper. Cut in the shortening with a pastry blender until the mixture is the texture of coarse meal. Add the cheese and toss to mix.

2. Drizzle the ice water over the surface of the dry ingredients, then mix briskly but lightly with a fork just until dough holds together.

3. Turn dough onto a lightly floured board and knead lightly 7 or 8 times. Roll dough to a thickness of about ½-inch, then cut in rounds with a 2¾-inch biscuit cutter.

4. Bake on an ungreased baking sheet in a hot oven (425°) about 20 minutes or until dappled with brown. Cool biscuits to room temperature, then split and sandwich together with slices of ham.

Cheese "Crackers"

Makes about 7½ dozen

A favorite hors d'oeuvre served at Middleton Place parties in the old days were these puffy, piquant cheese "crackers." You can make the cheese spread ahead of time, store in freezer or refrigerator, then take out and use as needed.

1 loaf thinly sliced firm-textured
   white bread
2 cups finely grated sharp Cheddar
   cheese

¼ cup butter, cut in small dice
½ teaspoon cayenne pepper

1. Trim crusts from bread, square up slices, then quarter each, or, if you prefer, cut small rounds from bread using a 1- to 1½-inch cutter. (Save bread trimmings and make into crumbs in an electric blender to use for casserole toppings, or for "crumbing" chicken, cutlets or chops.) Spread bread squares or rounds on a baking sheet, set in a very slow oven (300°) and let dry out for 15 to 20 minutes— just until crisp and pale golden.

2. Let the grated cheese stand at room temperature for an hour or two until very soft. Place in electric mixer bowl, add butter and cayenne and beat at high speed until thick and creamy.

3. Spread each bread square or round with cheese mixture—not too thin, but not too thick either; about a rounded ¼-teaspoon of the mixture per hors d'oeuvre is about right.

4. Arrange spread-side up on a baking sheet and bake in a hot oven (400°) for about 2 minutes, until puffed and lightly browned. Serve hot.

Benne Cocktail Biscuits

Makes about 4½ dozen

Benne seeds (more commonly known as sesame) grow in the South Carolina Low Country and are stirred into biscuits, cookies, and candies. One of the best benne recipes, we think, is this one of Mary's for peppery, bite-sized cocktail snacks.

½ cup sesame (benne) seeds
2 cups sifted all-purpose flour
2 teaspoons baking powder
½ teaspoon baking soda
1½ teaspoons salt
½ teaspoon cayenne pepper

⅓ cup hog lard or vegetable shortening
1 tablespoon butter or margarine
¾ cup buttermilk
¼ cup melted butter (optional)

1. Spread the sesame seeds out in a pie pan, place in a very slow oven (275°) and toast, stirring frequently, until a pale amber color—this will take about 10 minutes. Cool the sesame seeds to room temperature.

2. In a mixing bowl, stir together the flour, baking powder, soda, salt and cayenne pepper. Cut in the lard and butter with a pastry blender until mixture is the texture of coarse meal. Add the sesame seeds and toss to mix.

3. Make a well in the center of the dry ingredients, pour in the buttermilk and stir briskly but lightly with a fork just until dough holds together.

4. Turn dough onto a lightly floured board and knead lightly 7 or 8 times. Roll dough to a thickness of about ⅜-inch, then cut in 1-inch rounds with a small biscuit cutter or the cap of a screw-top bottle.

5. Bake on ungreased baking sheets in a hot oven (425°) for 15 to 20 minutes or until lightly browned. Serve hot. To make the biscuits extra-good, split them while hot and brush with melted butter. The biscuits may also be served at room temperature—plain or sandwiched together with bite-sized slices of baked ham.

Bacon-Flavored Corn Sticks

Makes 14 corn sticks

"This used to be one of Mr. Charles's favorites," Mary says of her bacon-flavored corn sticks. "So I'd make them almost every day for dinner." She is speaking of Charles H. P. Duell, a descendant of the original Middleton of Middleton Place and the plantation's present owner. He represents the fourth generation of Middleton descendants for whom Mary has cooked; his children are the fifth.

¼ cup warm bacon drippings, plus
   enough to grease pans
1 cup yellow corn meal
½ cup boiling water
2 eggs, well beaten

1 cup milk
1 cup sifted all-purpose flour
2½ teaspoons baking powder
2 teaspoons sugar (optional)
½ teaspoon salt

1. Brush two cast-iron corn-stick pans well with bacon drippings, then set in a moderately hot oven (375°) to heat while you prepare the corn-stick batter.

2. Place corn meal in a mixing bowl, pour in the boiling water and ¼ cup bacon drippings and stir well until thick. Beat in the eggs, then the milk. Sift together the flour, baking powder, sugar (if you want a slightly sweeter corn stick) and salt, then mix in lightly but thoroughly.

3. Remove pans from oven and spoon in batter, filling each depression until level with the rim of the pan.

4. Bake corn sticks in a moderately hot oven (375°) for about 30 minutes or until nicely browned on top. Serve straight away with plenty of butter.

Benne Cookies

Makes about 6½ dozen

Benne, the Low Country people believe, brings good luck—to those who grow the plant in their gardens and to those who eat the seeds. Benne Cookies are one of the specialities for which Charleston cooks are famous. Here is Mary's favorite recipe, one she worked out by trial and error. For best results, do not attempt this recipe in rainy or humid weather, because the cookies will not be crisp.

¾ cup sesame (benne) seeds
½ cup butter, at room temperature
1 cup firmly packed light brown sugar

1 egg
1 cup sifted all-purpose flour
¼ teaspoon salt
1 teaspoon vanilla

1. Spread sesame seeds out in a pie pan and toast in a very slow oven (275°) until a pale amber color—about 10 minutes. Remove from oven and cool.

2. Cream butter until light and fluffy, add sugar and again cream until light. Beat in egg; stir in flour, sesame seeds, salt and vanilla.

3. Drop dough in *slightly* rounded ½-teaspoonfuls (use a ½-teaspoon measuring spoon) onto greased baking sheets, spacing cookies 2½ to 3 inches apart. Do not attempt to get more than a dozen cookies on each large baking sheet—they spread considerably as they bake.

4. Bake in a moderate oven (350°) about 10 to 12 minutes or until cookies are a rich caramel color. Remove from oven, let cookies cool on baking sheets about 1 minute, then loosen carefully with a pancake turner. If the cookies are too hot, they will crinkle up as you try to loosen them from the baking sheet; if they are too cool, they will shatter. The 1-minute cooling period seems about right. Spread cookies out one layer deep on heavy brown paper and cool thoroughly before eating. Store in airtight containers.

Mrs. A. G. ("Miss Susie") Rankin, Sr.
of
Marengo County, Alabama

EVERYONE calls her "Miss Susie," even her own children—four grown sons, each of whom has a house on the family's 3,000-acre Cedarcrest Farms, and a grown daughter who lives in Yazoo City, Mississippi.

Miss Susie was born Susan Legg in Walker County, Alabama, in the mid-1890s—not on a farm but in the little town of Jasper where her father was an undertaker. Her late husband, Amzi ("they tell me that's a biblical name, but I've never seen it in the Bible"), was a town boy, too—from Marion in Perry County, which lies just east of Marengo County.

So how did this pair of town kids become one of Alabama's—indeed, one of America's—biggest breeders of registered Jersey cows?

"Well," says Miss Susie in her soft southern voice, "Amzi always did like farming. And he loved Jersey cows."

The Rankins went to farming soon after they were married in 1919, not on a place of their own but on a rented farm near Demopolis in Marengo County. "We farmed for a rich man in Birmingham," says Miss Susie.

Yes, they had Jerseys then, too. "With us it was always Jerseys. And we did real well with them." So well that by 1940 they were able to buy their own spread, then only a 2,200-acre tract. Today Cedarcrest Farms is a family corporation with each of the four sons carrying his full load. "One tends to the planting," explains Miss Susie. "The other three tend to the cows." But Miss Susie is the one all four turn to for guidance and support.

Whenever the boys have a tough decision to make, they will say, "We've got to go up to the big house." That's the old homestead where

Miss Susie lives, a Greek Revival white frame house built in 1831 that sits foursquare atop a green knoll overlooking miles of rolling pasturelands. The high-ceilinged, twenty-foot-square kitchen is the conference room. The boys settle around the big round dining table to talk things out. Miss Susie listens, refills the coffee cups, sets out some fresh-baked cookies or gingerbread and, before long, decisions are made.

The kitchen is the heart of Miss Susie's house and always has been, because she loves to cook. "I can't remember when I first started cooking," she says. "But I know it was *a-way* back. I just can't keep dates in my head anymore. I blame it on my hip. I had my hip operated on a couple of years ago and I say they took out my memory.

"But I *do* know that I've liked to cook always. I had five brothers and they would eat anything that I would fix. So Mama said to me when I was a girl, 'I'll sew if you will cook.' That's how I got started."

Miss Susie liked cooking so well that she majored in home economics at Alabama College in Montevallo, then took a post as a Home Demonstration Agent in Perry County during World War I. "They were called Tomato Clubs then, instead of Home Demonstration Clubs, because we mostly taught farm women how to can tomatoes."

It was while she was a home agent that Miss Susie met Amzi Rankin. "I lived in Marion," she explains, "and Marion was Amzi's home town."

"It wasn't hard for me to become a farmer's wife," she says. "I *liked* it. Of course, I always had help—nurses for the babies. I had my children *real* fast—one every year, it looked like. When the oldest one was five years old, I had four. And they had the best time together you ever saw. I waited nine years for the next child, so someone called him my postscript. Well, I *sure* have enjoyed my postscript!" She laughs and her blue eyes twinkle.

Today Miss Susie is surrounded by family. There are eighteen grandchildren and four great-grandchildren, all of them near enough to gather for picnics in summer, for Thanksgiving and Christmas. "And weddings," Miss Susie adds, brushing a silvery strand from her brow. "We had fifty-two people over here for a wedding not long ago."

Whenever the grandchildren or great-grandchildren come, Miss Susie remembers to cook the things they like best, despite the fact that her hip troubles her and she can't get around as well as she used to.

The recipes she likes best are the old family favorites—recipes her mother and grandmother handed down. Miss Susie has gathered them altogether in a big scrapbook, so that her grandchildren and great-grandchildren can pass them along to *their* grandchildren and great-grandchildren.

Deviled Eggs in Whipped-Cream Sauce

Makes 4 to 6 servings

Many of Miss Susie's recipes rely upon lots of butter, buttermilk, milk, and cream because, as she says, "we always have lots of rich Jersey milk on hand." We think her recipe here for deviled eggs smothered in whipped cream sauce one of the best we've eaten.

Deviled Eggs:
8 large eggs, hard-cooked, peeled and halved lengthwise
½ cup Cooked Dressing (see page 130) or mayonnaise
2 teaspoons spicy brown prepared mustard
½ teaspoon salt
Pinch of black pepper
2 teaspoons minced sweet pickle

Whipped-Cream Sauce:
⅔ cup heavy cream, whipped to soft peaks
⅔ cup mayonnaise
½ teaspoon salt
1 teaspoon Worcestershire sauce
Pinch of black pepper
3 to 4 dashes liquid hot red-pepper seasoning

1.   Scoop the hard-cooked egg yolks into a bowl and mash well with a fork. Blend in Cooked Dressing or mayonnaise, mustard, salt, pepper, and pickle. Stuff egg whites with the mixture, then arrange eggs one layer deep in a 9-inch round shallow casserole or *au gratin* dish.

2.   *For sauce:* blend together all sauce ingredients. Pour sauce over deviled eggs, cover with foil or plastic food wrap and chill several hours before serving.

Ham and Rice Loaf with Currant-Mustard Glaze

Makes 6 to 8 servings

Here's an imaginative way to use up leftover cooked ham and rice. Both go into this moist, sweet-sour ham loaf of Miss Susie's.

1½ pounds ground cooked ham
1½ cups cooked, unseasoned rice (measure firmly packed)
1½ cups soft breadcrumbs (not too firm)
1 medium-sized yellow onion, peeled and minced

1½ teaspoons dry mustard
1½ cups milk
4 eggs, lightly beaten

Glaze:
½ cup currant jelly
⅓ cup prepared mustard

1. Using your hands, mix together all ingredients except those for the Glaze. Pat the mixture into a high, rounded loaf in a 13- × 9- × 2-inch pan.

2. Bake uncovered in a moderate oven (350°) for 50 minutes. Meanwhile, whisk together the glaze ingredients until smooth. Brush the glaze liberally over the partially baked ham loaf, then bake uncovered for 20 minutes longer or until loaf is a glistening brown.

3. Remove ham loaf from oven and let cool 20 minutes before slicing.

Chicken Salad

Makes 6 servings

This recipe calls for diced cooked chicken, but it can just as easily be made with turkey. In fact, this is an unusually good way to use up turkey leftovers. How finely the chicken (or turkey) is cut depends upon whether you want to serve the salad as a main course or as a sandwich spread. Miss Susie also makes a meat-salad sandwich spread precisely the same way, substituting leftover roast beef or pork or ham for the chicken.

4 cups diced cooked chicken (cut the chicken in about ½-inch cubes if the salad is to be used as a main course; mince it fine if it is to be a sandwich spread)
1 cup finely minced celery
1 small yellow onion, peeled and finely minced (optional)
1 tablespoon minced sweet pickle
1 cup (about) Cooked Dressing (recipe follows)
1¼ teaspoons salt (or to taste)
⅛ teaspoon pepper

1. Mix all ingredients together, adding more dressing if needed—the chicken salad should be fairly moist.

2. Cover and store in the refrigerator until ready to serve. Just before serving, toss the salad well; if it seems to have dried out somewhat, add a little more dressing.

Cooked Dressing

Makes about 1 pint

"Now this is a real old dressing recipe," says Miss Susie, "and a real good one, too. I use it for making chicken or meat salad."

4 eggs
6 tablespoons cider vinegar
1 cup milk
2 tablespoons melted butter
1 teaspoon salt

2 tablespoons sugar
1 teaspoon dry mustard
1 teaspoon celery seed
½ teaspoon paprika

1. Using a wooden spoon, mix together all ingredients in the top of a double boiler.
2. Set over simmering—*not* boiling—water and heat, stirring constantly, until thickened and smooth. This will take about 10 minutes. When properly done, the dressing will have the consistency of a thin mayonnaise.
3. Pour dressing into a 1-pint jar, cap tightly and store in the refrigerator until you are ready to use it. The dressing is delicious, as Miss Susie says, in chicken or meat salads. It's also good when used to make coleslaw or potato salad.

Grits Casserole

Makes 6 to 8 servings

The Southerner's passion for grits is something few non-Southerners can understand, especially when those grits arrive on the breakfast plate as a flavorless puddle of gruel. But there are, of course, other ways to prepare grits, as this superlative casserole of Miss Susie's proves. It's something like a gnocchi, gratinéed with butter and grated cheese.

1 quart milk
¼ pound butter or margarine
1 teaspoon salt
⅛ teaspoon pepper
1 cup white hominy grits (*not* the instant type)

½ cup melted butter or margarine
3 tablespoons grated Parmesan cheese
1 cup fairly finely grated sharp Cheddar cheese
A sprinkling of paprika

1. Place the milk, ¼ pound butter, salt, and pepper in a large heavy saucepan and bring to a boil over moderate heat; reduce heat slightly, then add grits very slowly, beating hard with a whisk. Reduce heat to lowest point and continue whisking mixture until it is quite thick and smooth. Cover pan and simmer mixture very slowly 20 minutes, stirring now and then if necessary to keep it from sticking. Remove from heat and beat hard with an electric mixer for 3 to 4 minutes.

2. Pour grits mixture into a well-buttered 9- × 9- × 2-inch baking dish and chill several hours until very firm. Cut block of grits into ½-inch slices (you'll find the slicing easier if you periodically dip your knife in tepid water); then divide each slice into four domino-shaped pieces of equal size.

3. Arrange the grits "dominos" in rows in a buttered 9- × 9- × 2-inch baking dish, standing them on end but at an angle, domino-style. The rows should fit snugly with no space between them. Drizzle with melted butter, sprinkle with grated Parmesan, then with grated Cheddar. Add a blush of paprika.

4. Bake uncovered in a moderate oven (350°) for about 45 minutes or until bubbling and lightly browned. Serve oven-hot as a potato substitute.

Yellow Squash Casserole

Makes 4 to 6 servings

This moist, pudding-like casserole of Miss Susie's may be made with either yellow summer squash or zucchini. She prefers the yellow squash.

6 medium-sized yellow squash, trimmed, scrubbed and cut in ½-inch cubes
1 large yellow onion, peeled and coarsely chopped
⅓ cup water
1 teaspoon salt
⅛ teaspoon pepper
3 tablespoons butter, at room temperature

2 eggs, beaten until frothy
¾ cup fairly coarse soda-cracker crumbs
1 teaspoon sugar
⅛ teaspoon ground nutmeg (optional)

Topping:
½ cup fairly fine soda-cracker crumbs
4 teaspoons melted butter

1. Place squash, onion, and water in a very large saucepan, set over moderately low heat, cover and simmer about 25 minutes or until

very tender. Drain well, then mash squash and onion with a potato masher. Mix in salt, pepper, and butter. Quickly beat in the eggs, then the coarse crumbs and sugar and, if you like, the nutmeg.

2.   Spoon squash mixture into a well-buttered 6-cup casserole. *For the topping:* combine crumbs and melted butter and scatter over surface of squash.

3.   Bake in a moderate oven (350°) for 45 to 50 minutes or until topping is nicely browned. Serve oven-hot.

Note:

This casserole holds well. If, toward the end of baking, you reduce the oven temperature to 300°, you can delay serving as long as 30 to 40 minutes. And the casserole seems even better because it has a more caramel-like flavor.

Black-Eyed Peas with Bacon, Onion and Green Pepper

Makes about 6 servings

Black-eyed peas are about as staple to the South as corn bread. Here's an easy, old-fashioned way to prepare them. Just put everything in a pot and let bubble away for about three-quarters of an hour. That's all there is to it.

1 pound dried black-eyed peas, washed and sorted
2 slices lean bacon, diced
1 quart cold water
1 medium-sized yellow onion, peeled and chopped

1 medium-sized green pepper, cored, seeded and chopped
1½ teaspoons salt (or to taste)
¼ teaspoon pepper

1.   Place all ingredients in a heavy, large pot, set over moderate heat and bring to a boil. Lower heat so that water simmers gently, cover and cook about 45 minutes for *al dente* black-eyed peas or 1 hour for softer peas. Taste for salt and add more if needed.

2.   Ladle into soup bowls and serve as a vegetable. Or lift portions from kettle with a slotted spoon and serve on dinner plates.

Fried Green Tomatoes

Makes 4 to 6 servings

For best results, use only stone-ground corn meal for this recipe. Its texture is floury, so that the meal will adhere more firmly to the tomatoes than will a more granular corn meal. Firm-ripe tomatoes may also be fried the same way—just make certain they are good and firm. Soft tomatoes will be reduced to mush.

4 medium-sized green tomatoes	1½ teaspoons salt
⅔ cup stone-ground corn meal	½ teaspoon pepper
(either yellow or white)	3 to 4 tablespoons bacon drippings

1.   Wash the tomatoes and pat dry on paper toweling. Do not peel or core. Slice each about ½ inch thick, then pat cut surface dry on paper toweling.

2.   In a pie plate combine the corn meal, salt and pepper. Dredge the tomato slices in the seasoned corn meal, making sure each slice is well coated.

3.   Fry the tomatoes quickly in sizzling-hot bacon drippings in a large heavy skillet over moderately high heat. You need only brown the slices on each side—1 to 1½ minutes per side should do it. Serve straight away.

Buttermilk Spoon Bread

Makes 6 servings

Spoon bread is actually a sort of corn-meal soufflé—certainly this one is because it comes from the oven puffy, moist and fragile. This recipe *must* be made with stone-ground meal (Miss Susie prefers the white meal), which has a floury texture. The more granular meal is too heavy to make a good spoon bread and the mixture will sink to the bottom of the baking dish. The way to eat Spoon Bread is straight from the oven, with a fat chunk of butter tucked into each portion so that it sends golden rivulets throughout. Made as it is with buttermilk and soda, this particular Spoon Bread has unusually fine texture and a slightly tart flavor.

2 cups stone-ground corn meal
1 tablespoon sugar
1 teaspoon salt
⅛ teaspoon pepper
2½ cups boiling water

¼ cup butter
2 eggs, separated
1 teaspoon baking soda
1½ cups buttermilk

1. Combine the corn meal, sugar, salt and pepper. In a large heat-proof bowl, combine the boiling water and butter. As soon as the butter is melted, gradually add the corn-meal mixture, beating all the while until no lumps remain. A whisk is the best implement to use. Cover and let cool to room temperature.

2. Beat in the egg yolks. Stir the baking soda into the buttermilk and when it begins to froth a bit, mix into the corn-meal mixture.

3. Whip the egg whites to soft peaks, then fold in lightly but thoroughly. Spoon batter into a buttered 2½-quart soufflé dish, then bake in a moderately hot oven (375°) about 45 to 50 minutes or until puffed and lightly browned. Rush to the table and serve.

Jeff Davis Pie

Makes one 9-inch single-crust pie

This has to be the richest pie in all creation. There's nothing here to adulterate the rich, honest flavor of butter, sugar, eggs and cream—not even vanilla. Jeff Davis Pie is said to have been invented about the time of the Civil War by a talented Southern plantation cook, who when pressed for the name of the superlative pie, answered simply, "Why, I calls it Jeff Davis Pie" (because she was purported to be an admirer of Jefferson Davis).

1¾ cups sugar
1 tablespoon flour
½ cup butter, softened to room temperature
1 cup heavy cream

2 whole eggs
4 eggs, separated
Pinch of salt
1 9-inch baked pie shell (use your favorite piecrust recipe)

1. In the top of a double boiler, blend together 1¼ cups of the sugar, flour and butter. Mix in the cream, 2 whole eggs and 4 egg yolks.

2. Set over simmering—*not* boiling—water and cook and stir about 10 to 12 minutes or until thickened and smooth—about the consistency of a stirred custard. Remove from heat.

3. Beat the 4 egg whites and the remaining ½ cup sugar hard for about 5 minutes until thick and silvery—because of the high proportion of sugar, the egg whites will not froth up into a meringue.

4. Slowly fold egg whites into the custard mixture until no streaks of white or yellow remain.

5. Pour into the baked pie shell and bake in a moderately slow oven (325°) about 35 minutes or until puffed and a rich caramel brown on top. Cool pie to room temperature, then chill in the refrigerator about an hour or until filling is firm. Cut into small wedges and serve.

Alabama Buttermilk Pie

Makes one 9-inch single-crust pie

This tart, smooth, ivory-hued pie dates to the days when women churned their own butter and as a result had plenty of buttermilk on hand. The pie tastes somewhat of lemon although there is no lemon in it.

2 large eggs
1⅓ cups sugar
1 tablespoon flour
1⅓ cups buttermilk
⅓ cup melted butter

1 teaspoon vanilla
Pinch of salt
1 9-inch unbaked pie shell (use your favorite recipe)

1. With a wooden spoon, mix together the eggs, sugar and flour. Mix in the buttermilk, then blend in the butter thoroughly. Stir in vanilla and salt.

2. Pour filling into the unbaked pie shell and bake in a moderate oven (350°) for 10 minutes. Reduce heat to low (300°) and continue baking the pie for 40 to 45 minutes or until it is puffy and golden (but not brown). If you nudge the pie pan, the filling should quiver slightly in the center.

3. Remove pie from oven and cool to room temperature before serving. The filling will fall somewhat, but that is as it should be.

Miss Susie's Light Gingerbread
with Orange Sauce

Makes one 9- × 9- × 2-inch loaf

This particular recipe of Miss Susie's is so good that the Marengo County Extension Service mimeographed copies to share with others. The gingerbread is light in color and texture and keeps well for about a week although it's unlikely that you'll have any left after a day or two.

½ cup (1 stick) butter, at room temperature
½ cup sugar
2 eggs
1 teaspoon baking soda
½ cup molasses
1 teaspoon ground ginger

1 teaspoon ground cinnamon
¼ teaspoon salt
1½ cups sifted all-purpose flour
½ cup cold water

Topping:
1 recipe Orange Sauce (recipe follows)

    1.   Cream butter and sugar until fluffy-light; beat in the eggs.

    2.   Stir soda into molasses and when it foams and lightens, stir into the creamed mixture.

    3.   Sift together the ginger, cinnamon, salt and flour, then add to the creamed mixture alternately with the cold water, beginning and ending with the dry ingredients; stir just enough to blend.

    4.   Pour batter into a well-greased 9- × 9- × 2-inch baking pan and bake in a moderately slow oven (325°) for 35 minutes or until gingerbread is springy to the touch and begins to pull from sides of pan. Cool about 10 minutes before cutting.

    5.   Cut into large squares and top with hot Orange Sauce.

Orange Sauce

Makes about 1½ cups

Store any leftover sauce in the refrigerator. Warm slowly in the top of a double boiler before serving, adding, if necessary, 1 to 2 tablespoons hot water to thin the sauce.

½ cup (1 stick) butter, at room temperature
1 cup sugar
½ cup orange juice (about 1 large orange)

Finely grated rind of 1 large orange
1 egg, well beaten
1 tablespoon hot water

1.   Place butter and sugar in the top of a double boiler, set over simmering water and cook, stirring, until butter melts and sugar dissolves.

2.   Lift double-boiler top to a counter, and quickly whisk in orange juice, rind and beaten egg. Set once again over double-boiler bottom —the water should be simmering, *not* boiling—and heat, stirring constantly, until thickened and smooth, about 5 minutes.

3.   Just before serving, stir in the 1 tablespoon hot water. Use as a sauce for Miss Susie's Light Gingerbread (recipe precedes).

Brown-Sugar Poundcake with Walnut Glaze

Makes one 10-inch tube cake

Most poundcakes have no frosting. This one is drizzled with a buttery walnut glaze, which gives the cake a nice finish. As for the cake batter, Miss Susie says, "Lick the pan yourself!"

1 cup butter, softened to room temperature
½ cup vegetable shortening
1 pound light brown sugar (press out all lumps)
1 cup granulated sugar
5 eggs
3 cups sifted all-purpose flour
1 teaspoon baking powder
½ teaspoon salt
1 cup milk
1 teaspoon vanilla

1 cup finely minced walnuts (black walnuts are especially good)

Walnut Glaze:
1 cup confectioners (10X) sugar
2 tablespoons butter, at room temperature
6 tablespoons light cream, at room temperature
½ teaspoon vanilla
½ cup *very* finely minced walnuts (again, black walnuts are best)

1.   Cream the butter and shortening hard until very fluffy; add the brown sugar gradually, creaming all the while until light, then add the granulated sugar the same way. Beat the eggs in, one at a time.

2.   Sift the flour with the baking powder and salt. Combine the milk and vanilla. Add the sifted dry ingredients to the mixture alter-

nately with the milk, beginning and ending with the dry ingredients and mixing only enough to blend. Fold in the walnuts.

3.   Pour batter into a well-greased-and-floured 10-inch tube pan and bake in a moderate oven (350°) for about 1 hour and 15 minutes or until cake pulls from sides of pan and when it is pressed lightly with a finger, the imprint vanishes slowly.

4.   Remove cake from oven and cool upright in its pan on a wire rack for 15 minutes. Loosen cake from sides of pan and around central tube with a thin-bladed spatula, then invert pan on a large round plate and turn cake out.

5.   *For the walnut glaze:* Stir together all glaze ingredients, then spoon over still-warm cake. Scoop up any glaze that "puddles" on the cake plate, and reapply it to the sides of the cake for a thicker glaze. Let glaze harden before cutting the cake.

Mama's Teacakes

Makes about 8 dozen cookies (including re-rolls)

"Any time I want to do something nice for a child," Miss Susie says, "I'll bake Mama's Teacakes. I've cut the recipe down for people who want to make things quick. The old recipe calls for 7 cups of flour. Now, that is just a *world* of work to mix in. I tried the recipe again recently and found that you can mix the dough with your mixer, using about 5½ cups of flour. That's a-plenty. I put the dough in a bowl and set it in the refrigerator. Then whenever I want teacakes, I just get me a gob of dough and roll it out."

1 cup butter, at room temperature	2 eggs
2 cups sugar	1 teaspoon baking soda dissolved
3 teaspoons ground nutmeg	in ½ cup buttermilk
1 teaspoon vanilla	5½ cups sifted all-purpose flour

1.   Cream together the butter, sugar, nutmeg and vanilla until light and fluffy. Add eggs and mix just until blended. Stir in soda-buttermilk mixture, then, with mixer set at low speed, beat the flour in, a cup at a time.

2.   Divide dough in four equal parts, flatten each into a large round on a sheet of heavy-duty foil, then wrap and chill several hours until firm enough to roll. Or freeze the dough for later use.

3. Roll dough out, ¼ at a time on a lightly floured pastry cloth, making it about as thin as piecrust. Cut with a 2¾- to 3-inch round cutter. Bake cookies on lightly greased baking sheets in a moderately hot oven (375°) for 8 to 10 minutes or until pale tan.

4. Remove cookies from oven and transfer while warm to wire racks to cool.

Mrs. James ("Miss Tootie") Guirard
of
St. Martin Parish, Louisiana

*At a Cajun picnic, the cook
is the most highly regarded person—
the* cher chérie—*in the crowd.*

"WHEN did I learn to cook?" The question puzzles Mrs. James Guirard of St. Martinville, Louisiana—but only for a second. *"Chère,"* she answers (beginning with the French term of endearment, then switching easily to English), "Cajuns are *born* knowing how to cook!"

Mrs. Guirard (born Leona Martin but called "Tootie" ever since she was a baby) is Cajun and proud of it. She is a descendant of Claude Martin, one of the thousands of French living in Acadia (now Nova Scotia) who were given an ultimatum by the British some 220 years ago: Swear allegiance to the British Crown or be deported. The Acadians chose deportation.

So they were herded aboard ships only to be cast ashore at ports up and down the Atlantic coast. Families were separated, as were friends and lovers (including the star-crossed couple whose story was immortalized by Longfellow in *Evangeline*). The French-speaking Acadians (today more often called "Cajuns") were miserable in the alien land and those who could do so made their way to the French colony of Louisiana, not to New Orleans but to the bayous and swamps 140 miles west of it.

Claude Martin arrived on the banks of Bayou Teche in 1765 and stayed. Today there are Martins all over St. Martin Parish. At a recent reunion "with just the Martin side of the family," says Miss Tootie, "we were sixty-four."

Miss Tootie's mother, also Cajun with a dab of Pennsylvania Dutch mixed in, was an excellent cook. She was, in fact, one of the first home economics students at the University of Southern Louisiana (USL) in Lafayette and "taught kindergarten to just about everybody in the Parish." Miss Tootie now lives with her husband, Jim, in what she calls "a funny little house" on the fringe of the Atchafalaya Swamp some six or seven miles out of St. Martinville. The house began as a one-room cabin, built by Miss Tootie's father, then grew "like Topsy" over the years. "It's a happy home," she says, "but I'm telling you, the floors and the walls slant—there's not one corner that's square."

The house stands on the old family plantation, divided up after her father's death among Miss Tootie, her two brothers and one sister. It is a working plantation with cane and rice fields, a sawmill, two crawfish farms and some thirty head of Brangus cattle grazing on the levee. (The Brangus, a cross between Angus and Brahman, provide the Guirards with all the meat they can eat.)

Miss Tootie and Jim moved to the house by the levee from St. Martinville not long after they were married (in the late 1930s). They had known one another all their lives. Jim's family, although French, is not Cajun; his ancestors immigrated to Louisiana directly from France. "I fell in love with Jim when I was seventeen," says Miss Tootie. "We paired off one day at a picnic on Bayou Teche, rode in a pirogue practically all day and I decided, 'By golly, this is who I am going to marry.'"

And marry Jim she did. But not until she was twenty-four (in the interim, Miss Tootie attended USL, then taught elementary school in nearby Catahoula Lake). "It was *very* elementary," she remembers. "Everybody went barefoot and on rainy days we had no lessons. We acted out fairy stories and made pulled candy and pralines on the little wood stove. Nobody *ever* missed school—it was too much fun."

When Miss Tootie and Jim first went to housekeeping, it was in a little house just behind the big white house in St. Martinville where she grew up. Before long, however, they moved out to the little cabin by the swamp, put a few cows up on the levee and loved the country life so much they decided to stay. It was here that their two sons grew up. "We were so isolated in those days that neither one of our boys spoke English until he went to grammar school. We spoke French amongst ourselves, so that is what they learned first."

Both boys are married and on their own now. But every summer they come home to the bayou, bringing their wives and six children. "And do we have fun!" says Miss Tootie.

Fun in Acadiana (as southwestern Louisiana is called) is synonymous with good food. And of that there is always plenty. "It seems like the children spend the whole summer cutting up okra," says Miss Tootie. "We freeze fifty-two bags of it every year so that we can have gumbo once a week." She also preserves figs and kumquats, which grow on the farm. And she ferments sweet cherries into Cherry Bounce, a sweet liqueur with considerable kick. In summer there are plenty of garden-fresh tomatoes to enjoy, and sweet corn, cucumbers and peppers. "We grow five kinds of peppers," she continues. "Both the sweet and the hot. We put peppers in just about everything except ice cream. Onions, celery, and parsley, too.

"Cajuns," she points out, "don't ever follow written recipes. It's all in our heads. We just put in a pinch of this and a fistful of that. We're just *born* knowing how. And, of course, we learn by watching and helping our mothers. Cajun mothers are easy-going and don't mind if their children come in and mess up the kitchen. Even my little granddaughter who is ten makes delicious cake and pralines. And my brother, Dr. Murphy Martin, is the best cake baker in the family."

What are her own specialties? "Well, gumbo, of course. And crawfish. You know, crawfish and Cajuns are a lot alike. We're both getting to be stylish.

"Just look at the thousands of people who come to the Acadian House Museum in St. Martinville." (Miss Tootie was for years curator of that museum, a two-story early Cajun house located in the Longfellow Evangeline State Park.) "So many of them come from France and from French-speaking Canada because they want to see how the Cajuns are doing. We speak to them in French—we're completely bilingual at the museum—but we've been stuck back in the swamps so long that our French is more like what would have been spoken in France two hundred years ago."

Cajun recipes reflect the French heritage; indeed the titles of many *are* French: *Pain Perdu* ("Lost Bread," which is nothing more than stale bread imaginatively rejuvenated by dunking in beaten egg and frying), *Chicken à la Gros Oignon* (chicken smothered with a great big sweet onion), *grattons* (crackling), *boudin* (homemade link sausage), *café au lait* ("coffee-milk," of which, according to Miss Tootie, every Cajun has two cups before getting out of bed in the morning).

Roux is a French word, too. It means "russet," which is exactly the color a properly cooked roux (blend of fat and flour) should be. "Just about everything Cajun begins with a roux," says Miss Tootie. "All the different kinds of gumbo. Rice dressing, too. On a rainy day when I'm not doing anything else, I'll make a whole pot of roux. Then I'll put it in little containers and stick it in the deep-freeze. That way I'm done with the whole business and can have some fun.

"Now you talk about something that's fun," she continues. "That's Pie Day. We hold it every Good Friday. Back in the old days, Cajuns were so isolated they didn't have their own priests. They knew they were supposed to do something on Good Friday—fast or feast—but they didn't know which, so they decided to do both. So they'd have coffee-milk, then they'd fast in the morning. But all the while they'd be busy making pies—crawfish pies, tuna pies, chicken pies, mince pies, sweet dough pies, all kinds of pies. Then everyone would get together and eat nothing but pie.

"Last year the whole family came out here for Pie Day, then we got in our boats and rode all the way down the bayou to New Iberia. We got to my cousin's house about three in the afternoon. And, of course, we kept right on eating after we got there. It was *such* fun, *chère!*

"You simply *cannot* separate a Cajun from fun," says Miss Tootie.

Or, it would seem, from good food either.

Shrimp (or Crawfish) Gumbo

Makes 6 to 8 servings

"There are all kinds of gumbo," explains Miss Tootie. "Chicken and sausage gumbo, gumbo *z'herbes* (a green gumbo made with spinach and turnip greens), shrimp or crawfish gumbo. Like most Cajuns, she will serve gumbo once a week "and sometimes twice. I love gumbo thickened with okra" (instead of with filé powder). "But it must be thickened with *cooked* okra. If you just cut it up and slip it in at the end as they so often do in New Orleans, it gets slimy. Don't ever cook okra in an iron pot," she cautions, "or it will turn black." Here, then, is a shrimp or crawfish gumbo made the Cajun way. It begins with a roux, and you must work the roux very slowly in a very heavy pot for at least half an hour, until it turns a rich rusty brown. "Any time I see a recipe that says to cook the roux five minutes," says Miss Tootie, "I know it's no good."

Okra Thickening:
4 tablespoons lard (hog lard, not vegetable shortening)
1 pound fresh okra, washed, stemmed and sliced tissue thin
1 can (8 ounces) tomato sauce

Roux:
3 tablespoons lard (again hog lard)
5 tablespoons all-purpose flour (don't use the instant-type flour—it won't work; and don't use self-rising flour, either)

Gumbo:
2 medium-sized yellow onions, peeled and chopped fine
1 large sweet green pepper, cored, seeded and chopped fine
3 large celery stalks, finely diced
1 clove garlic, peeled and crushed
2½ quarts cold water
2 teaspoons salt (or more to taste)
½ teaspoon cayenne pepper (¼ teaspoon if you don't like things "hot")
Pinch of black pepper
1½ pounds medium-sized raw shrimp in the shell (or crawfish, if available)
1 gallon boiling water mixed with 1 tablespoon salt
¼ cup thinly sliced scallion tops (green part only)
3 tablespoons minced parsley (preferably the flat-leafed Italian parsley, which is more flavorsome)

1. *Begin the okra thickening first:* it must cook several hours and be ready to add to the gumbo when the gumbo is ready for it. Pick a very heavy saucepan—enameled cast-iron is particularly good because it holds and distributes the heat evenly. Melt the lard over moderately high heat, add the okra and sauté 10 to 12 minutes until golden, not brown. Okra is pesky to work with because it is so sticky, but keep at it, scraping recalcitrant slices from the spoon and sides of the pan down into the lard. Lower heat and continue sautéing okra, uncovered, very slowly for ½ hour. Add tomato sauce and cook uncovered for about 2 hours, stirring now and then, until, as Miss Tootie says, "it is very dry and just comes together in one big ball." At the end pour off any fat that has oozed out.

2. *While okra cooks, prepare the roux:* Melt lard in a very large heavy kettle over fairly high heat, blend in flour, reduce heat and keep stirring and working the roux for ½ hour. You don't have to stir non-stop, but "don't take your eyes off the pot," cautions Miss Tootie. The roux should mellow and brown slowly, so raise and lower the heat as needed. It will first turn a honey color, then butterscotch, and finally a rich rust-brown. And it should have a nice sheen, or "halo," as Miss Tootie describes it.

3. Mix onions, green pepper, celery and garlic into the roux, turn the heat off and as soon as they stop sizzling, clap the lid on the kettle and "just leave them alone for 15 minutes."

4. Blend 1 quart of the cold water into the roux, turn heat under kettle to moderate and heat and stir until thickened—about 3 minutes. Add the remaining 1½ quarts cold water and boil gently, uncovered, until reduced by about one-half. "You want the roux-water to cook

down, down, down," says Miss Tootie. This will take 30 to 40 minutes.

5.   Mix in the reserved okra thickening, the salt, cayenne and black peppers and simmer uncovered over low heat for 1 hour, stirring occasionally.

6.   Meanwhile, boil the shrimp or crawfish in their shells for 1 minute exactly in the boiling salted water. Drain, rinse under cool water, then shell and devein. Halve any shrimp or crawfish that are large.

7.   Add to the gumbo and cook, uncovered, for 10 minutes. "Don't ever cover a pot that's got shrimp in it—crawfish, either," warns Miss Tootie, "or they will fall apart." Add the scallion tops and simmer uncovered for 5 minutes, stir in the parsley and simmer uncovered 5 to 10 minutes longer. Keep the heat low or the shrimp will toughen. Taste the gumbo and add more salt, if needed.

8.   To serve, spoon hot cooked rice into big soup bowls, then ladle the gumbo on top. "If you're serving the gumbo to company," advises Miss Tootie, "make it up the day before, cool to room temperature, then cover and refrigerate. Reheat just before serving and the gumbo will be even better than if made and served the same day."

Chicken à la Gros Oignon

Makes 4 servings

"I guess you'd call this smothered chicken," says Miss Tootie, "because it's nothing more than chicken smothered with a great big sweet onion" (*gros oignon*). It is an easy recipe to make and an economical one, too.

1 3- to 3½-pound broiler-fryer, disjointed	2 tablespoons lard (hog lard)
	¼ cup cold water
¾ teaspoon salt	1 very large Spanish onion, peeled
⅛ teaspoon black pepper	and cut in slim wedges

1.   Rub chicken pieces well on both sides with salt and pepper, then let stand at room temperature for ½ hour.

2.   Heat the lard in a very large heavy skillet over high heat until ripples show on the surface, then add all pieces of chicken (except giblets and neck) and brown well on both sides—12 to 15 minutes. Lower the heat if chicken browns too fast or lard begins to smoke. When chicken is a nice topaz brown, drain off excess drippings. Add heart and liver (save neck and gizzard for soup or stock).

3. Pour in water (it will sputter, so stand back), cover skillet snugly, reduce heat to moderately low and cook 35 minutes. Uncover, push chicken well to one side of skillet, increase heat slightly and let accumulated drippings cook down until they just cover bottom of skillet. Add onion and stir-fry about 10 minutes until golden and touched here and there with brown. Rearrange chicken pieces so that they're well distributed among the onion pieces and cook uncovered about 5 minutes longer or until a fork will pierce the chicken easily. Serve with hot cooked rice.

Miss Tootie's Bacon-Studded Roast Turkey with Green-Pepper Gravy

Makes about 10 servings

"To me," says Miss Tootie, "turkey is as tasteless as a chip. I don't cook it at all unless I do it this way. When I tell people that I poke holes all over the outside of the turkey and tuck in little pieces of bacon, they are horrified. 'What!' they say. "All the juices will run out!" "Certainly not!" is Miss Tootie's reply. She does not stuff the turkey either—"except," she explains, "with a few strips of bacon." But she does make up a big pot of Rice Dressing (recipe follows) to serve on the side. As for basting, she uses the pan drippings *only*. "If we have wine," she says, "we drink it."

1 small (10- to 12-pound) turkey (if frozen, thaw completely)
1 tablespoon salt
1 large bay leaf, crumbled very fine
½ teaspoon black pepper
2 small yellow onions, peeled and minced fine
½ medium-sized sweet green pepper, cored, seeded and minced fine
1 large celery stalk, finely diced
1 clove garlic, peeled and crushed

2 teaspoons bacon drippings
1 pound sliced *lean* bacon

Green-Pepper Gravy:
Turkey pan drippings
1 medium-sized yellow onion, peeled and minced fine
½ medium-sized sweet green pepper, cored, seeded and minced fine
1 large celery stalk, finely diced
2½ cups cold water
Salt and pepper to taste (if needed)

1. Freeze turkey giblets and neck to use in making soup or stock. Rub both the body and neck cavities of the turkey well with a mixture of salt, crumbled bay leaf and black pepper; reserve remaining seasoned salt. With a sharp knife, make deep ½- to 1-inch-long slits on the fleshiest parts of the turkey back, cutting right down to the bone

(about 2 slits on each side of the back), then make 3 cuts on each breast and 1 on each drumstick, again in the fleshiest parts, cutting all the way to the bone. Enlarge each hole by poking an index finger in and working round and round, then rub the inside of each hole with the remaining seasoned salt.

2. Stir-fry the onions, green pepper, celery and garlic in the bacon drippings 3 to 5 minutes, just until no longer crisp and raw. Cool until easy to handle, then stuff about 1 teaspoon (heaping) of the mixture into each hole, packing it in firmly. Then stuff into each hole ½ strip of bacon, rolled up, again packing in firmly. Finally, tuck 1 bacon strip into the neck cavity and 3 strips into the body cavity. Do not lace up the openings, but do fold the neck skin flat against the back and truss the turkey if it is not a "tucked turkey" (with the legs thrust underneath a flap of tail skin).

3. Place the turkey breast-side up in a shallow roasting pan (Miss Tootie does not use a rack) and drape bacon strips, overlapping, across the breast, covering it completely. Roast the turkey, uncovered, in a moderate oven (325°) about 20 minutes per pound, basting with pan drippings about every ½ hour, until you can move a drumstick easily in its socket. About 45 minutes before the turkey is done, remove the bacon strips from the breast (reserve for soup or scrambled eggs) so that the turkey will brown (raise oven temperature to about 350° these last 45 minutes if needed to brown the turkey nicely).

4. When the turkey is done, remove from pan, place on a hot platter, cover loosely with foil and keep warm while making the gravy.

5. *To make gravy:* pour all pan drippings into a large, heavy skillet (don't forget to scrape up the browned bits in the bottom of the roasting pan), add the onion, green pepper and celery and heat and stir about 5 minutes over fairly high heat until vegetables are limp and golden brown. Add the water and boil vigorously, uncovered, about 5 minutes until slightly reduced. Taste for salt and pepper, and add if needed. Pass the gravy at the table so that everyone may spoon some over the turkey.

Rice Dressing

Makes about 8 servings

Rice dressing is made much like jambalaya; in fact, it *becomes* jambalaya if you increase the amount of meat to about 1 pound (or in the case of leftovers, to 2 to 2½ cups). Jambalaya is of course a main dish, and an economical one. Miss Tootie says it doesn't much matter what kind of meat you use for making rice dressing or jambalaya. It can be leftover cooked chicken, turkey or ham, it can be minced giblets, it can be hamburger or sausage. Or you can use a mixture of meats. The method is the same regardless of the meat used. This recipe makes a whopping potful, but if you like rice dressing as much as Cajuns do, it will disappear fast. You can reheat any leftovers by forking up well, placing in a casserole, dotting well with butter, then cooking, covered, for 20 to 30 minutes in a moderate (350°) oven.

Roux Mixture:

1 tablespoons lard (hog lard)
3 tablespoons all-purpose flour (don't use the instant-type flour)
1 large yellow onion, peeled and minced (1 cup)
1 small sweet green pepper, cored, seeded and minced
1 large celery stalk, finely diced
6 cups cold water
¼ pound ground chuck (ir if you prefer, sausage meat or diced smoked ham or 1 cup diced cooked chicken, turkey or giblets)
1 teaspoon lard (for browning meat)
½ cup chopped pimiento-stuffed green olives

Rice Mixture:

5 cups cold water
½ teaspoon onion salt
½ teaspoon garlic salt
½ teaspoon celery salt
¼ teaspoon cayenne pepper
⅛ teaspoon black pepper
1 bouillon cube (beef or chicken, depending upon whether you are making the dressing with meat or fowl)
2½ cups uncooked converted rice
3 tablespoons very thinly sliced scallion tops (green part only)
2 tablespoons minced parsley
3 tablespoons butter

1. Make a roux by heating and stirring the 1 tablespoon lard and the flour together over low heat in a very large heavy kettle about 30 minutes, until roux is a rich rust-brown (for detailed directions, see Shrimp Gumbo, page 143).

2. Stir the onion, green pepper and celery into the roux and when they stop sizzling, turn heat off, cover and let stand 15 minutes. Mix in 2 cups of the cold water, turn heat to moderate and cook and stir until thickened, about 3 minutes. Add the remaining 4 cups cold water, reduce heat to low and let simmer uncovered, stirring now and then, until mixture has cooked down by three-fourths, is thick and brown and about the consistency of gravy. This will take 3 to 4 hours of slow simmering, but the kettle does not have to be watched every second. Check it every hour or so and give it a good stir. You should have, in the end, about 1½ cups of roux mixture.

3. Meanwhile, brown the ground chuck in the 1 teaspoon lard and set aside. (If you are using sausage meat, you will not need to add extra fat, but you will need to drain the browned sausage of excess drippings.)

4. When roux mixture is nice and thick, stir in browned meat and chopped olives and set aside.

5. *For the rice mixture:* Place water in a large heavy saucepan, add flavored salts, cayenne and black peppers and bouillon cube and bring to a rolling boil. When bouillon cube has dissolved, stir in the rice and let boil vigorously, uncovered, for 3 to 4 minutes. Lower heat so that liquid bubbles gently, add scallion tops and continue cooking uncovered until rice is tender and all liquid absorbed—about 15 to 20 minutes. The rice will not be fluffy and soft but will be *al dente,* somewhat firm with every grain distinct.

6. Fork parsley and butter into rice, and as soon as the butter melts, combine the rice and roux mixtures and toss lightly but thoroughly. Let mellow 2 to 3 minutes over low heat, then serve.

Red Beans and Rice

Makes 6 to 8 servings

"You don't fool with time on Mardi Gras," says Miss Tootie. "You just stick everything together in one big pot and the easier the better. You're too busy having a good time to worry about cooking, but at the same time you do need something substantial to eat." That's why red beans and rice are traditional Mardi Gras foods. The red beans cook most of the day and barely need to be stirred. And the rice, of course, can be boiled at the last minute.

1 pound dried red kidney beans, washed and sorted
2 quarts cold water
2 medium-sized yellow onions, peeled and chopped (1 cup)
1 medium-sized sweet green pepper, cored, seeded and chopped
2 celery stalks, finely diced
¼ pound smoked ham, finely minced
2 teaspoons salt (or more to taste)
½ teaspoon cayenne pepper (reduce to ¼ teaspoon if you are sensitive to "hot" food)

⅛ teaspoon black pepper
3 tablespoons very thinly sliced scallion tops (green part only)
3 tablespoons minced parsley (preferably the flat-leafed Italian parsley)
2½ cups converted rice, cooked by package directions (for extra flavor, Miss Tootie will plop a fat lump of butter—about 2 tablespoons—down in the rice, let it melt, then fork the rice up a few times to mix)

1. Place beans in a very large heavy kettle, add water, cover and soak overnight.

2.   Next day, add onions, green pepper, celery, ham, salt, cayenne and black peppers to the beans and their soaking water, bring to a boil over high heat, reduce heat so that liquid ripples gently, cover and simmer 2½ hours. Uncover, stir well, turn heat to lowest point and cook uncovered about 3 hours longer, stirring now and then, until beans are very soft and mixture is about the consistency of chili.

3.   Stir in scallion tops and cook uncovered 10 minutes, then mix in parsley and cook for 10 minutes more.

4.   Dish up the red beans and rice separately and put out big bowls so that people can help themselves to as much rice as they want, then ladle the red beans on top.

Mardi Gras Potato Salad

Makes 8 to 10 servings

If Red Beans and Rice are not being served for Mardi Gras, you're sure to have cold sliced ham and potato salad, both of which can be prepared the day before so as not to interfere with the merrymaking. "I like to add olive salad [chopped pimiento-stuffed green olives] to my salad because I think pimiento helps the taste of potato salad," Miss Tootie says. This potato salad keeps well for 2 to 3 days in the refrigerator; be sure to cover it snugly so that it does not absorb other refrigerator odors.

10 medium-to-large Irish potatoes, peeled and quartered (the waxy Maine or Eastern potatoes are best because they hold their shape)
6 cups water
1 celery top, or ½ teaspoon celery salt
1 small yellow onion, peeled, or ½ teaspoon onion salt
1 clove garlic, peeled, or ½ teaspoon garlic salt
1½ teaspoons salt (use *only* if using the celery top, whole onion and garlic instead of the flavored salts)
½ medium-sized sweet green pepper, cored, seeded and minced fine

⅓ cup very thinly sliced scallion tops (green part only)
2 tablespoons minced parsley
½ cup chopped pimiento-stuffed green olives
6 hard-cooked eggs
¼ cup cider vinegar
3 tablespoons water
2 teaspoons sugar
1 tablespoon olive oil
1 tablespoon prepared mustard (preferably the spicy brown mustard)
1 teaspoon onion salt
½ teaspoon garlic salt
½ teaspoon celery salt
⅛ teaspoon black pepper
1 pint mayonnaise

1. Put the potatoes in the water in a covered large saucepan together with the celery top, onion and garlic clove and 1½ teaspoons salt (or, if you prefer, the celery, onion and garlic salts; with no additional salt). Boil until potatoes are firm-tender (about 20 minutes). When potatoes are done, drain well (save cooking water, if you like, for making soup; also the celery top, onion and garlic). Potatoes should be very dry, so if they seem moist, shake pan over low heat a few seconds to drive off excess moisture. Cool potatoes to room temperature, then cut in ½- to ¾-inch cubes.

2. Place potatoes, green pepper, scallion tops, parsley and olives in a very large bowl and set aside.

3. Peel the eggs, halve, scoop out yolks and press through a fine sieve; reserve. Mince the egg whites very fine and reserve also.

4. In a medium-sized mixing bowl, blend vinegar with water, sugar, olive oil, mustard, flavored salts and pepper. Blend in mayonnaise until creamy, then stir in sieved egg yolks and minced egg whites.

5. Pour dressing over potato mixture and toss well to mix. Taste for salt and pepper and add more, if needed. Mixture will seem soft at this point but will firm up in the refrigerator. Cover and chill several hours before serving.

Green Beans with Pecans

Makes 4 to 6 servings

Green beans and almonds are a combination known to most of us. But green beans and pecans? Even better! Sugar may seem an odd seasoning but, according to Miss Tootie, "just a little dab of sugar will help most any vegetable."

2 pounds green beans, washed and tipped	¼ cup (½ stick) butter
	½ teaspoon sugar
2 cups water	1 teaspoon salt
1 cup fairly finely chopped pecans	⅛ teaspoon black pepper

1. Cook the beans, covered, in the water about 15 minutes or until just crisp-tender (or a few minutes longer until done the way you like them).

2. Meanwhile, brown the pecans lightly in the butter 3 to 4 minutes over low heat—and reserve.

3.   When beans are done, drain well, return pan to heat and shake gently to drive off excess moisture. Add browned pecans, sugar, salt and pepper and toss gently to mix. Let mellow over low heat 2 to 3 minutes before serving.

Pain Perdu ("Lost Bread")

Makes 4 to 6 servings

This recipe gets its name from the fact that it's made with stale bread, bread that might otherwise be pitched out. It is a Cajun breakfast favorite, dusted with confectioners sugar and smothered with pure cane syrup (a dark sugar syrup that tastes somewhat like molasses). Use maple syrup, if you prefer. Traditional accompaniments are browned link sausages and, of course, *café au lait.*

1 large, stale but not hard loaf of French Bread (it should measure about 20 inches in length and 4 inches in diameter)
4 large eggs, beaten lightly
½ cup sugar
Rind of 1 lemon, very finely grated

¼ teaspoon vanilla
Cooking oil for deep fat frying (about 1 quart)
Confectioners (10X) sugar for dusting
Nutmeg (optional)

1.   Slice the bread 1 inch thick (don't use the heels). You should have about 14 slices.
2.   Beat eggs, sugar, lemon rind and vanilla until very thick and lemony. Dip slices of bread into egg mixture, 3 to 4 at a time, letting them soak in the mixture for 15 seconds on each side. Transfer to a waxed-paper-lined tray or baking sheet and let stand at room temperature ½ hour or until egg has soaked well into the bread. Or better, cover loosely with waxed paper and refrigerate 2 to 3 hours.
3.   Heat oil in a large deep skillet or broad-bottomed deep-fat fryer to 380° on a deep-fat thermometer. Fry the bread, about 3 slices at a time, until a nice golden brown on each side. This will take about 1 to 2 minutes per side. Keep the oil temperature as nearly at 380° as possible by raising and lowering burner heat as needed.
4.   Set browned slices on a paper-towel-lined baking sheet to drain; place uncovered in a very slow oven (250°) to keep warm while you fry the remainder (leave oven door ajar).

5.   When all slices are browned and drained, dust lightly with 10X sugar and, if you like, sprinkle each slice with a small pinch of nutmeg. Serve piping hot with cane or maple syrup.

Groom's Cake

Makes one 9-inch two-layer cake

"You talk about something that was different," says Miss Tootie. "That was an old-time Cajun wedding. When an Acadian boy first decided he liked a girl, he had his mama make him a little corncob doll to give her. It was a very crude thing with pumpkin seeds for eyes, but still it was a doll and it was a girl's first gift from a boy. When the couple got serious, they would go together and announce their marriage plans to relatives. This, of course, was before telephones, so to spread the word, the girl's family would hang a blue quilt with a big white star on it from the gallery. It meant 'wedding in the making—come see what's going on.' On the wedding day, the boy gave a big dinner for his family at his house and the girl gave one for her family at her house. Then the boy and his family all went over to the girl's house and together everyone paraded to the church—none of this business of not seeing the bride before the wedding. After the ceremony, there was a big reception at the girl's house with a groom's table and a bride's table. The Groom's Cake was always chocolate (ask any man what kind of cake he likes and he will say chocolate) and the Bride's Cake was white.

⅔ cup sifted cocoa (not a mix)	¾ cup butter (1½ sticks)
2 cups sifted all-purpose flour	1⅔ cups sugar
1¼ teaspoons baking soda	3 eggs
½ teaspoon baking powder	1½ teaspoons vanilla
1 teaspoon salt	1⅓ cups milk

1.   Grease two 9- × 1½-inch layer-cake pans well, then dust with a little sifted cocoa so that bottoms and sides are lightly but evenly coated; tap out excess cocoa.

2.   Sift the cocoa with the flour, soda, baking powder and salt onto a piece of waxed paper and set aside.

3.   In a mixer, cream butter until pale and light, add sugar gradually, creaming all the while. Beat eggs in, one at a time, add vanilla,

then beat at moderately high speed for 5 minutes until very fluffy, stopping now and then to scrape the sides of the bowl down.

4. Add the sifted dry ingredients alternately with the milk, beginning and ending with the dry ingredients and beating only enough to blend.

5. Divide batter between the two prepared pans, then bake cake layers in a moderate oven (350°) 35 to 40 minutes until cakes pull from sides of pans and tops spring back slowly when pressed with a finger.

6. Cool layers upright in their pans on wire racks 10 minutes, loosen around edges with a thin-bladed spatula, then turn out on wire racks. Cool layers thoroughly (about 2 hours), then fill and frost with Groom's Frosting (recipe follows).

Groom's Frosting

Makes enough to fill and frost one 9-inch two-layer cake

This is a rich, satin-smooth, cooked fudge frosting. Because it is quite heavy and thick, make sure that the cake layers are completely cold before you frost them, otherwise they may break apart. Also, after spreading the bottom layer and setting the top layer in place, anchor the two together by sticking four wooden toothpicks down through both layers about 2 inches in from the edge of the cake. When the cake is completely frosted, pull the picks out and discard. Let the frosting harden for at least 2 hours before cutting the cake.

3 cups sugar
¾ cup sifted cocoa (not a mix)
¼ teaspoon salt
1 cup plus 2 tablespoons milk

3 tablespoons light corn syrup
6 tablespoons butter
1½ teaspoons vanilla

1. Mix sugar, cocoa and salt in a very large, heavy, deep saucepan, pressing out all cocoa lumps. Blend in milk and corn syrup, insert a candy thermometer and set over moderately low heat.

2. Boil mixture slowly *without stirring* to 234° on the candy thermometer (a drop of hot syrup should form a very soft ball in cold water), then remove from heat and drop in butter and vanilla—do not stir. Let cool slowly to 110° without stirring.

3. Remove candy thermometer and beat at high speed until frost-

ing is a good spreading consistency and begins to lose its sheen—about 8 to 10 minutes.

4. Set bottom layer of cake on a circle of cardboard cut to fit on a lazy Susan. Spread frosting over bottom layer, set top layer in place and anchor with 4 wooden toothpicks. Spread sides of cake thinly with frosting, then the top, and add a second, thicker layer after the first layer has hardened. Swirl the final layer of frosting into peaks and valleys on top of the cake. If frosting should become too firm to spread, beat in about 1 tablespoon of milk—enough to make it a good spreading consistency again. When cake is frosted, discard wooden picks. Let frosting harden several hours before cutting the cake.

Pralines

Makes about 20

Pecans and sugar cane both grow in Cajun country, so pralines, understandably, are a favorite sweet. Some Cajun cooks make pralines by boiling down pure cane syrup, which produces a dark, molasses-flavored praline. Others prepare them the more classic way, by boiling white sugar with milk and butter until they are thick and honey-brown. You must choose a dry, sunny day for making pralines, otherwise they may turn gritty as they harden or may not harden at all. You must also use a very heavy saucepan about three times the volume of the ingredients put into it so that the praline syrup has plenty of room to boil up without boiling over.

3 cups sugar
1⅓ cups milk
Pinch of salt

2 tablespoons butter
2 cups coarsely chopped pecans

1. Place sugar, milk and salt in a large, deep, very heavy saucepan and stir well to mix. Drop in butter; insert a candy thermometer. Set over moderately low heat and bring slowly to the boil without stirring. Lower heat slightly and continue cooking, without stirring, until a drop of the hot syrup forms a soft ball when dropped in cold water (238° on the candy thermometer). This will take an hour at least, so have patience—if you try to hurry the cooking the pralines will not be as fine-grained as they should be. And don't be alarmed if the syrup seems too white; it will begin to color after the temperature reaches 225°, then brown quite rapidly toward the end of cooking.

2.   When the syrup has reached 238°, remove from heat at once and stir in the pecans. Beat hard with a wooden spoon for 30 seconds, then pour onto large buttered strips of aluminum foil set on baking sheets or on the counter top. You must work quickly at this point because the syrup hardens fast. Simply pour it out, making each praline about 2½ inches in diameter. Don't try to make the circles perfectly round—pralines should be irregular in shape.

3.   Let pralines harden thoroughly (about 1 hour), then peel from the foil and arrange one layer deep on a large platter.

Mrs. Jake R. Hatfield
of
Washington County, Arkansas

SHE *says* she doesn't care about cooking. But don't you believe it!

Anyone who bakes yeast breads from scratch, who finds it "no trouble at all" to feed twenty or thirty at a clip, who in some sixty years of cooking has never served a TV dinner, scarcely fits the image of someone who doesn't like to cook.

And certainly no one has ever accused Mrs. Jake Hatfield of Fayetteville, Route 4, of being a bad cook. Quite the contrary.

"My grandchildren say, 'You just cook so good we don't know why you say you don't like to.' Well," Mrs. Hatfield continues, "I guess what I don't like is planning the meals. I just don't enjoy sittin' down and figurin' out what I'm gonna serve.

"I'd rather be out in the yard," she explains. "I *like* outside work. I was one of my Daddy's helpers in the field when I was little. We had two or three hundred head of cattle. First dairy cows, then beef. And I had to milk twenty to thirty head a day—*twice* a day."

She was also both her mother's and her sister's helper in the kitchen. "I learned to cook when I was a small child," she says. "*Real* small. My mother was sick, and my sister and I had to cook" (she and her sister were the oldest of four children). "Saturday was our day to bake, to do the wash, to iron and everything like that.

"Being older, my sister did most of the cooking. She dirtied the dishes and I washed them. Mother used to say that she could dirty dishes faster than I could wash them. And I reckon it was so."

Today Mrs. Hatfield lives only a few miles from the place she grew up, in the early 1900s, as Catherine Rebecca Dowell. "Our old farm is where the by-pass cut through around Fayetteville," she says. "Where you see that new apartment complex."

Except for a couple of times during the Depression when Mr. Hatfield took whatever work he could find to support his wife and their two sons, they have always lived on the farm.

Their new red-brick house, which they themselves designed and built, nestles amid forty-two acres of the greenest pastures you ever saw. Mrs. Hatfield also designed her huge, airy kitchen, which opens into the dining ell off the living room. She's a wizard with a measuring tape, making every inch of shelf and counter space work.

Adjoining the kitchen is Mrs. Hatfield's equally carefully planned pantry, its shelves laden with jars of fruits and vegetables, pickles and preserves. How much does she put up each year? "My land," she says, "I couldn't begin to tell you.

"Stuff grows so good here," she says. "So fast. Last year I had potatoes that weighed a pound and a quarter each."

Mr. Hatfield, who sits in a rocker by the window as we talk, interjects, "She takes a blue ribbon at the fair every year for her produce. And for her canned goods, too."

He and Mrs. Hatfield have known each other since they were children. They lived in the same community, "within a half mile of each other"; they attended the same Presbyterian church and the same high school. They were married in 1922 when both were still teenagers. "She was eighteen when we got married," Mr. Hatfield says. "I was seventeen. That's the reason she 'drives the boss' all the time—'cause she's older."

Mrs. Hatfield laughs. Clearly theirs is a strong marriage. They are proud of their two sons, both now grown up (the older son works with a big corporation in Pennsylvania, the younger one lives within "hollering distance" on a chicken, dairy and cattle farm of his own). The Hatfields are proud, too, of their six grandchildren and two great-grandchildren.

They all have recipe favorites and whenever they're coming to dinner, Mrs. Hatfield will accommodate as many of them as possible. There will be fresh-baked rolls and cinnamon rolls for sure. ("I just stir 'em up and let 'em rise"), a jar brimming with cookies, and possibly a butternut squash pie. Mr. Hatfield likes the simple things best —his wife's pot roast, for example, her fried squash, or her slow-simmered soups.

Did he know, at seventeen, that he was marrying such a good cook?

Mrs. Hatfield laughs. "My sister and I always cooked together so I don't reckon Jake ever knew which one of us cooked what."

He knows today, of course. And he has no complaints, for Mrs. Hatfield is a superlative cook whether she admits it or not.

Beef and Vegetable Stew
with Rice and Macaroni

Makes 10 to 12 servings

The Hatfields raise their own beef cattle and usually slaughter one steer each year. "All we have to do," says Mr. Hatfield, who boasts that he can see his herd from any window in the house, "is load the steer on the truck and carry it to the slaughterhouse. They do everything else." For making this stew, Mrs. Hatfield uses any good meaty soup bone. We call for beef shanks, which make a supremely rich and flavorful broth.

4 pounds beef shank, cut in 1- to 2-inch chunks	2 medium-sized potatoes, peeled and diced
1 small onion, peeled and chopped	1 cup sliced carrots
2½ quarts (10 cups) water	1 cup green peas
2 cups canned tomatoes (Mrs. Hatfield would use those she has grown and canned herself)	1 cup elbow macaroni
	½ cup converted rice
	1 tablespoon salt (or to taste)
	¼ teaspoon pepper (or to taste)

1. Simmer the beef shank with the onion in the water in a large, covered kettle over moderately low heat about 4 to 4½ hours or until beef falls from the bones. Remove bones and discard. Cool kettle mixture to room temperature, then cover and refrigerate overnight.

2. Next day, skim off and discard layer of fat on top. Add tomatoes and simmer uncovered over moderately low heat about 1 hour, breaking up clumps of tomatoes with a spoon.

3. Add potatoes, carrots, and peas, cover and simmer 30 minutes; add macaroni, rice, salt, and pepper, raise heat so that kettle liquid boils gently, cover and simmer 20 to 25 minutes longer or until macaroni and rice are tender. Taste for salt and pepper and add more if needed. Ladle into soup bowls and serve.

Oven Pot Roast with Carrots and Potatoes

Makes 6 to 8 servings

Like many Southerners and Midwesterners, the Hatfields like their beef well done. Mrs. Hatfield believes the best way to deal with the less-than-tender cuts is to make this pot roast, which literally cooks itself.

1 blade roast, cut about 4 inches thick and weighing about 5 pounds
1 teaspoon salt
⅛ teaspoon pepper
1 cup water
6 medium-sized carrots, peeled and cut in 2-inch chunks

6 medium-sized potatoes, peeled and quartered
3 medium-sized onions, peeled and quartered, or, if you prefer, 12 whole, peeled small white onions (*Note:* Mrs. Hatfield usually omits the onions because her husband doesn't care for them)

1. Sprinkle the roast well with salt and pepper, place in a very large roasting pan, add water, cover, and roast in a moderately slow oven (325°) for 1½ hours.

2. Uncover, arrange vegetables around roast in pan, re-cover, and roast 2½ to 3 hours longer, until meat and vegetables are both fork-tender. When serving, be sure to ladle some of the pan juices over each portion.

Arkansas Sausage Scrapple

Makes about 6 servings

Scrapple is usually considered a Pennsylvania Dutch dish, yet it's popular in the Ozarks, too. Here is Mrs. Hatfield's favorite recipe, which she serves for breakfast drizzled with maple syrup or spread with peanut butter.

½ pound sausage meat
½ teaspoon salt
⅛ teaspoon pepper
1 teaspoon rubbed sage or poultry seasoning

2½ cups chicken or beef stock or water
1 cup yellow corn meal
2 to 3 tablespoons bacon drippings, butter or margarine (for frying the scrapple)

1. Stir-fry the sausage in a large heavy skillet (not iron) over moderate heat about 5 minutes, breaking up large clumps. Blend in salt, pepper and sage or poultry seasoning, then add stock and bring to a boil.

2. Very gradually whisk in the corn meal, beating vigorously lest the corn meal lump. Turn heat to lowest point, cover skillet and let cook very slowly 15 minutes, stirring occasionally.

3. Pack the scrapple mixture into an 8½- × 4½- × 2½-inch loaf pan (the lightweight foil loaf pans that you buy in sets in dime stores work

well). Lay a piece of foil on top of scrapple, press down, then chill
for several hours or overnight until firm.

4.   Unmold scrapple, slice about ¼ inch thick, then brown quickly
on both sides in bacon drippings, butter or margarine. Serve hot
topped with syrup.

Fried Yellow Squash

Makes 6 servings

"The best way we like squash is fried," Mrs. Hatfield says. Her method
of frying is an easy one—simply dip the sliced squash in seasoned corn
meal, then brown in a skillet. You must use, however, the floury-
textured stone-ground meal for dredging the squash. Coarser meal is
far too gritty.

6 medium-sized yellow squash,   2 teaspoons salt
   washed, trimmed and sliced about   ¼ teaspoon pepper
   ⅜ inch thick   ¼ cup vegetable oil (about)
1 cup stone-ground corn meal

1.   Dredge the squash in the corn meal, which has been mixed with
the salt and pepper. The best way to do this, according to Mrs. Hatfield, is to put the seasoned meal in a pie plate, then to press the cut
sides of the squash slices in the meal so that it adheres. Shake off any
excess.

2.   Heat oil in a large heavy skillet over moderately high heat until
a drop of water will sputter in it. Lay the squash slices in the hot fat
and fry until nicely browned on each side—about 2 minutes per side.

3.   As squash is browned, drain on several thicknesses of paper
toweling, then transfer to a paper-toweling-lined baking sheet and
set uncovered in a very slow oven (about 250°) to keep warm while
you fry the remaining squash.

Spinach and Radish Salad with Honey Dressing

Makes 4 to 6 servings

Mrs. Hatfield grows spinach, radishes, and scallions in her garden—the three essentials of this crisp, vitamin-packed salad. The dressing is her own invention—equal parts honey, vinegar, and oil. You may find the dressing a bit sweet, but that's easily rectified; simply reduce the quantity of honey to 2 tablespoons.

Honey Dressing:
2 to 4 tablespoons honey (depending on how sweet you like things)
¼ cup cider vinegar
¼ cup vegetable oil or olive oil
1 teaspoon salt

Salad:
1 pound tender young spinach leaves, trimmed, washed well, then patted dry on paper toweling

4 large radishes, trimmed, washed and sliced tissue-thin (you'll find a swivel-bladed vegetable knife the handiest gadget for slicing the radishes)
Tops of 3 scallions (green part only), washed and sliced tissue-thin

1.   Place all dressing ingredients in a 1-pint jar, screw lid down tight and shake well to blend. It's best to make the dressing several hours ahead of time so that the flavors mellow. Shake again well before using.

2.   Pile all salad ingredients in a large bowl, drizzle lightly with dressing, then toss to mix. Taste and add a touch more dressing if needed—also, if needed, add a sprinkling of salt and pepper. Toss again and serve.

Note:
Any leftover dressing can be saved to dress other green salads later.

Pinto Bean Salad with Sour-Cream Dressing

Makes 6 to 8 servings

Now here's an unusual salad—cooked dried beans marinated in a creamy sweet-sour dressing. Mrs. Hatfield says that almost any dried beans may be used for this recipe, but she prefers either pinto beans or white beans (great northern or navy). The salad is equally good made with cooked green beans, she adds. And the dressing may also be used to dress potato salad or coleslaw.

1 pound dried pinto, great northern, navy or kidney beans, washed, sorted, and cooked by package directions
1 small yellow onion, peeled and minced (optional)
2 tablespoons finely minced parsley (optional)
1½ to 2 teaspoons salt (about)
⅛ teaspoon pepper (about)

Sour-Cream Dressing:
⅔ cup sugar
1 tablespoon flour
1 teaspoon salt
½ teaspoon dry mustard
Pinch of pepper
1 egg
1 cup cider vinegar
1 tablespoon butter, at room temperature
1 cup sour cream, at room temperature

1.   Drain beans well and place in a large mixing bowl. Add, if you like, the onion and parsley. Add 1½ teaspoons salt and the pepper; toss well and set aside.

2.   *For the dressing:* In the top of a double boiler, blend sugar, flour, salt, mustard and pepper, pressing out all lumps. Blend in egg, then add vinegar, stirring until smooth. Drop in the butter.

3.   Set over simmering (*not* boiling) water and cook and stir until smooth and about the consistency of a thin white sauce. This will take 5 to 8 minutes. Remove from heat and let cool 10 minutes. Whisk in the sour cream.

4.   Pour about 1 cup of the still-warm dressing (the recipe makes about 2½ cups total) over beans and toss well. Taste salad and add remaining ½ teaspoon salt, if needed. Also add a bit more dressing if salad seems dry. Cover and let marinate in the refrigerator for 1 to 2 hours before serving. Refrigerate remaining dressing and save to dress other salads—it will keep well for about a week.

No-Knead Yeast Rolls

Makes about 2 dozen dinner rolls

"I always make hot rolls when my grandchildren are here 'cause dinner just wouldn't be dinner without them." This recipe is an easy one because the dough needs no kneading at all. Simply let it rise, then shape it any way you wish—into cloverleaves or Parker House rolls or pan rolls. If you like, shape half the dough into dinner rolls, the remaining half into Cinnamon Rolls (recipe follows). You'll get a dozen dinner rolls and a dozen and a half Cinnamon Rolls.

1 package active dry yeast	2 tablespoons sugar
¼ cup very warm water	1 cup boiling water
¼ cup vegetable shortening	1 egg, lightly beaten
1¼ teaspoons salt	4½ cups sifted all-purpose flour

1. Sprinkle yeast over very warm water in a large bowl (very warm water should feel comfortably warm when dropped on wrist). Stir until yeast dissolves.

2. Combine shortening, salt and sugar with boiling water, stirring until shortening melts and sugar dissolves. Cool mixture to 105° to 115°.

3. Add shortening mixture to yeast, then beat in egg. Mix in flour, about 1 cup at a time, to make a soft dough.

4. Place dough in a warm greased bowl and turn greased side up. Cover with a clean, dry cloth and let rise in a warm, draft-free place until doubled in bulk—1½ to 2 hours.

5. Punch dough down and let rest 10 minutes. Working on a well-floured board (make sure hands are well-floured, too, because the dough is sticky), shape into your favorite rolls. Cover and again let rise until doubled in bulk—about 1 to 1½ hours.

6. Bake in a hot oven (425°) for about 20 minutes or until rolls are nicely browned and sound hollow when thumped with your finger. Serve hot with plenty of butter.

Cinnamon Rolls

Makes about 3 dozen rolls

"My grandchildren don't just request my Cinnamon Rolls, they *demand* them," Mrs. Hatfield says, obviously pleased.

1 recipe No-Knead Yeast Roll dough (recipe precedes)	½ cup sugar blended with 1½ teaspoons cinnamon
½ cup butter, softened to room temperature	

1. Prepare the yeast dough as directed in the preceding recipe through Step 4.

2. Punch dough down and let rest 10 minutes. Divide dough in half, then roll out one half on a well-floured pastry cloth into an oval about 20 inches long and 12 inches wide. Spread with half the softened butter and sprinkle with half of the cinnamon-sugar.

3. Roll the dough up snugly jelly-roll style, beginning at one long side so that you have a roll about 20 inches long. Make sure that the seam is on the bottom of the roll.

4. Slice about 1¼ inches thick, then arrange the slices, not quite touching and cut sides up, in a well-greased 9-inch round layer-cake pan. Repeat with remaining half of dough.

5. Cover the two pans of rolls with a clean dry cloth and let rise in a warm, draft-free spot until doubled in bulk—about 1 to 1½ hours.

6. Bake in a hot oven (425°) for about 20 minutes or until nicely browned. Serve oven-hot.

Butternut Squash Quick Bread

Makes one (9- × 5- × 3-inch) loaf

Of all the winter squashes, Mrs. Hatfield likes butternut best. "It's a good keeper," she explains. The family likes it as a vegetable, but even better when baked into this dark, sweet bread.

1 cup granulated sugar
½ cup firmly packed light brown sugar
1 cup cooked, mashed, unseasoned butternut squash (you may use, if you like, 1 cup thawed, frozen commercial winter squash)
½ cup vegetable oil
2 eggs
2 cups sifted all-purpose flour
1 teaspoon baking soda
½ teaspoon salt
½ teaspoon ground cinnamon
⅛ teaspoon ground nutmeg
¼ teaspoon ground ginger
¼ cup water
1 cup seedless raisins
½ cup chopped black walnuts, California walnuts or pecans (Mrs. Hatfield uses black walnuts, which grow wild on the farm)

1. Place granulated sugar, brown sugar, squash, oil and eggs in large mixer bowl and beat at medium speed 1 to 2 minutes until smooth.

2. Sift flour with soda, salt and spices and mix in alternately with the water, beginning and ending with the dry ingredients. Fold in raisins and nuts.

3. Pour batter into a well-greased-and-floured 9- × 5- × 3-inch loaf pan and bake in a moderate oven (350°) for 60 to 65 minutes, until bread pulls from sides of pan and is peaked and springy to the touch.

4. Cool bread upright in its pan on a wire rack for 10 to 15 minutes, then loosen with a thin-bladed spatula, turn out on rack and cool to room temperature before cutting.

Ozark Pudding

Makes 6 servings

Mrs. Hatfield doesn't know whether or not Ozark Pudding originated in the Ozarks where she grew up. But she does know that it's an old Arkansas favorite. The best way to serve it is topped with gobs of whipped cream.

1 egg, well beaten
¾ cup firmly packed light brown sugar
¾ cup *unsifted* all-purpose flour
1½ teaspoons baking powder

½ teaspoon ground cinnamon
1 teaspoon vanilla
¾ cup finely chopped peeled apples
½ cup finely chopped pecans or black walnuts

1. Beat egg and sugar well in a small mixing bowl; sift flour with baking powder and cinnamon and mix in. Stir in vanilla, apples and nuts.

2. Spoon batter into a well-greased-and-floured 8- × 8- × 2-inch baking pan and bake in a moderate oven (350°) for 30 minutes or until crusty-brown on top.

3. Let pudding cool about ½ hour before serving. To serve, cut in large squares and top each with a drift of whipped cream.

Butternut Squash Chiffon Pie

Makes one 9-inch single-crust pie

The Hatfields prefer this spicy, butter-smooth squash pie to pumpkin pie. It looks much the same but has a more nutlike flavor.

1 envelope unflavored gelatin
1 cup sugar
½ teaspoon salt
½ teaspoon ground cinnamon
½ teaspoon ground nutmeg
¼ teaspoon ground ginger
2 eggs, separated
1 cup light cream or evaporated milk

2 cups cooked, mashed, unseasoned butternut squash (you may use, if you like, 2 cups thawed, frozen commercial winter squash)
1½ teaspoons finely grated orange rind
1 9-inch baked pie shell with a high fluted edge

1. In the top of a double boiler combine gelatin, ¾ cup of the sugar, salt, spices, egg yolks and cream. Set over simmering water and cook, stirring constantly, about 10 minutes or until thickened and smooth. Remove from heat, blend in squash and orange rind and cool to lukewarm.

2. Beat the egg whites until soft peaks form, then add the remaining ¼ cup sugar gradually, beating all the while to stiff peaks. Fold the egg whites into the squash mixture thoroughly so that no streaks of white or yellow remain.

3. Spoon into pie shell and chill several hours until firm.

Chopped-Apple Cake

Makes one 8- × 8- × 2-inch loaf cake

There is no liquid in this uncommonly light and moist cake other than that supplied by the chopped apples. And the flavoring is vanilla, not spice. Because the cake is so very tender, it's best to let it cool to room temperature before serving.

½ cup (1 stick) butter, at room temperature
1 cup sugar
1 egg

1½ cups coarsely chopped peeled apples (McIntosh or Jonathan preferably)
1½ cups sifted all-purpose flour
1 teaspoon baking soda
1 teaspoon vanilla

1. Cream butter and sugar until fluffy-light; beat in egg, then stir in apples. Combine flour and baking soda and mix in (batter will be quite stiff). Stir in vanilla.

2. Spread batter in a well-greased-and-floured 8- × 8- × 2-inch loaf pan and bake in a moderate oven (350°) for 40 to 45 minutes or until cake pulls from sides of pan and is nicely browned, or until a finger pressed gently in the center of the cake leaves an imprint that vanishes slowly.

3. Cool cake upright in its pan on a wire rack for 20 to 25 minutes, then cut into large squares and serve.

Raisin-Oatmeal Cookies

Makes about 4 dozen cookies

"I reckon I been making these cookies since I was married," says Mrs. Hatfield. She adds that she's bound to keep her cookie jar filled, not only for the grandchildren who stop by but also for her younger son who heads straight for it every time he sets foot in the kitchen.

2 cups quick-cooking rolled oats	1 teaspoon baking soda dissolved in
2 cups sifted all-purpose flour	¼ cup milk
1 cup sugar	1 teaspoon ground cinnamon
1 cup vegetable shortening	¼ teaspoon salt
1 cup seedless raisins	1 teaspoon vanilla
2 eggs	

1. Place all ingredients, in the order listed, in large mixer bowl without stirring. Beat well about 2 minutes or until thoroughly blended.

2. Drop cookies by rounded teaspoonfuls onto greased cooky sheets, spacing about 2 inches apart.

3. Bake in a moderately hot oven (375°) 10 to 12 minutes until browned around the edges. Remove while warm to wire racks to cool.

Variation:

Chocolate Raisin-Oatmeal Cookies: Prepare as directed but add, after the vanilla, 5 tablespoons cocoa. Drop and bake the cookies as directed in Steps 2 and 3.

Rolled and Cut Sugar Cookies
Makes 6½ to 7 dozen

This is an old, old family recipe, given to Mrs. Hatfield by her mother. She loved the cookies as a child, her children did, and now her grandchildren do. Because of the recipe's high proportion of fat, the cookies are somewhat tricky to roll and cut. You cannot manage it successfully in hot weather, or, for that matter, in a steamy kitchen; the dough will be much too soft. It's a good idea to keep the dough well chilled—or frozen—and roll out small amounts at a time before the heat of your hands makes the dough sticky.

3⅔ cups sifted all-purpose flour
1 teaspoon baking powder
½ teaspoon salt
1¼ cups sugar

1 cup butter, margarine or vegetable shortening
3 eggs
1½ teaspoons vanilla

1. Place flour, baking powder, salt and sugar in a large mixing bowl and stir well. Add butter, margarine or vegetable shortening and cut in, using a pastry blender, until mixture is uniformly crumbly—about the texture of coarse meal.

2. Add the eggs and vanilla and beat in briskly. Divide dough in 4 equal parts and wrap each in foil. Chill several hours in the refrigerator—until firm enough to roll. Or, if you prefer, freeze the dough.

3. Roll the dough out, ¼ at a time, on a lightly floured board or pastry cloth, making it about as thin as piecrust. Cut with a round cutter 2½ to 3 inches in diameter. Place cookies about 2 inches apart on lightly greased baking sheets.

4. Bake in a moderately hot oven (375°) about 8 minutes or until pale tan.

5. Remove cookies from baking sheets while warm and transfer to wire racks to cool.

Quince's Peanut Brittle

Makes about 1½ pounds

"I got this recipe from my cousin who says it is the best peanut brittle she ever ate," says Mrs. Hatfield. The baking soda, added at the last minute, makes it light—both in texture and in color.

1 cup water
1 cup light corn syrup
2 cups sugar

¼ teaspoon salt
1½ cups roasted unsalted peanuts
1 tablespoon baking soda

1.   In a large heavy saucepan, combine water, corn syrup, sugar and salt. Insert a candy thermometer, set over moderate heat and let cook, without stirring, until thermometer registers 280°.
2.   Stir in peanuts and continue cooking until thermometer registers 300°. Remove from heat and quickly stir in soda. The syrup will bubble and foam.
3.   Pour out as thin as possible on a well-buttered baking sheet. For even thinner brittle, pull and stretch the candy out with a spatula while it is still hot. Cool until hard, then break the brittle into bite-sized chunks.

Ozark 13-Day Pickles

Makes about 8 pints

"I've been using this pickle recipe almost as long as I can remember," says Mrs. Hatfield. "It's our favorite because the pickles are so nice and crisp and spicy."

1 gallon small, fresh, *firm* pickling cucumbers, washed and drained well
1⅓ cups pickling salt dissolved in 3 quarts cold water (brine)
6 quarts boiling water (you will need 3 quarts at a time)
½ ounce alum mixed with 3 quarts boiling water

Pickling Syrup:
1 quart white vinegar
1½ cups cold water
4 cups sugar
1 tablespoon mixed pickling spices
2 teaspoons celery seed
1 teaspoon caraway seed
1½ teaspoons whole allspice
3 cinnamon sticks, each broken into several pieces

1. Place cucumbers in a very large ceramic bowl or deep crock, pour in brine, set a large plate on top, weight down with a quart preserving jar filled with water (screw jar lid down tight), then let cucumbers stand 7 full days in a cool spot. About every other day skim off the scum that collects and stir brine well. Make sure, however, that cucumbers are submerged in brine at all times.

2. On the 8th day, drain cucumbers well, cover with 3 quarts boiling water and let stand 24 hours.

3. On the 9th day, drain cucumbers, cover with alum and boiling water mixture and let stand 24 hours.

4. On the 10th day, drain cucumbers, cover once again with 3 quarts boiling water and let stand until cool. *Meanwhile, prepare pickling syrup as follows:* Place vinegar, cold water and 1 cup of the sugar in a large stainless steel or enamel saucepan and stir to mix. Bundle all spices in a cheesecloth bag and drop into saucepan. Set over moderately high heat and bring to a boil, stirring until sugar has dissolved. Drain cucumbers well, then pour in boiling hot syrup (spice bag, too), weight pickles down and let stand 24 hours.

5. On the 11th day, drain off the pickling syrup, pour it into a large saucepan, add spice bag and 1 cup sugar. Bring to a boil, pour over pickles, weight down and let stand 24 hours.

6. On the 12th day, repeat Step 5, again heating the syrup and spice bag with an additional 1 cup sugar. Let pickles stand, weighted down, in syrup 24 hours.

7. On the 13th day, drain off pickling syrup, pour it into a large saucepan, add spice bag and the final 1 cup sugar. Bring to a boil. Pack pickles in 8 1-pint preserving jars, pour in boiling syrup, leaving ¼-inch head space. Run a thin-bladed spatula around inside edge of jars to release air bubbles, seal jars, then process in a boiling water bath (212°) for 10 minutes. Remove from water bath, cool to room temperature, check seals, then label jars and store on a cool, dark, dry shelf. Let the pickles "season" for about a month before serving.

The Midwest

Mrs. Reuben Shoemaker
of
Ross County, Ohio

"I *had* to cook as a child," says Blanche Shoemaker, settling into an easy chair by a window festooned with spider plants. "There were only fourteen in my family, the Pollocks. Fourteen *children*. I was along about number ten. My dad farmed and of course my older brothers helped him. So I helped Mother. There was a big breakfast every morning. Why, I remember my mother getting up early and baking our bread. We hardly knew what a store-bought loaf was!"

There were big dinners, too, eaten at midday and followed by hearty suppers. But luckily the Pollock farm, only about five miles from where Mrs. Shoemaker now lives, produced all the milk, eggs, meats, fruits and vegetables the family needed. "We raised sorghum and made our own molasses. We tapped our maple trees. My dad even made his own home brew . . . he couldn't afford to buy beer."

The Pollocks not only relied on what they could grow, they also gathered wild greens, mushrooms, nuts and berries in the woodlands and "pasture fields," a practice the Shoemakers follow today.

This particular day, in fact, Mrs. Shoemaker has just returned from gathering wild lettuce (it is soaking in the sink as she talks), and her husband has just set off for the ridge behind the house in search of mushrooms.

Though their house, a trim white-wood structure a story-and-a-half high, sits smack on Route 50-South (the main street) in the little town of Bourneville, they are only minutes in any direction from the fields and woodlands that are their foraging grounds. Moreover, enough property surrounds the house for a big vegetable garden and a flock of forty chickens.

It was to this house that Mrs. Shoemaker moved as a bride of seventeen in 1937. And it was here that her six children—all girls—grew up. They are all married now, with families of their own, giving the Shoemakers twelve grandchildren and one great-grandchild.

"Reuben, my daughters and I all went to the same school," Mrs. Shoemaker says. "Of course, Reuben was older and ran around with my older brothers. I was just a kid sister, I guess." But, as it happened, Mrs. Shoemaker's best girl friend in high school was Reuben Shoemaker's niece. "I said to her one day, 'I'd give anything for a date with Reuben,' and she said, 'I'll get you one.'" She did, and six months later Blanche Pollock and Reuben Shoemaker were married.

In the early years of their marriage, Mr. Shoemaker worked in a paper plant in Chillicothe some dozen miles away. "But he never did like indoor work," Mrs. Shoemaker explains, "so he got him a job as a conductor with the B & O Railroad and has worked there ever since."

Mrs. Shoemaker worked, too—for ten years as the head cook in the local high school cafeteria—yes, the same school that she, Reuben and their daughters attended. Her years of helping her mother feed such a large family on the farm prepared her well, as did her years of home economics in high school.

"I can tell you," she says, "after setting off at five-thirty of a morning to fix lunch for four hundred children, I didn't feel much like cooking when I came home." But cook she did, especially on the days that Reuben was home.

"Reuben tells me I have never set before him anything he didn't like," she says. "Except *once*. That was when I opened up a can of beans we'd gotten on special at the store. He took one bite and said, 'Where'd we get this?' I told him and he said, 'Well, it is terrible!'"

Fortunately, none of the Shoemakers had to settle for canned or packaged foods. Like her mother before her, Mrs. Shoemaker cooks almost everything the old-fashioned way. "My mother didn't cook by recipe. She never measured a thing. I remember that she had this great big granite dishpan, and when she'd go to making bread, she'd just dump the flour out of a twenty-five pound bag. She knew just how much she needed. Then she'd just add handfuls of this and that. She was a wonderful cook. She could take nothing and make something out of it. I don't guess that in my own mind I will ever measure up to her standards."

Most of Mrs. Shoemaker's recipes are in her head, too, although she does keep a handwritten file of the old family favorites, together with "interesting-sounding"recipes that she has obtained from friends and the Bourneville Home Demonstration Club to which she belongs.

She doesn't cook as much as she once did—her husband has been ill lately and is on a diet. And she herself has to watch what she eats.

Still, whenever the children, grandchildren and great-grandchild gather at Christmas, she covers the table with a whopping feast. "I roast turkey and ham, both," she says. "The girls always ask if they can't bring something, but it's easier just for me to cook. Besides, Reuben is always there in the kitchen with me, peeling the potatoes or cleaning the vegetables."

Now that Mr. Shoemaker is about ready to retire, the two of them are looking forward to spending more time together, to traveling about the country and visiting their daughters (the farthest from home lives in California).

"Reuben told me," she continues, "that he was going to retire early so that he could spend a little time with me. He said, 'I've spent two-thirds of my married life away from home. You have raised our six children practically by yourself. And now I'm going to try to make up for that.'"

Oxtail Soup

Makes about 8 servings

A soup that the Shoemakers are especially fond of is Oxtail Soup. The vegetables that Mrs. Shoemaker adds to the soup depend upon what she has on hand. "Sometimes in the fall I shell out my green beans," she says, "and I would add some shell beans to the soup." Most of the time, however, this is the way she prepares it. The soup will be better if you begin it one day and finish it the next.

4 pounds oxtail, cut crosswise in 1- to 1½-inch chunks
8 cups water
2 medium-sized yellow onions, peeled and cut in very slim wedges
2 medium-sized carrots, peeled and sliced about ¼ inch thick
2 medium-sized celery ribs, sliced about ¼ inch thick

2 cups thinly sliced cabbage
2 cups canned tomatoes (Mrs. Shoemaker would use home canned)
2 large potatoes, peeled and diced
2 tablespoons minced fresh parsley
1 tablespoon salt (or to taste)
¼ teaspoon pepper (or to taste)

1. Simmer the oxtail in the water in a large, heavy, covered kettle over low heat 5½ to 6 hours or until meat all but falls from bones. Cool to room temperature, then refrigerate overnight.

2. Next day, skim off and discard all fat that has solidified on top of the soup. Warm the soup just until liquid (it will have congealed in the refrigerator). Lift out all pieces of oxtail, then using your fingers, separate the meat from the bones. Also discard bits of fat. Reserve the meat. For a more attractive soup, strain the beef broth and return to kettle.

3. To the kettle add onions, carrots, celery, cabbage and tomatoes; cover and simmer 1 hour. Add all remaining ingredients, including reserved meat, cover and simmer 40 to 45 minutes longer or until all vegetables are tender. Taste the soup for seasoning and add additional salt and pepper if needed. Ladle into soup bowls and serve as a main dish.

Soup Beans with Pork

Makes about 8 servings

"I like to cook my beans with fresh pork," says Mrs. Shoemaker. This recipe, a family favorite, is really more a soup than a vegetable. Serve it for lunch on a cold winter's day.

1 pound dried navy or pea beans, washed and sorted
6 cups cold water
1 pound lean, meaty spareribs, divided into individual rib sections
2 medium-sized yellow onions, peeled and cut in slim wedges
2½ teaspoons salt
¼ teaspoon pepper

1. Soak the beans in the cold water overnight in a large heavy kettle.

2. Next day add all remaining ingredients to kettle, set over moderate heat and bring to a boil; reduce heat so that water ripples gently, cover and simmer about 1½ hours or until beans are very tender and pork falls from bones. Remove and discard bones; cut pork into bite-sized pieces and return to kettle.

3. Simmer, uncovered, over lowest heat about 20 minutes longer, stirring occasionally to keep mixture from sticking. Ladle into soup bowls and serve.

Batter-Browned Mushrooms

Makes about 4 servings

The Shoemakers like to go mushrooming. "We get a lot of morels," Mrs. Shoemaker says, "also some little white mushrooms that look like those you buy in the store." We're not recommending that *you* go mushrooming, which is rather like Russian roulette unless you know precisely what you're doing. But we do recommend that you try Mrs. Shoemaker's way of cooking wild mushrooms with those you buy at the market.

1 pound medium-sized mushrooms, wiped clean with a damp cloth, trimmed of coarse stem ends and then sliced about ⅜-inch thick
1 cup *unsifted* all-purpose flour
1½ teaspoons salt

¼ teaspoon pepper
2 eggs well beaten with 2 tablespoons milk
4 tablespoons butter
4 tablespoons vegetable oil

1. Shake the mushrooms, a few at a time, in a mixture of the flour, salt and pepper in a brown paper bag to dredge.
2. Dip quickly in the egg mixture (a slotted spoon is the handiest implement to use); let excess drain off, then brown the mushrooms, about a third of them at a time, on both sides in a very large heavy skillet in the butter and oil. With the burner heat set at moderately high, the mushrooms will take about 1 to 2 minutes per side to brown.
3. Drain on paper toweling and serve hot.

Bacon-Dressed Dandelion Greens

Makes 4 to 6 servings

For the Shoemakers, dandelion greens are a great delicacy—as are the blossoms, which Mrs. Shoemaker fries in deep fat (recipe follows). Because dandelion greens are apt to be pungent, you may want to do as Mrs. Shoemaker often does—that is, use about half dandelion greens and half young spinach, turnip or mustard greens.

3 quarts young and tender dandelion greens, or 6 cups dandelion greens and 6 cups tender young spinach, turnip or mustard greens
5 cups water

1 teaspoon salt (or to taste)
3 to 4 tablespoons melted bacon drippings
⅛ teaspoon pepper

1. Trim greens of coarse stalks and blemished leaves; wash in a sinkful of tepid water by gently lifting the greens up and down in the water so that the grit stays behind in the bottom of the sink. Drain greens and rinse out sink. Again fill sink with tepid water, add 2 tablespoons of salt and let greens soak in the salt water 10 to 15 minutes. Drain greens; rinse once again, this time in cool water. Drain.

2. Place greens in a very large kettle, add 4 cups of the water and bring to a boil. Boil 1 minute, then drain greens in a colander (this is to extract some of the bitterness).

3. Return greens to kettle, add remaining 1 cup water and the salt and bring to a boil. Adjust heat so that water bubbles gently, cover and cook 15 to 20 minutes or until greens are tender. Drain well, return kettle to burner and shake gently 1 to 2 minutes to drive off excess moisture. Add 3 tablespoons of the melted bacon drippings and the pepper and toss well. Taste and add the additional 1 tablespoon of bacon drippings if needed, also a little additional salt. Dish up and serve.

Batter-Fried Dandelion or Pumpkin Blossoms

Makes about 4 servings

Dandelion blossoms are not something most of us think of cooking—or pumpkin blossoms, either. But Mrs. Shoemaker likes to deep-fry both, jacketed in an egg batter. If you intend to gather pumpkin blossoms, she cautions, you must do so early in the morning. "They close up tight in the heat of the day."

2 quarts dandelion or pumpkin blossoms, washed and stemmed (be sure to leave the green caps on the blossoms)
1 cup *unsifted* all-purpose flour
1 teaspoon salt
¼ teaspoon pepper
2 eggs beaten well with 2 tablespoons milk
Vegetable oil or shortening for deep-fat frying (you'll need about 2 inches of fat in the deep-fat fryer)

1. Soak the blossoms for about 10 minutes in a sinkful of cool water to which you have added 1 tablespoon of salt. Drain, spread blossoms out on several thicknesses of paper toweling and let "air-dry" about 15 minutes.

2. To dredge the blossoms, shake—very gently—a few at a time, in a mixture of the flour, salt and pepper in a brown paper bag. Using a

slotted spoon, dip blossoms into the egg mixture, letting excess run off.

3.   Deep-fry at about 365° to 375° until golden and crisp—this will take only a minute or two. Drain blossoms on paper toweling, then serve straightaway as a vegetable.

Sweet-Sour Coleslaw with Carrots and Olives
Makes about 8 servings

"I like to make my coleslaw early of a morning," Mrs. Shoemaker says, "then let it sit in the refrigerator until supper time." That way, she explains, the flavors "get together." She shreds the cabbage fairly fine —the second coarsest side of a four-sided grater will give the cabbage about the right texture. "My daughter shreds hers in the blender," Mrs. Shoemaker said, "but I think that makes it too mushy."

8 cups fairly finely shredded cabbage (about 1 medium-sized
  head, trimmed)
2 medium-sized carrots, peeled and
  shredded
1 small yellow onion, peeled and
  minced
½ cup chopped pimiento-stuffed
  green olives

Dressing:
1 cup mayonnaise
¼ cup cider vinegar
3 tablespoons sugar
1 tablespoon prepared mustard
1 teaspoon salt
½ teaspoon celery seed
⅛ teaspoon pepper

1.   Place all slaw ingredients (except Dressing) in a large bowl and toss to mix.

2.   Combine all dressing ingredients, whisking with a fork to mix. Pour over slaw and toss well again.

3.   Cover slaw and chill several hours in the refrigerator before serving. Toss once again just before dishing up.

Wilted Wild Lettuce

Makes about 4 to 6 servings

The wild green that the Shoemakers like best is the tender young lettuce that flourishes in lowlands and along creek banks. "But you can substitute the lettuce that you grow in your garden," says Mrs. Shoemaker. "*Leaf* lettuce rather than iceberg."

4 slices lean smoked bacon
3 quarts tender young wild lettuce or leaf lettuce, trimmed of coarse stalks and blemished leaves
3 scallions, sliced tissue-thin (include green tops)

¼ cup cider vinegar
4 teaspoons sugar
¾ teaspoon salt
⅛ teaspoon pepper

1.   Fry the bacon until crisp; crumble. Reserve both the crumbled bacon and the drippings.

2.   Wash lettuce by gently lifting it up and down in a sinkful of tepid water. Drain well. Rinse out sink, fill with cool water and mix in 1 tablespoon salt. Soak greens in the salt water 10 minutes, drain well, then spread out between several thicknesses of paper toweling to absorb excess moisture. You can, if you like, bundle the greens up in the paper toweling at this point and store them in the refrigerator until serving time. In fact, the greens will be crisper if you do.

3.   To wilt the greens, heat the bacon drippings in the skillet, add sliced scallions and sauté 2 to 3 minutes until limp. Add vinegar, sugar, salt and pepper to skillet and bring to a boil.

4.   Pile greens in a large salad bowl, pour the boiling skillet mixture over all, then toss to mix. Add the reserved bacon crumbles, toss lightly again, then serve as a salad.

Butter Horns

Makes about 3 dozen rolls

Mrs. Shoemaker is so famous for her Butter Horn rolls that she was once asked to make six hundred of them for the local high school's Athletic Banquet. "The hardest part of the whole thing," she says, "was having to stand up at the end of the banquet and be recognized."

3 packages active dry yeast
¼ cup very warm water
1 cup milk, scalded
½ cup sugar
2 teaspoons salt

½ cup (1 stick) butter or margarine
5½ cups sifted all-purpose flour
3 eggs, well beaten
½ cup melted butter

1. Sprinkle yeast over very warm water in a large bowl (very warm water should feel comfortably warm when dropped on wrist). Stir until yeast dissolves.

2. Combine scalded milk with sugar, salt and butter or margarine, stirring until sugar dissolves and butter melts. Cool mixture to 105° to 115°.

3. Add milk mixture to yeast, then beat in 2 cups of the flour. Beat in the eggs, then beat in the remaining 3½ cups of flour to make a very soft dough. Place dough in a well-greased bowl (grease the top of the dough also), cover with a clean dry cloth and let rise in a warm, dry spot until doubled in bulk—about 1 hour.

4. Punch dough down and let rest 5 minutes. Turn out on a well-floured board. Flour your hands well also and begin kneading the dough, adding additional flour to the board and to your hands as needed to keep dough from sticking. You'll find the dough very soft and sticky at first, but persist and before long it will become satiny and elastic. You should knead the dough about 10 minutes total.

5. Divide the dough into 3 equal parts, then roll, 1 part at a time, on a well-floured pastry cloth into a circle about 12 inches in diameter. Brush the circle of dough well with melted butter, then cut into 12 pie-shaped wedges of as nearly equal size as possible. Beginning at the base of each wedge, roll up jelly-roll style toward the point. Repeat until all dough is rolled and shaped. Place the rolls, with the points on the bottom, about 2 inches apart on ungreased baking sheets.

6. Cover the rolls with a clean dry cloth and let rise in a warm spot until doubled in bulk—about 40 to 45 minutes.

7. Bake the rolls in a moderately hot oven (375°) for 12 to 15 minutes or until nicely browned on top. Serve oven-hot with plenty of butter.

Note:

These rolls freeze well. Simply cool to room temperature, bundle into heavy-duty plastic bags, twist necks and secure with twist-bands. Pop into the freezer and store until ready to use. To reheat, thaw rolls, then warm about 5 minutes in a slow oven (300°).

Vinegar Meringue Pie

Makes one 8-inch single-crust pie

This unusual pie is one that Mrs. Shoemaker got from her husband's sister, the late Grace Curtis, who was a Methodist preacher. It might be called "mock lemon pie," for it tastes surprisingly like lemon meringue pie.

1 cup sugar
3 tablespoons flour
3 large egg yolks
1 cup water
2 tablespoons butter

4 tablespoons cider vinegar
1 8-inch baked pie shell

Meringue:
3 large egg whites beaten to stiff peaks with 6 tablespoons sugar

1.   Blend sugar and flour in a small saucepan, pressing out all lumps. Add egg yolks and water and stir briskly to mix; drop in butter. Set over low heat and cook, stirring constantly, until smooth and quite thick—about 8 to 10 minutes. Remove from heat and add vinegar in a slow stream, beating all the while.

2.   Spoon vinegar filling into baked pie shell, then spread meringue on top, making sure that it touches the pastry all around. For a more attractive meringue, swirl into peaks and valleys, using a thin-bladed spatula or table knife.

3.   Bake in a moderate oven (350°) for 8 to 10 minutes or just until meringue is lightly browned.

4.   Cool pie to room temperature before serving.

Lemon Cracker Cookies

Makes about 6½ dozen cookies

Proof that this cookie recipe is a very old one is the fact that the leavening called for is baker's ammonia, which was used before the days of commercial baking powders. You can buy chunks of baker's ammonia at drug stores, also oil of lemon, the flavoring called for in this recipe. Mrs. Shoemaker says that she remembers her mother making these cookies in huge batches, then storing them in airtight tins. "They just seem to get better and better the longer they stand," she says. The cookies are not as sweet as we tend to like cookies today, but they are crisp and good.

1 tablespoon finely crushed baker's ammonia

1 cup milk

½ cup butter or lard (Mrs. Shoe-maker says that her mother used lard)

1½ cups sugar

1 egg

1½ teaspoons oil of lemon

5 cups sifted all-purpose flour

1. Combine the baker's ammonia and milk and let stand overnight in the refrigerator. This is so that it will dissolve thoroughly. Stir mixture well just before using.

2. Next day, cream the butter and sugar until light, then beat in egg and oil of lemon. Add the flour alternately with the ammonia-milk mixture, beginning and ending with the flour.

3. Divide dough in half and roll, half at a time, on a well-floured board into a large rectangle that is about the thickness of piecrust. Cut into 2-inch squares and space about 1½ inches apart on ungreased baking sheets. Roll and cut the remaining half of the dough the same way (also reroll and cut trimmings). Prick the top of each cookie well with a floured fork.

4. Bake in a moderately hot oven (375°) about 8 to 10 minutes—just until cookies are pale tan and firm. Cool on wire racks, then store in airtight canisters.

Sassafras Tea

Makes 4 to 6 servings

Sassafras trees abound in the forests of southern Ohio as they do over much of the United States. Whenever Mrs. Shoemaker goes mush-rooming or gathering wild greens, she will also cut a young and tender sassafras root to brew into a bracing tea.

1 young sassafras root (about 2 to 3 inches long)

1 quart water

1. Scrub the sassafras root well with a brush under a stream of tepid water, then peel off the outer "skin."

2. Boil the root in the water for about 20 minutes or until the "tea" has a strong aromatic flavor. Dilute to suit your taste with boiling water, then sweeten or not as you like.

Mrs. Russell Harris
of
McLean County, Illinois

"I GREW up in the Depression and when I'd want to cook, my mother would say, 'Well . . . we have to be careful. I just can't let you waste.' So there were a lot of things I wanted to make as a girl that I couldn't," says Mrs. Russell Harris, who lives today on the black, tabletop farmland of central Illinois about halfway between the little towns of Colfax and Cooksville.

"I married in 1943," she continues. "The war was on, so I had to be careful *then*, too, because things were sugarless."

Mrs. Harris finds today that her early training in frugality carries over, also her experiences as a girl on a dairy farm in southern Illinois. Born Marian Wilhelm near Edwardsville, she was the oldest of four children—three girls and a boy.

"I had to do a lot of canning as a girl," Marian Harris says. "And I do a lot of it today. I also do a lot of freezing." She has two whopping freezers, in fact, to accommodate the fruits and vegetables she grows ("plus what we get from family and friends"), not to mention the beef and hogs they slaughter.

"The steers you see here now," she continues, "are left over from Georgia's 4-H projects." Georgia is her youngest daughter, who now works in northern Illinois. Her older three children, all married, are away from home, too.

Mrs. Harris and her husband now run their 320-acre farm as a team (they don't own the farm but rent from an absentee landlady who lives in Ohio). "I help Russell with the planting in spring," Mrs. Harris says. "Then in the fall we hire people to help with the harvesting." (They grow about equal parts corn and soy beans.)

They've lived for seventeen years on the farm known locally as "the old Henline place." The house, a white-brick, two-story Victorian Gothic structure, all bay windows, stained glass and inlaid woods, has been declared a historic site by the McLean County Bicentennial Arts Festival Committee. The original part of the house (which now contains Mrs. Harris's modern kitchen worked out in mahogany, avocado green, and harvest tones) was built in 1837. The later addition—actually the main house—was put up during the 1880s. It's unique in that its white glazed bricks were all imported from Italy, then set in red mortar and trimmed around the arched windows and doorways with red brick.

The Harrises have put considerable love and effort into the old house—refinishing, papering, and painting. "We love the house so much that we offered to buy it a few years back," Mrs. Harris says. "But the owner didn't want to sell. Still, she lets us do just about anything we want in the way of fixing it up."

Mrs. Harris effervesces as she talks and her hazel-brown eyes fairly glow. She looks a good ten to fifteen years younger than she is (late fifties), maybe because of her freckles and curly, close-cropped sandy hair, but more likely because she has so many interests and outside activities. She has been a 4-H Club leader for more than twenty years, she is involved in the Homemakers Extension Association and in church activities. (It was at church that she met her husband in the early 1940s in Bloomington where she had gone to work for State Farm Insurance.) Until recently, Marian Harris also assisted a caterer and, to help put her children through college, sold eggs to customers in both Bloomington and Normal.

"For fifteen years, I delivered eggs every week . . . sometimes as many as a hundred and forty dozen a week. We have just a few chickens now—just enough for ourselves. Chickens are a lot of work, and once the children were through college, I decided that it was time I rested a bit."

Not that she is sitting back and taking life easy. In addition to all of her other activities, she still plants a vegetable garden every spring. "It's only about twenty by forty feet," she says, "but I plant my things real close together so I don't have to hoe so much in between. Everybody teases me about my narrow rows, but I say, 'Well all that extra space just gives me a lot more room for weeds to grow.'"

Mrs. Harris is also known as one of the best country cooks in McLean County, one who, for the most part, does things "from scratch." If she has a specialty, it is probably the German recipes she learned as a child.

"My family was of German descent," she explains. "My husband's mother's family, too. And the recipes I like best today are the old standbys. My mother was quite a baker of breads. I like to bake bread, too, and cookies.

"Of course, cooking is so much easier today. I remember having to do everything by hand. Creaming the sugar and lard for cakes. And whipping up angel-food cakes with a wire whip. Oh, I had some flops in my day."

Like her children, Mrs. Harris was in the 4-H Club as a girl. And she credits the club with teaching her most of the basics of cooking. "Certainly the club taught me about seasonings and sauces," she says. "Twice I won trips to the State Fair," she continues, "once for my cooking projects, once for clothing."

She still makes most of her own clothes and tries, every Christmas, to make something for each of her seven grandchildren. As for her own children, she makes their gifts, too. Last year each received a rug that she had crocheted.

"You know," she adds, "the Depression still has an effect on us. We just didn't buy things in those days. We *made* them. And this has kind of become a tradition with me. I think this is what makes a home.

"I remember seeing a quote that my daughter Georgia had pasted in one of her college notebooks—'Home is where the feet may leave but the heart never.' I think of that often these days. It seems so true of our four children. They all have their own homes now, but they do really seem to enjoy coming home to the farm.

"It's a feeling they're passing along to their children. And one that I hope *their* children will pass along, too."

Mustcohola

Makes 6 servings

"Not many people know about this recipe," Mrs. Harris says. "It's one I learned while I was in high school. Our farm was seven miles from town and since we didn't have buses in those days, I stayed with a family in Edwardsville for two years, working for my room and board. The family was Bohemian—the wife had come from Bohemia as a child; her husband, too, I think. Anyway, Mustcohola is something this lady made often as a main dish. I liked it so well that I took the recipe down."

2 tablespoons bacon drippings
2 large yellow onions, peeled and chopped
2 sweet green peppers, cored, seeded and chopped
¼ pound mushrooms, wiped clean and sliced thin
¾ pound lean ground beef
¼ pound ground pork (or sausage meat)

1 tablespoon chili powder
¾ teaspoon salt
⅛ teaspoon pepper
2 cups canned tomatoes (preferably home-canned)
½ pound shell or elbow macaroni, cooked by package directions and drained well

1. Heat bacon drippings in a large heavy Dutch-oven-type kettle over moderate heat, add onions and green peppers and stir-fry about 5 minutes until limp. Push to one side, add mushrooms and stir-fry 5 minutes. Add beef and pork and stir fry, breaking up clumps with a spoon, about 5 minutes—just until no longer pink. Blend in chili powder, salt and pepper.

2. Add tomatoes and simmer, uncovered, about ¾ to 1 hour until slightly thickened. Mix in drained macaroni, spoon into a 2½-quart casserole, then set uncovered in a moderate oven (350°) and bake, stirring now and then, about 45 minutes or until sauce is no longer soupy and flavors are blended. Serve as a main course.

Spicy Meat and Sausage Loaf

Makes 6 to 8 servings

Marian Harris more or less improvises with her meat loaves. "The recipes are in my head," she explains.

1½ pounds ground beef (not too lean)
1 pound sausage meat or, if you prefer, ground pork
1 cup uncooked rolled oats
1 medium-sized yellow onion, peeled and chopped
1 teaspoon salt

¼ teaspoon pepper
1 tablespoon prepared mustard
¼ cup ketchup
2 eggs, lightly beaten
¾ cup milk or tomato juice (the tomato juice will make a moister, softer loaf)
¼ cup cold water

1. Mix all ingredients together well, using your hands. Pack in a well-greased 9- × 5- × 3-inch loaf pan.
   Note:
Wash hands thoroughly in hot soapy water after handling the raw pork, paying particular attention to any bits that may have lodged underneath your fingernails.

2. Bake loaf in a moderate oven (350°) for 1½ hours. Remove from oven and let loaf cool upright in its pan about 10 minutes before turning out and slicing. This is to allow the loaf time to "firm up" so that it will slice more neatly.

Hurry-up Scalloped Corn

Makes 4 servings

"Sometimes," Marian Harris says, "you have to cook things fast. I do this with whole-kernel corn that I've frozen, and Russell likes it a lot."

4 cups frozen whole-kernel corn
½ cup water
2 tablespoons butter
2 teaspoons sugar

½ cup light cream
½ teaspoon salt (or to taste)
Pepper to taste
4 to 6 soda crackers

1. Place corn, water, butter and sugar in a heavy saucepan, set over moderate heat and bring to a boil. Reduce heat so liquid bubbles gently, cover and cook 5 minutes or until corn is tender and no raw starch flavor remains.

2. Mix in cream, and salt and pepper to taste, and bring to a simmer. Remove from heat and crumble in just enough soda crackers to give corn a "spoon soup" consistency. Ladle into soup bowls and serve.

Pickled Beets

Makes 6 to 8 servings

What makes Mrs. Harris's Pickled Beets different is that she uses brown sugar in the pickling syrup. It gives the beets a mellower flavor.

5 pounds uniformly small beets, trimmed of all but 1 inch of the tops and scrubbed well (do not peel and be sure to leave the root ends on so that the beets don't fade as they cook)
Water (for cooking the beets)

Pickling Syrup:
2 cups firmly packed light brown sugar
2 cups cider vinegar
2 cups water
2 teaspoons salt
1 tablespoon whole allspice
1 cinnamon stick, broken in several pieces

1. Place beets in a very large kettle, add just enough water to cover, then set over high heat and bring to a boil. Reduce heat so that water boils gently, cover and cook about 20 to 25 minutes or until beets are firm-tender. Drain, cool beets just until easy to handle, then slip off the skins, trim off tops and root ends. Set aside.

2. Rinse out kettle well, then add all pickling syrup ingredients and bring to a boil. Add the beets and cook about 10 to 15 minutes longer or until a fork pierces them easily. Serve hot, or chill the beets in the pickling syrup and serve cold. The beets will keep well in the refrigerator for about 1 week.

German Coleslaw

Makes 6 to 8 servings

"You'll not go wrong in making the German sweet-sour dishes," says Mrs. Harris, "if you use equal parts sugar, water and vinegar." It's a lesson she learned from her mother and one she uses today whether she is pickling beets or making coleslaw, lettuce or potato salad.

8 cups moderately finely shredded cabbage
½ medium-sized sweet green pepper, cored, seeded and minced
1 medium-sized yellow onion, peeled and chopped fine

Dressing:
3 tablespoons sugar
3 tablespoons hot water
3 tablespoons cider vinegar
½ teaspoon celery seed
½ teaspoon salt
Pinch of pepper
¼ cup vegetable oil

1. Place cabbage, green pepper and onion in a large bowl and toss well to mix.

2. *For the dressing:* Combine sugar and hot water, stirring until sugar dissolves; stir in vinegar, celery seed, salt and pepper. Pour vinegar mixture over slaw and toss well; drizzle in oil and toss well again.

3. Cover slaw and let marinate in the refrigerator 2 to 3 hours before serving. Toss well again before dishing up.

Zucchini Light Bread
Makes one 9- × 5- × 3-inch loaf

"This is really like a fruit-nut bread," Mrs. Harris says. It is, and deliciously moist and full-flavored.

3 eggs
¾ cup vegetable oil
1½ cups sugar
2 cups peeled, moderately coarsely shredded zucchini (you'll need about 3 smallish zucchini; for best results in shredding, use the second coarsest side of a four-sided grater)
1 teaspoon finely grated lemon rind
½ teaspoon vanilla
½ teaspoon orange extract
3 cups sifted all-purpose flour
¾ teaspoon salt
½ teaspoon ground cinnamon
¼ teaspoon ground ginger
2 teaspoons baking powder
1 teaspoon baking soda
½ cup fairly finely chopped pecans

1. Beat eggs with electric mixer at moderate speed until frothy. Add oil slowly, beating all the while. Add sugar and beat hard until creamy and light. Stir in zucchini, lemon rind, vanilla and orange extract.

2. Combine flour with salt, cinnamon, ginger, baking powder and soda, then stir into mixture, 1 cup at a time, beating only enough to blend. Fold in nuts.

3. Spoon into a well-greased-and-floured 9- × 5- × 3-inch loaf pan, then bake in a moderate oven (350°) for 1 hour or until bread pulls from sides of pan and is nicely browned. Cool bread upright in its pan on a wire rack for 15 minutes, then turn out and cool before slicing.

Basic Sweet Dough
Makes enough for one 10-inch tea ring plus 1½ dozen sticky buns

This light and rich yeast dough can be used for making all kinds of sweet breads. "Sometimes I just shape the dough into bowknots and put a gob of jelly in the center of each," Mrs. Harris says. But more often, she will make half of the dough into an Apricot-Pecan Tea Ring and the other half into Sour Cream-Butterscotch Sticky Buns, one of her mother's specialties. Recipes for the tea ring and the sticky buns follow.

2 packages active dry yeast
½ cup very warm water
1 cup milk, scalded
½ cup sugar
¼ cup butter or margarine

2 teaspoons salt
5 to 5½ cups sifted all-purpose flour
2 eggs
1 teaspoon finely grated lemon rind
¼ teaspoon ground mace

1. Sprinkle yeast over very warm water in a large bowl (very warm water should feel comfortably warm when dropped on wrist). Stir until yeast dissolves.

2. Combine scalded milk with sugar, butter and salt, stirring until sugar dissolves and butter melts. Cool mixture to 105° to 115°.

3. Add milk mixture to yeast, then beat in 2 cups of the flour. Beat in the eggs, then the lemon rind and mace. Mix in the remaining 3 to 3½ cups of flour, 1 cup at a time, to make a soft but manageable dough.

4. Turn dough out on a well-floured board (you'll find the dough very sticky at first, so keep your hands well floured, too). Knead the dough lightly for about 5 minutes or until smooth and elastic.

5. Place dough in a warm buttered bowl; turn greased side up. Cover and let rise in a warm, draft-free place until doubled in bulk—about 1½ hours.

6. Punch dough down and let rest for 10 minutes. Divide the dough in half, and use half for preparing the Apricot-Pecan Tea Ring and the other half for Sour Cream-Butterscotch Sticky Buns (both recipes follow). If you prefer to make two tea rings or to use all the dough for sticky buns, simply double the quantities given in the recipes for each.

Apricot-Pecan Tea Ring

Makes one 10-inch tea ring

½ recipe Basic Sweet Dough (recipe precedes)
¼ cup butter or margarine, at room temperature

½ teaspoon ground cinnamon
1¼ cups sieved apricot preserves (about)
¾ cup finely chopped pecans

1. After the Basic Sweet Dough has risen, been punched down, then rested for 10 minutes, roll on a lightly floured pastry cloth into a rectangle about 22 × 12 inches. The rolled-out dough should be between ⅛- and ¼-inch thick.

2. Spread sheet of dough with butter, sprinkle with cinnamon, then spread evenly with preserves. Sprinkle pecans on top. Roll the dough up snugly jelly-roll style, beginning at one long end so that you have a roll about 22 inches long. Make sure that the seam is on the bottom of the roll.

3. Transfer roll to an ungreased baking sheet, then bend into a ring, tucking one end into the other and pinching seam well to seal. With sharp kitchen shears, snip into the top of the ring every 2 inches or so, making V-shaped cuts. Turn points of V's toward outer edge of ring, exposing filling underneath.

4. Cover the ring with a clean dry cloth, then let rise in a warm, draft-free spot until doubled in bulk—about ¾ hour to 1 hour.

5. Bake the ring in a moderate oven (350°) about 25 to 30 minutes or until top is nicely browned and ring sounds hollow when thumped with your finger. Remove from oven, cut into wedges and serve hot with plenty of butter.

Sour Cream-Butterscotch Sticky Buns

Makes 1½ dozen buns

½ recipe Basic Sweet Dough (page 192)

¼ cup butter or margarine, at room temperature

½ cup firmly packed light brown sugar

¾ cup finely chopped pecans

½ teaspoon ground cinnamon

Glaze:

Light brown sugar (about ¾ cup firmly packed)

Sour cream (about ¾ cup)

Finely chopped pecans (about ¾ cup)

1. After the Basic Sweet Dough has risen, been punched down, then rested for 10 minutes, roll on a lightly floured pastry cloth into a long thin strip measuring about 30 × 9 inches; the rolled-out dough should be between ⅛- and ¼-inch thick.

2. Spread butter over surface of dough; sprinkle evenly with brown sugar, pecans and cinnamon. Roll the dough up snugly jelly-roll style, beginning at one long end so that you have a roll about 30 inches long. Make sure that the seam is on the bottom. Let rest for a minute while you prepare the pans.

3. Butter 18 muffin-pan cups well, then, into each, spoon—in this order—2 teaspoons light brown sugar, 2 teaspoons sour cream and 2 teaspoons finely chopped pecans.

4. Slice the roll of dough about 1¼ inches thick, then place one slice, cut-side up, into each muffin-pan cup, pressing down very lightly. Cover rolls with a clean dry cloth and let rise in a warm, draft-free spot until doubled in bulk—about ¾ hour to 1 hour.

5. Bake the rolls in a moderate oven (350°) about 20 to 25 minutes or until they are nicely browned and glaze bubbles up around sides. Remove from oven and invert rolls at once on sheets of waxed paper. Serve hot.

Open-Face Dutch Apple Pie

Makes one 9-inch single-crust pie

"This is a recipe my mother-in-law taught me," Mrs. Harris says. (And we might add that the taste-testers for this cookbook thought it about the best apple pie they'd ever eaten because the apples are held together in a rich, creamy sauce.) The pie's secret? Heavy cream is drizzled over the half-baked pie, then the pie finishes baking. "I remember seeing my mother-in-law take a fork and kind of ooze the cream in so that it ran down between the apples," Mrs. Harris says. "I do it that way, too."

1 cup sugar
2 tablespoons plus 1 teaspoon flour
½ teaspoon ground cinnamon
6 cups sliced raw apples (about 6 to 8 medium-sized all-purpose or cooking apples)

1 9-inch unbaked pie shell with a high fluted edge
2 tablespoons butter or margarine
¼ cup heavy cream beaten with 1 egg yolk

1. Place sugar, flour and cinnamon in a large mixing bowl and mix well. Add apples and toss well until apples are evenly coated with sugar mixture.

2. Fill pie shell with apple mixture, mounding apples up in the center, then dot well with butter. Bake in a hot oven (400°) for about 30 minutes or until crust begins to brown and apples are tender. Remove pie from oven and reduce oven temperature to moderate (350°).

3. Drizzle cream–egg yolk mixture evenly over surface of pie, pressing apples lightly with a fork so that cream oozes down into the filling.

4. Return pie to oven and bake about 15 minutes longer or until crust is nicely browned and filling bubbly. Cool pie to room temperature before cutting.

Farm-Style Apple Crisp

Makes about 6 servings

"This recipe," says Marian Harris, "is another one I got from my mother-in-law. I don't make my apple crisp quite as sweet as she does, but otherwise the recipe's the same. The crisp is delicious served with a scoop of vanilla ice cream or a dab of whipped cream or just with plain milk poured over it."

6 cups sliced raw apples (you'll need 6 to 8 medium-sized apples; Mrs. Harris usually uses Jonathans or Grimes Goldens but any all-purpose apples will do)
1 cup sugar
2 tablespoons flour
½ teaspoon ground cinnamon

2 tablespoons butter or margarine

Topping:
1 cup sugar
1 cup sifted all-purpose flour
1 teaspoon baking powder
1 teaspoon ground cinnamon
½ teaspoon salt
1 large egg, slightly beaten

1. Mix the apples with the sugar, flour and cinnamon; place in a well-buttered 8- × 8- × 2-inch baking dish and dot well with butter.
2. *For the topping:* Place sugar, flour, baking powder, cinnamon and salt in a mixing bowl, stir to mix, then make a well in the center and put in the egg. Fork together briskly until crumbly.
3. Scatter topping over apples, then bake in a moderately slow oven (325°) for about 1 hour or until bubbly and touched with brown. Serve warm or cold.

French Cookies

Makes about 2½ dozen bars (approximately 1 × 2 inches)

"When the corn shellers come here, I make a batch of these cookies," Marian Harris says. "And, oh, they just love them!" The "cookies" are more like brownies, although they are studded with raisins and flavored with cinnamon and coffee in addition to chocolate. They're easy to make, too. You just dump everything in one bowl, *then* mix.

2 cups firmly packed light brown sugar
2 eggs
3 cups sifted all-purpose flour
1 cup vegetable shortening or lard
1 cup strong hot coffee
1 cup seedless raisins
1 teaspoon ground cinnamon
1 teaspoon baking soda

1 teaspoon baking powder
¼ teaspoon salt
3 tablespoons cocoa

Icing:
1 pound confectioners (10X) sugar
3 tablespoons cocoa
8 tablespoons (about) heavy or light cream
1 teaspoon vanilla

1. Place all but icing ingredients in largest mixer bowl in the order listed without stirring. Beat at low speed until lightly mixed, then at medium speed for about 30 seconds.

2. Spread batter evenly over a well-greased jelly-roll pan (15½- × 10½- × 1 inch) and bake in a moderate oven (350°) for about 30 minutes or until springy to the touch.

3. *Meanwhile, prepare the icing:* Combine confectioners sugar and cocoa in a small mixing bowl, pressing out all lumps, then add about 6 tablespoons of the cream and stir to mix. Add the remaining 2 tablespoons of cream if necessary to make a thick but spreadable icing. Stir in vanilla. Set aside.

4. When "cookies" are done, remove from oven and cool upright for about 5 minutes on a wire rack. Then spread the icing evenly on top. Cool to room temperature, then cut into bars.

Date-Pecan Pinwheels

Makes about 5 to 5½ dozen cookies

If you're to have success with these cookies, you must make them on a cool dry day, and in a cool kitchen. The filling and dough are both so sticky that they become completely unmanageable in muggy weather. Even under the best conditions, you may find that you have to chill the dough often as you work it; the heat of your hands will soften it faster than you think possible. But if you persevere, you will be rewarded by some of the very best cookies you've ever eaten. The recipe comes from Mrs. Harris's mother and is one Mrs. Harris remembers fondly as a child. Nowadays she likes to make the dough ahead of time and freeze rolls of it so that she has on hand homemade slice-and-bake cookies.

1 cup butter, lard or vegetable shortening, at room temperature
2 cups firmly packed light brown sugar
3 eggs, well beaten
4 cups sifted all-purpose flour
½ teaspoon salt
½ teaspoon baking soda

Filling:
2¼ cups coarsely chopped dates (you'll find it easiest to snip the dates with kitchen shears; for this amount you'll need about ¾ pound dates)
1 cup sugar
½ cup water
1 cup finely chopped pecans (Mrs. Harris often uses wild hickory nuts, which grow on the farm)

1.   Cream the butter and sugar until fluffy-light; beat in the eggs. Combine flour with salt and soda and beat in, 1 cup at a time. Divide the dough in half, wrap in foil and chill several hours.

2.   *While dough chills, make the filling:* Simmer dates, sugar and water in a small heavy saucepan over low heat, stirring frequently, about 10 minutes or until thick. Remove from heat, mix in nuts, then set aside.

3.   When dough is firm enough to roll, take out half at a time and roll on a well-floured strip of waxed paper into a rectangle about 20 × 10 or 11 inches. The sheet of dough should be very thin—about like piecrust. Spread half the filling over the dough, leaving ½-inch margins all around. Arrange the sheet of dough so that the long side parallels the counter's edge, then lifting the ends of waxed paper nearest you, let the dough roll up on itself, jelly-roll style, so that you have a snug roll, about 20 inches long. Cut roll in half crosswise, then wrap each half in foil and refrigerate or freeze. Repeat with remaining dough.

4.   When ready to bake, slice the cookies as thin as possible—and no more than ¼-inch thick. Space about 2 inches apart on greased baking sheets and bake in a moderate oven (350°) 8 to 10 minutes or until lightly browned. Remove from oven and transfer while warm to wire racks to cool.

Dilled Green Tomatoes

Makes about 8 quarts

According to Mrs. Harris, this same basic recipe may be used for making dill pickles as well as Dilled Green Tomatoes. Simply substitute an equivalent weight of small pickling cucumbers, leave the cucumbers whole instead of quartering them, then proceed as directed.

12 pounds firm, medium-sized green tomatoes, washed and stemmed	2 teaspoons powdered alum
	8 grape leaves, washed
	16 umbels of fresh dill (umbels are the bud clusters)
3 quarts water	8 cloves of garlic, peeled
1 quart white vinegar	8 small hot red peppers, washed
1 cup pickling salt	

1. Quarter the tomatoes but do not peel or core. Bring water, vinegar, salt, and alum to a full rolling boil for the pickling liquid.

2. Pack hot 1-quart jars as follows: Place 1 grape leaf in the bottom of each jar, then 1 umbel of dill, 1 garlic clove and 1 hot red pepper. Pack tomatoes in jars, arranging as attractively as possible and filling to within ¼-inch of the tops. Pour in enough boiling pickling liquid to cover the tomatoes, leaving ¼-inch head space. Tuck in a second umbel of dill. Run a thin-bladed spatula around inside of jar to free air bubbles, wipe jar rims and seal jars.

3. Process jars for 20 minutes in a boiling water bath (212°).

4. Remove jars from water bath, cool to room temperature and check seals. Label jars and store on a cool, dark, dry shelf. Let pickles "season" for about 6 weeks before serving.

Lime Pickles

Makes 12 pints

Last year alone, Mrs. Harris put up about fifty quarts of pickles—dill pickles, bread-and-butter pickles, and these Lime Pickles, which she says are real favorites because they are so crisp and spicy. "I thought my cucumbers would never stop bearing. Even after the first frost they were *still* hanging on the vine!"

8 pounds small-to-medium pickling cucumbers, washed well	8 cups sugar
	1 tablespoon pickling salt
2 cups hydrated lime (calcium hydroxide) mixed with 2 gallons cold water	1 teaspoon celery seeds
	1 teaspoon whole cloves
	1 teaspoon mixed pickling spice
2 quarts white vinegar	

1. Slice cucumbers ¼-inch thick or, if they are very small, halve lengthwise. Place in a large, deep stainless-steel or enamel kettle and cover with the lime-water solution. Cover and let stand 24 hours.

Drain off lime water, rinse cucumbers well, then cover with fresh cold water and soak 3 hours. Drain well again.

2. In a large stainless-steel or enamel saucepan, bring vinegar, sugar, salt and all spices to a boil. Pour boiling hot over drained cucumbers, cover and let stand overnight.

3. Next day, set kettle of pickles over moderately low heat and simmer uncovered for 35 minutes.

4. Pack pickles in hot 1-pint preserving jars, filling to within ¼-inch of the tops; pour in just enough pickling liquid to cover the pickles, leaving ¼-inch headspace, then run a thin-bladed spatula around inside of jars to release trapped air bubbles. Wipe jar rims, seal jars, then process for 10 minutes in a boiling water bath (212°).

5. Remove jars from water bath, cool to room temperature, then check seals. Label jars and store on a cool, dark, dry shelf. Let pickles "season" for at least a month before serving.

Spring's Best Strawberry-Rhubarb Preserves

Makes about 6 to 8 half-pints

"My mother always told me that whenever I wanted to make preserves, I should use equal parts—*by weight*—of prepared fruit and sugar. I've used this recipe almost since I was old enough to know how to make preserves, and I find that I can count on it pretty well. It works for all kinds of fruit—peaches, pears, berries, rhubarb. Of course, you should make certain that part of your prepared fruit— maybe a fourth of it—is slightly *underripe*. Then you can be sure there is enough pectin for the preserves to jell."

2 pounds washed and hulled straw-   2 pounds washed and trimmed rhu-
   berries   barb, cut in 1-inch chunks
                                        4 pounds sugar

1. Place all ingredients in a large heavy stainless-steel or enamel kettle, crush berries slightly, then let stand at room temperature until the berries have given up some of their juice—about 1 hour.

2. Set the kettle over moderately high heat and boil, stirring constantly, for 20 minutes. You must keep stirring the kettle, Mrs. Harris cautions, otherwise the preserves may stick.

3. Skim froth from preserves, then pour into hot, sterilized half-

pint preserving jars, filling to within ⅛-inch of the tops. Seal with a thin layer of melted paraffin. Label jars and store on a cool, dark, dry shelf.

Old-Fashioned Peach or Pear Preserves

Makes about 6 to 8 half-pints

4 pounds thinly sliced fresh peaches or coarsely ground fresh pears (about ¼ of the fruit should be slightly underripe)

4 pounds sugar
Juice of 1 lemon

1. Place all ingredients in a large heavy stainless-steel or enamel kettle, stir to mix, then let stand at room temperature for 1 hour.

2. Set kettle over moderately high heat and boil, stirring *constantly,* for 20 minutes.

3. Skim froth from preserves, then pour into hot, sterilized half-pint preserving jars, filling to within ⅛-inch of the tops. Seal with a thin layer of melted paraffin. Label jars and store on a cool, dark, dry shelf.

Mrs. Godfrey Kaupang
of
East Polk County, Minnesota

"WHEN I was getting married and leaving home in 1931," says Myrtle Kaupang, "my sister copied down Mama's old recipes in a ledger and gave them to me."

They were Norwegian recipes, for the most part, because both of Mrs. Kaupang's parents were Norwegian (her maiden name was Hogenson). Her mother was born in Minnesota, but her father came to this country from Hardanger at the age of eight. Shiploads of Norwegians, including her father and his parents as well as Godfrey Kaupang's people, arrived during the late nineteenth century to homestead the Midwestern wilderness.

"I expect about ninety-five percent of the people in East Polk County are Norwegian," Mrs. Kaupang continues, "although there are some Swedes up north of Winger.

"I didn't learn to speak English until I started to school at the age of five. If the teachers caught us speaking anything *but* English, we'd be made to stay in during recess. Otherwise we never would have learned English. Maybe that's why we didn't teach Norwegian to our two sons, Byron and Marls."

Fortunately, she has not forgotten the Norwegian recipes of her childhood—the sweet soup and spritz, the *lefse* and flat bread, the Christmas cookies and molasses cake.

"Mother was a good cook," she continues, "but she didn't cook like we cook today. Her recipes call for a pinch of this and a pinch of that and butter the size of an egg. Of course, we cooked with what we had on the farm. Father brought eleven children up on a hundred and sixty acres. Think of it! You wouldn't do that today, that's for sure.

"I learned to do outside chores, to sew and cook. But I didn't learn how to bake until after I married. It's funny Godfrey didn't starve on my bread. I would get permission as a little girl to tend the loaves, but Mama always did the mixing and shaping."

Now that her two sons (aged forty-one and thirty-seven) are married with families of their own (they have five sons between them), Mrs. Kaupang does not bake yeast bread as often as she once did. She is more apt to make *lefse*, a thin Norwegian potato pancake, which she describes as "sort of like a taco." She is so adept at it, in fact, that she has been called upon to demonstrate the art of making *lefse* at local Homemaker's Clubs (farm women's groups affiliated with the Minnesota Agricultural Extension Service).

"We have always been farmers," she says. "I grew up on a farm in this county and so did my husband, although we were from different townships." The Kaupangs did not know each other until they were both "quite grown up" (they met at a party in the little town of Winger).

For the first eight years of their marriage, the Kaupangs lived on a farm that had been in his father's family. Then they moved to their present farm, some 400 acres devoted altogether to alfalfa, wheat and pinto beans. "We don't even keep a cow," Mrs. Kaupang says, "or hogs or chickens, although one of our sons has some beef cows."

Both of their sons are now carrying on as farmers in the family tradition. Each has his own farm just down the sandy country lane from their father's farm, and each is teaching the business to his own sons. "I have *only* grandsons," Mrs. Kaupang says. "There hasn't been a girl in the Kaupang family for fifty-three years and that's a fact.

"Farming isn't like it used to be," she continues. "Everything is so specialized today. And there is all this modern machinery. My father farmed with horses and Godfrey's father drove a team of oxen. My sons both have CB radios in their tractors so that they can keep in touch with their families. Their wives take lunch out to them in the fields and the CB is the only way they know which fields the boys are working."

The boys work not only their own farms but also help with their father's now that he is semiretired. Mr. Kaupang spends more time these days around the trim white story-and-a-half farmhouse that he has remodeled over the years. His favorite room—and his wife's— is the huge country kitchen done up in cheerful pinks and reds.

From almost any room in the house, Mr. Kaupang can see the undulating fields of grain that comprise his farm. He can see, too, his wife's showy flower beds and the vegetable garden where she puts in plenty of peas and beans, cucumbers and onions, beets and Swiss chard, melons and corn.

"You know," Mrs. Kaupang says, reminiscing about the old days, "this used to be all forest" (the only trees remaining, save an occasional stand of timber, are the huge shade trees engulfing the Kaupang's house). "Why, I remember as children that we used to hear wolves howling as we walked home from school. If it was getting dark we'd be scared and hurry up home.

"Today it's all farmland—open fields."

Just so, because of the dedication and pluck of Scandinavian immigrants like the Kaupangs and Hogensons who set ax to the north woods wilderness and carved from it a new and more comfortable life.

Scandinavian Sweet Soup

Makes about 8 servings

Although called a soup, this is actually a fruit pudding dessert. "It is considered a great delicacy," says Mrs. Kaupang. "In the old days, we always brought a big container of sweet soup to new mothers. Now people just buy gifts."

1 cup pitted prunes
½ cup dried apricots
½ cup dried peaches
1 cup seedless or sultana raisins
7 cups water
1 cup sugar (or more to taste)

1 cinnamon stick, broken in several places
¼ cup quick-cooking tapioca
⅓ cup medium-dry wine (port, Madeira, sherry, or Marsala)

1. Place prunes, apricots, peaches, raisins, 4 cups of the water, ½ cup of the sugar and the cinnamon stick in a large heavy saucepan. Cover and simmer over moderately low heat 10 to 12 minutes—until fruits are tender. Remove from heat and let stand, covered, until mixture cools to room temperature. This is to allow the fruits to plump. Remove cinnamon stick.

2. In a separate saucepan combine the remaining 3 cups water and ½ cup sugar with the tapioca. Let stand 5 minutes, then set over moderate heat and cook, stirring constantly, until mixture comes to a full boil and tapioca is transparent. Remove from heat and cool 20 minutes, stirring occasionally.

3. Combine fruit and tapioca mixtures, then stir in wine. Taste for sweetening and add slightly more sugar if needed to suit your taste. Serve warm or cold as a dessert.

Casserole of Chicken, Carrots, Peas and Pasta

Makes 4 to 6 servings

At the top of this recipe in Mrs. Kaupang's notebook of favorites is written, "Very good." The casserole, moreover, is a splendid way to use leftover cooked chicken, chicken gravy, and snippets of cooked carrots and peas.

2 to 2½ cups diced cooked chicken (or turkey)

2 cups cooked, well-drained egg noodles or elbow macaroni

¾ cup chicken gravy (use leftover gravy or substitute medium white sauce, seasoned to taste)

½ cup finely diced celery

½ cup diced, drained, cooked carrots

½ cup cooked, drained green peas (you may substitute green beans, whole-kernel corn or limas, if you like)

1 tablespoon finely grated onion

½ teaspoon salt

⅛ teaspoon pepper

Topping:
¾ cup soft fine breadcrumbs mixed with 1 tablespoon melted butter or margarine

1. Combine all ingredients except the breadcrumb topping and toss lightly to mix.

2. Place in a buttered 6-cup casserole, scatter topping evenly over all and bake uncovered in a moderate oven (350°) for 40 to 45 minutes or until browned and bubbly.

Fried Northern Pike

Makes 4 servings

"One of our boys ice-fishes in winter," says Mrs. Kaupang. "Whitefish is what he gets mostly . . . he smokes it and it tastes just like cisco" (a particularly delicate variety of whitefish). Northern pike is another of the Kaupangs' favorites, especially when Mrs. Kaupang deep-fries it. She selects small fish, those weighing about a pound, and fries them whole—bones and all. You may prefer to have the fish filleted.

4 small pike (about 1 pound each), cleaned, dressed, and filleted

¾ cup milk

¾ cup unsifted all-purpose flour

Vegetable oil or shortening for deep-fat frying

Salt and pepper to season

1. Dip the fish fillets in the milk, then in flour so that they are nicely coated on each side.

2. Deep-fry in hot fat (375° on a deep-fat thermometer) about 3 to 4 minutes, just until a rich golden brown on each side. Drain on paper toweling.

3. Sprinkle with salt and pepper and serve with lemon wedges.

Scalloped Carrots

Makes 4 to 6 servings

"I scallop carrots just the way I scallop corn," Mrs. Kaupang says. "I cook the carrots first, dice them, then mix them with butter, cream and egg and top with buttered saltine crumbs."

2 tablespoons butter or margarine
2 tablespoons flour
⅛ teaspoon ground nutmeg
1⅓ cups light cream or milk
1 teaspoon salt
⅛ teaspoon pepper
1 egg, lightly beaten

3 cups finely diced well-drained cooked carrots
1 cup fairly coarse soda-cracker crumbs mixed with 2 tablespoons melted butter or margarine (topping)

1. In a medium-sized heavy saucepan, melt 2 tablespoons butter or margarine over moderate heat. Blend in flour and nutmeg, add light cream or milk and heat, stirring constantly, until thickened and smooth—about 3 minutes. Stir in salt and pepper. Mix a little of the hot sauce with the egg, then stir back into pan.

2. Combine sauce with carrots, pour into a buttered 6-cup casserole and scatter the cracker-crumb topping evenly on top.

3. Bake uncovered in a moderate oven (350°) for 30 to 35 minutes or until browned and bubbling.

Creamed New Turnips

Makes 4 to 6 servings

"We used to pull turnips in the spring while they were still very small and cream them like new potatoes. Oh, they were good!"

1½ pounds small, young turnips (they should be about the size of new potatoes)
1½ cups boiling water
4 tablespoons butter or margarine
4 tablespoons flour

2 cups milk or light cream
1 teaspoon salt (about)
⅛ teaspoon pepper (about)
⅛ teaspoon ground nutmeg (about)

1. Trim stem and root ends from turnips and discard; scrub turnips well in cool water, then put into the boiling water in a covered saucepan and boil about 30 to 35 minutes, just until you can pierce a turnip easily with a fork. Drain well.
2. While turnips cook, melt the butter in a separate saucepan and blend in flour. Add milk, salt, pepper and nutmeg and cook and stir over moderate heat just until thickened and smooth. Turn heat to lowest point and let sauce mellow while turnips finish cooking. Taste for seasoning and add more salt, pepper and nutmeg, if needed.
3. Pour sauce over drained turnips, toss lightly and serve.

Sauerkraut Salad

Makes about 3 cups

"You serve this like a relish, not a salad," says Mrs. Kaupang. "It goes real good with meat, especially steak."

½ cup cider vinegar
1 cup sugar
2 cups (about 1 pound) sauerkraut, rinsed and drained

1 cup finely diced celery
¼ cup minced onion
¼ cup minced sweet green pepper
¼ cup minced sweet red pepper

1. Boil vinegar and sugar uncovered in a small heavy saucepan 4 to 5 minutes or until slightly syrupy. Cool 15 minutes.

2.   Place sauerkraut, celery, onion and peppers in a large bowl, pour in syrup and toss well to mix. Cover and refrigerate several hours before serving. This relish keeps well for about two weeks, if refrigerated.

Homemade White Cheese

"Here's a very good cheese recipe that I got from Godfrey's mother," says Mrs. Kaupang. "It's not a cottage cheese because she made it in a mold. She used unpasteurized milk, of course, and I'm not sure whether or not it would work with pasteurized milk." Here, then, just as she dictated it, is Mr. Kaupang's mother's recipe for white cheese:

"Have 3 gallons of milk in a large kettle on the stove with the heat no hotter than the hand can be held at the bottom of the kettle. Let stand until milk curdles. Pour into cloth and strain off the whey. Let the curds stand 20 minutes. Crumble well. Add 1 teaspoon soda, ½ cup butter and let stand 2 hours. Put in double boiler and add ½ cup cream and 1 teaspoon salt and cook until thick, about 45 minutes. Pour into a form and let stand 7 days before using."

Lefse (Norwegian Potato Pancakes)

Makes about six 12-inch, thin pancakes

"Some people put cream in *lefse,* but I never do," Mrs. Kaupang says of these tissue-thin potato pancakes. "It makes them tough." She learned how to make *lefse* as a little girl but admits that "it took a little while" to master the art of rolling them thin, then transferring them to the griddle without tearing them. She uses a 15-inch round griddle for making *lefse* (and rolls them exactly that size), but we suggest that you try the recipe with the more widely available 12-inch griddle. Moreover, a 12-inch tissue-thin circle of dough is somewhat easier to handle than one 3 inches larger. How does one eat *lefse?*

"With sugar and butter," Mrs. Kaupang says. "Of course, they're good spread with jam and good with fruit sauce, too." They are eaten as an accompaniment to the main course and are traditional at Christmastime along with *lutefisk* (cod that has been treated with lye).

3 cups hot, unseasoned mashed potatoes
1 tablespoon melted butter

1½ teaspoons sugar
1 to 1¼ cups sifted all-purpose flour

1. In a large mixing bowl, beat potatoes with butter and sugar until well blended. Cool to room temperature. Mix in 1 cup of flour to make a stiff dough (if it seems sticky or too soft to knead, mix in the additional ¼ cup of flour).

2. Turn onto a lightly floured board and knead 3 to 5 minutes or until elastic. Pinch off chunks of dough and shape into balls about the size of tennis balls.

3. On a floured pastry cloth, roll the balls of dough, one at a time, into tissue-thin circles about 12 inches in diameter, using a floured, stockinette-covered rolling pin.

4. Lay rolling pin across center of a circle of dough, carefully lop half of it over the rolling pin and ease onto a lightly greased, hot, 12- to 15-inch round griddle set over high heat (Mrs. Kaupang uses a 15-inch electric griddle set at 500°). Let bake 1 to 2 minutes—surface of pancake will rumple into hills and valleys. With a pancake turner, check underside. When it is dappled with brown, carefully turn pancake over and lightly brown the other side. Bake the remaining circles the same way. Serve hot or cold.

Norwegian Flat Bread

Makes about six 12-inch, thin pancakes

Like *lefse*, Norwegian Flat Bread is a tissue-thin pancake that requires dexterity with the rolling pin. It is a shorter dough than *lefse*, hence it is even more difficult to handle, especially when it comes to flipping it on the griddle. Unlike *lefse*, it bakes slowly so that it will dry as it browns. Mrs. Kaupang says that the implement to use when rolling the dough is a corrugated rolling pin. You can, however, roll it with a regular rolling pin, then prick the pancake with a fork as it bakes on the griddle. This is to release steam so that the flat bread will become fairly crisp.

¼ cup sugar
1 cup buttermilk
½ teaspoon salt
½ cup *unsifted* stone-ground corn meal

½ cup *unsifted* Graham flour
½ teaspoon baking soda
¼ cup melted lard (hog lard, not vegetable shortening)
2 cups sifted all-purpose flour

1. In a large mixing bowl, combine sugar, buttermilk, and salt. Mix in corn meal. Combine Graham flour with soda and mix in also. Stir in lard, beating until it is thoroughly incorporated. Blend in the all-purpose flour, 1 cup at a time, to make a stiff dough.

2. Turn onto a lightly floured board and knead 2 to 3 minutes or until elastic. Pinch off chunks of dough and shape into balls about the size of tennis balls.

3. On a floured pastry cloth, roll the balls of dough, one at a time, into tissue-thin circles about 12 inches in diameter, using a corrugated rolling pin (or if you don't have one, a stockinette-covered rolling pin), lightly floured.

4. Lay rolling pin across center of a circle of dough, carefully lop half of it over the rolling pin and transfer to a lightly greased 12- to 15-inch round griddle set over low heat. Let the flat bread bake 2 to 3 minutes, and if you have not rolled it with a corrugated rolling pin, prick the surface lightly with the tines of a fork. Carefully flip the bread over, using a pancake turner, and let crispen and dry for 4 to 5 minutes longer. Bake the remaining circles the same way. Serve hot or cold, with or without butter and jam.

Note:
If the flat bread does not seem crisp—or if the weather is humid and it loses its crispness—set uncovered in a very slow oven (250°) for 8 to 10 miuntes. The bread will quickly crispen.

Molasses Cake Made with Coffee

Makes one 13- × 9- × 2-inch loaf cake

"This is an old, old recipe that my mother got from her mother," Mrs. Kaupang says. It is a rich, dark, and moist loaf cake that tastes much like gingerbread although it contains no ginger.

4 eggs
1 cup sugar
1 cup melted butter
1 teaspoon ground allspice
1 cup molasses
4¼ cups sifted all-purpose flour

1 cup very strong hot coffee in which 2 teaspoons baking soda have been dissolved (use a 2-cup measure for combining the coffee and soda because mixture will froth up and overflow a 1-cup measure)

1. Beat eggs and sugar until frothy-thick; add butter slowly, beating all the while. Mix in allspice and molasses.

2. Add flour alternately with the coffee mixture, beginning and ending with the flour and beating after each addition only enough to mix.

3. Pour batter into a greased 13- × 9- × 2-inch baking pan and bake in a moderately hot oven (375°) for 30 to 35 minutes or until cake begins to pull from sides of pan and feels springy to the touch.

4. Cool cake upright in its pan on a wire rack for at least 15 minutes before cutting into squares and serving.

Note:

This cake needs no frosting.

How to Make Cake Flour

"You know, in the old days," says Myrtle Kaupang, "we couldn't get cake flour. So we'd make our own." Here, just as she dictated it, is the way it was done:

"To make a cup of cake flour, first place 2 level tablespoons of cornstarch in a 1-cup measure. Then fill up the measure with sifted bread flour. This makes the equivalent of 1 cup of *unsifted* cake flour. Sift 3 times before using."

Norwegian Christmas Cookies

Makes about 5 dozen cookies

"You cut these in little squares," Mrs. Kaupang says of these crisp cookies that are baked in a thin, solid sheet. "The thinner you can press them, the better." We might add that it's important to keep the thickness of the dough as uniform as possible, especially about the edges so that they do not brown before the center is done.

1 cup butter, at room temperature	2 cups *unsifted* all-purpose flour
1 cup sugar	1 cup finely minced walnuts or pe-
1 egg, separated	cans
½ teaspoon ground cinnamon	

1. Cream butter, sugar and egg yolk until light; mix in cinnamon. Add flour and beat just enough to blend.
2. Press the dough out on a lightly greased large baking sheet until uniformly ⅜-inch thick.
3. Beat the egg white lightly, then with a pastry brush, brush evenly over surface of dough. Scatter nuts on top, distributing as uniformly as possible. Again press dough out with your hands—the nut coating makes it easier to press because it does not stick to your hands—until ⅛- to ¼-inch thick. The dough will almost cover the baking sheet.
4. Bake in a moderately hot oven (375°) 15 to 20 minutes or until very lightly browned and dough seems fairly firm to the touch. Remove from oven and mark into 1- to 1½-inch squares, but do not separate squares. Let cookies cool about 10 minutes, then separate the squares and transfer to wire racks to cool. Store in airtight canisters.

Spritz

Makes about 5 dozen cookies

Spritz are usually thought of as being German, but these buttery, egg-yolk-rich cookies, squirted out of a cooky press into fancy shapes, are also a great favorite among Norwegians, according to Mrs. Kaupang. Her recipe—an old family one—is somewhat unusual in that it contains finely ground almonds.

1 cup butter, at room temperature	4 blanched almonds, very finely
⅔ cup sugar	ground
3 egg yolks	2½ cups sifted all-purpose flour
	½ teaspoon ground cardamom

1. Cream butter, sugar and egg yolks until light; blend in almonds.
2. Add the flour, 1 cup at a time, beating well after each addition. Mix in the cardamom. If dough seems soft, chill until it will hold its shape when put through a cooky press.
3. Press dough into fancy designs by putting through a cooky press directly onto ungreased baking sheets, spacing the cookies about 1 inch apart. Mrs. Kaupang likes to use the star tip of the press, squirting the dough into little ridged logs about 2½ to 3 inches long, which she then bends into little horseshoes.
4. Bake in a moderately hot oven (375°) for 8 to 10 minutes or until cookies are firm to the touch but not brown.
5. Cool 2 to 3 minutes on baking sheets, then transfer to wire racks and cool to room temperature. Store in airtight canisters.

Chokecherry Syrup

Makes about 1 pint

Chokecherries abound in northern Minnesota and to Scandinavians, homesick for the lingonberries of the old country, they are a good substitute. Mrs. Kaupang says that her family used to make chokecherry wine, also a syrup much like this one to serve over pancakes.

1 pint (2 cups) chokecherry juice made by boiling chokecherries in just enough water to cover until berries are mushy, then straining the juice through cheesecloth)

3 cups sugar
½ cup light corn syrup

1. Simmer all ingredients together, uncovered, over moderately low heat in a very large heavy enamel or stainless-steel saucepan about 15 minutes or until mixture is thick and syrupy.
2. Pour into a heatproof pitcher and serve in place of maple syrup on pancakes.

Swiss Chard Pickles

Makes about 4 half-pints

"We raise a lot of Swiss chard," says Mrs. Kaupang. "It's easy to grow around here. We like it just boiled and buttered. And I like to make these pickles with it. They're very unusual and good."

4 cups Swiss chard stalks, cut in 1-inch pieces
2 cups coarsely chopped yellow onions
2 cups sugar
1 tablespoon salt
1 teaspoon pepper
3 cups cider vinegar
1 tablespoon mixed pickling spices, tied in cheesecloth
3 tablespoons cornstarch
2 teaspoons dry mustard
1 tablespoon ground turmeric
⅓ cup cold water

1. Place the chard, onions, sugar, salt, pepper, vinegar and spice bag in a large heavy enamel or stainless-steel kettle, cover and boil 10 to 15 minutes or until chard is crisp-tender. Remove spice bag and discard.

2. Meanwhile, blend cornstarch, mustard and turmeric, then mix with the cold water to make a smooth paste.

3. Blend a little of the hot kettle mixture into cornstarch paste, stir back into kettle and cook, stirring, for 5 minutes or until thickened and clear.

4. Using a wide-mouthed canning funnel to facilitate jar filling, ladle boiling hot pickles into half-pint jars, filling to within ⅛-inch of the tops. Run a thin-bladed knife around inside edges of jars to release air bubbles. Wipe jar rims with a damp cloth and seal jars.

5. Process jars for 10 minutes in a boiling water bath (212°). Lift jars from water bath, complete seals if necessary and cool to room temperature. Check seals, label jars and store on a dark, cool, dry shelf. Allow the pickles to mellow and season about 4 to 6 weeks before serving.

Beet Wine

"There used to be so many fruits and berries around here that we always made wine," says Mrs. Kaupang. "We even made wine out of beets." Here's the recipe, copied just as it was set down in Mrs. Kaupang's notebook of hand-written family receipts:

"Boil 8 or 9 large beets, peeled and sliced, in 4 quarts of water. Strain. Stir in 8 cups of sugar and one-half of a 5-cent cake of yeast. Let stand 10 days. Strain and bottle. This will make about 4 quarts of wine."

The Plains and Southwest

Mrs. Serafin Gomez
of
Hidalgo County, Texas

THE chili parlors scattered across the United States have created more than one misconception about "Tex-Mex" cooking. "So have a lot of magazine articles," says Albesa Gomez of San Juan, Texas. "Most people have the wrong idea about what we eat and how we cook."

When she says, "we," she is speaking of the thousands of Texans of Mexican descent who live, as she does, in the Rio Grande Valley. Although her husband was born in Monterrey, south of the border, Albesa (whose maiden name was Villarreal) can trace her own Texas roots back for three generations.

Continuing her discussion of the misconceptions about "Tex-Mex" cooking, she says, "I don't make chili very often. And I don't use much red pepper in cooking. Our dishes are *not* hot. I guess you could say that our favorite seasonings are *comino* (cumin), *cilantro* (coriander), cinnamon, and garlic."

Yes, she does make tortillas every day. She also makes guacamole fairly often (a surprisingly bland version), but the great dietary staple in her house, as in many others, is the *frijole* (dried pinto bean) prepared in half a dozen different ways.

"I love to bake," she continues, adding that she didn't learn how until after she was married in the spring of 1949. "I wish now that I *didn't* like to bake so much. My older daughter has to go on a diet." (She has four sons and two daughters, ranging in age from late twenties down to seven.) "Then, too," she adds, "my doctor wants me to lose *so* many pounds."

Now in her late forties, Albesa Gomez may not have the trim figure she did when she married at eighteen, but she is hardly obese. Her skin has the deep olive tones of perpetual suntan but is remarkably unlined; her hair, cut short and curled, is a lustrous black, and her eyes are a warm cinnamon brown. "It's funny," she says, "my sons are all so slim. So is my littlest one"—a girl—"but my older daughter and I both have to watch what we eat."

It's difficult. Her children are all unmarried and living at home ("we *still* claim them," she says, laughing). And of course, the foods they like best are the lusty Mexican dishes on which they were brought up.

"I learned to cook most of them when I was a girl," Albesa says. "There were six children in my family, so we had to do our share of the work." She remembers learning how to roll and shape tortillas, how to cook *frijoles*. "They're easy to burn," she explains. "But I learned as a girl that if they *start* to burn, what you have to do is take the beans off the top and put them in another pot. If you add water to the burned beans, the flavor will get through all the beans and ruin the whole pot."

Albesa was born and brought up only a few miles from where she lives today—in the little town of Alamo where her father had a grocery business. And she has spent most of her life in "the valley," as she calls it. This is citrus country, and the orange and grapefruit groves stretch for miles across the alluvial flatlands, their arrow-straight rows marching toward the horizon.

The Rio Grande (not particularly impressive at this point), meanders through, forming the Texas-Mexico border. Reynosa is the Mexican border town, and it is to the big, roistering central market here that Albesa goes to buy many of her groceries "because things are so much cheaper in Mexico." She knows precisely what she is and isn't allowed to bring back into the United States, and she shops accordingly.

Although the distance from Albesa's house to Reynosa is less than twenty miles, the minute you cross over the bridge into Mexico you feel as if you're a thousand miles away. Changes are abrupt. The town is built in the old Spanish style around a green plaza. Streets and sidewalks are narrow, and the buildings fronting them are either faced with pop-art tiles or washed in pastel shades of pink and green and gold. The lilt of Spanish is heard everywhere (there is no decompression zone as there is in certain other border towns). But Albesa, who is as fluent in Spanish as in English, feels completely at ease as she bargains with the fruit and vegetable vendors. (Her husband is bilingual, too, as are her six children.)

"I didn't study Spanish in school," she says. "But we spoke it at home. I stopped school in the tenth grade," she says, then adds with a laugh, "I guess I'm one of the drop-outs." Although her own children are all studying Spanish in school (even the littlest one who is in the grammar grades), English is what the Gomezes speak at home. "My older daughter doesn't like to speak Spanish," she continues. "But she will if she has to."

The whole family had to during their five-year stay in Venezuela in the late 1950s and early 1960s. "My husband was helping to build an oil refinery there," she explains. "We liked living in Venezuela, but we did get homesick for some of the foods we have here." Also, it might be added, for the new house they had just bought in San Juan. "We rented the house while we were away," Albesa explains. "But we didn't live here until we came back in 1962." (It was then that her husband went into business for himself—he sells used construction equipment.) Serafin Gomez is extremely handy with a hammer and saw and shortly after the family moved into the new house he knocked out the carport walls to give Albesa a bigger kitchen and the family a TV room (the two now open into each other).

The kitchen is where you'll find most of the action at the Gomezes, especially at the big round dining bar that encircles one of the old carport pillars. "This was my husband's idea," Albesa says, pointing to the dining bar. And an excellent one, it turns out, for such a busy family; they rarely settle down for a meal together except in the evening.

Dinners always included some of the particular family favorites—*tacos* heaped with *carne* (meat filling), *pollo en salsa* (chicken in tomato sauce), a big bowl of *frijoles* that have simmered slowly most of the day, a guacamole salad, perhaps, and, of course, a plate piled high with tortillas, fresh from the griddle.

Caldo de Pollo (Chicken Soup)

Makes 6 to 8 servings

Whenever Mrs. Gomez prepares one of the family's favorite chicken dishes, she saves the skimpy pieces—backs, necks, wings—along with the hearts and gizzards to make into soup. Her chicken soup, Mexican in origin, is seasoned with coriander and chock full of potatoes, carrots, sweet pepper, and green peas.

2 chicken necks
2 chicken backs
4 chicken wings
2 chicken gizzards
2 chicken hearts
2 quarts water
2 medium-sized carrots, peeled and sliced thin
2 celery ribs, washed and sliced thin
1 medium-sized yellow onion, peeled and chopped

½ medium-sized sweet green pepper, cored, seeded, and minced
1 small garlic clove, peeled and crushed (optional)
3 medium-sized potatoes, peeled and cubed
1 cup green peas (fresh, frozen, or canned)
1 tablespoon minced fresh coriander leaves, or ¼ teaspoon ground coriander
¼ teaspoon cumin seeds, crushed
2 teaspoons salt or to taste

1.   Place all chicken parts and water in a large heavy kettle and simmer, covered, about 2 hours or until meat falls from bones. Remove and discard bones and skin. Chop gizzards and hearts and any large chunks of meat; reserve.

2.   To kettle, add carrots, celery, onion, green pepper and, if you like, the garlic, cover and simmer 30 minutes. Add all remaining ingredients and the reserved chopped chicken meat, cover and simmer 30 to 40 minutes longer or until all vegetables are tender and flavors well balanced. Taste for salt and add more if needed. Ladle into soup bowls and serve.

Pollo en Salsa (*Chicken in Tomato Sauce*)

Makes 6 to 8 servings

Chicken is Mrs. Gomez's favorite meat, which she often prepares as *Pollo en Salsa* (chicken in a spicy tomato sauce). "People always say we do a lot of casseroles," Mrs. Gomez says. "Actually what we do are skillet dishes."

2 young broiler-fryers (about 2½ to 3 pounds each), disjointed (reserve and freeze giblets and neck to use later in soups or stews)
4 tablespoons vegetable oil
1 medium-sized yellow onion, peeled and minced
1 medium-sized green pepper, cored, seeded, and minced

1 garlic clove, peeled and minced
¼ teaspoon cumin seeds, pulverized
3 tablespoons flour
1½ teaspoons salt
⅛ teaspoon pepper
2 medium-sized ripe tomatoes, peeled, cored and chopped (include all juices)

1.   Brown the chicken (undredged) in the oil in a *very* large heavy skillet over fairly high heat; drain chicken on several thicknesses of paper toweling and keep aside. Pour all but 2 tablespoons oil from skillet.

2.   Add onion, green pepper and garlic to skillet and stir-fry about 5 minutes over moderate heat until limp. Blend in cumin and flour and heat, stirring, about 2 minutes. Mix in salt, pepper, and tomatoes and cook, stirring, about 5 minutes. Mixture will be quite thick—but it will thin considerably as the dish cooks.

3.   Return chicken to skillet, spoon sauce over each piece, cover and simmer very slowly about 1 hour or until chicken is tender. Uncover and simmer about 15 minutes longer to thicken the sauce a bit, then serve with fluffy boiled rice.

Carne (Meat) for Tacos

Makes enough to fill 6 to 8 tacos

This taco filling can be made with any leftover roast—beef, pork, even chicken or turkey. Simply mince enough meat to measure about 2 cups, then use it in place of the ground beef in the recipe. In filling their tacos, the Gomez family usually add first some shredded crisp lettuce, then a heaping spoonful or two of the *carne,* then a sprinkling of grated sharp Cheddar.

1 pound lean ground beef	3 tablespoons flour
1 tablespoon vegetable oil	¼ teaspoon cumin seeds, pulver-
1 small yellow onion, peeled and minced	ized
	1 teaspoon salt
1 small garlic clove, peeled and crushed	⅛ teaspoon pepper
	1 cup cold water

1.   Brown the beef in a large heavy skillet in the oil about 5 minutes over moderately high heat; add onion and garlic and stir-fry mixture over moderate heat about 5 minutes. Blend in flour, cumin, salt and pepper, then add water and cook and stir about 3 minutes or until thickened.

2.   Turn heat under skillet to lowest point, cover skillet and simmer *very* slowly for 30 to 40 minutes. Check the skillet every now and then and give the mixture a stir so that it doesn't stick. If you have an

asbestos flame-tamer, put it underneath the skillet during the slow simmering so that the mixture does not dry out too much.

Note:

This taco filling is also very good spooned into hamburger buns.

Machacado (*Eggs Scrambled with Beef*)

Makes about 6 servings

If you want to break the boring breakfast routine, try *Machacado*, eggs scrambled with meat. A true *Machacado* should be made with jerky (dried meat), but according to Albesa Gomez, you can substitute leftover roast beef or pork. And she, in fact, often does. The way her family likes *Machacado* best is rolled up inside tortillas.

2 cups finely minced leftover roast beef (or 1 cup shredded jerky)
2 tablespoons vegetable oil
⅓ cup finely minced yellow onion
2 medium-sized ripe tomatoes, peeled, cored, and finely chopped (include juice)

1 teaspoon salt
2 *chiles serranos*, seeded and minced fine, or ¼ to ½ teaspoon crushed, dried red chili peppers (depending upon how hot you like things)
6 eggs, lightly beaten

1.   Stir-fry the meat in the oil in a large heavy skillet (not iron) over moderately high heat about 5 minutes, until frizzled and browned. Reduce heat to moderate, add onion and stir-fry about 5 minutes, until onion is limp and golden. Add tomatoes and their juice, salt and chili peppers and cook uncovered, stirring, about 25 to 30 minutes or until mixture is thickened and sauce-like.

2.   Pour in the eggs and scramble until eggs are softly set or cooked the way you like them. Dish up and serve at once with tortillas.

Mexican-Style Rice

Makes 6 servings

When Albesa Gomez speaks of serving rice, she means Mexican-style rice, which is very much like Spanish Rice except for two additions—garlic and cumin. "They are our most important seasonings," she explains ("our" meaning Texans of Mexican descent). Sometimes she will make this recipe with tomato juice, sometimes with a chopped fresh tomato, or "if I want the rice real red, with tomato sauce."

⅓ cup finely chopped onion
⅓ cup finely chopped sweet green pepper
½ small garlic clove, peeled and minced
1 cup rice (*not* quick-cooking)
2 tablespoons vegetable oil or olive oil

1 can (8 ounces) tomato sauce
1¾ cups water
¼ teaspoon cumin seeds, pulverized
½ teaspoon salt
⅛ teaspoon pepper

1.   Stir-fry the onion, green pepper, garlic and rice in the oil in a large heavy saucepan over moderate heat about 5 minutes—until onion and pepper are limp and rice golden.

2.   Stir in all remaining ingredients, bring to a boil, then reduce heat so that liquid bubbles gently, cover tight and simmer about 25 to 30 minutes or until rice is tender and all liquid absorbed. Serve as a potato substitute with beef, pork, or chicken.

Frijoles

Makes about 6 servings

Frijole is the Spanish word for bean, and in the Southwestern United States, where many Americans are of Spanish or Mexican descent, *frijoles* are a dietary staple. The *frijole* Albesa Gomez likes best is the pinto bean, beige with dark speckles when dried, coral red when cooked. "I always soak my *frijoles* before I cook them," she explains. "That way I get bigger beans."

2 cups dried pinto beans, washed and sorted
5 cups cold water

⅛ pound lean slab bacon, cut in 3 to 4 chunks
2 teaspoons salt
⅛ teaspoon black pepper

1.   Soak the beans in the water overnight in a large heavy kettle. Next day add bacon, salt and pepper, bring kettle to a boil over moderate heat, then reduce heat so that water barely ripples, cover and cook slowly for about 2 to 2½ hours or until beans are very soft and most of the water is absorbed.

2.   Remove about half the beans, mash well with a potato masher and stir into unmashed beans. Serve as a side dish. Save any leftover beans for that other great favorite of the Gomezes, *Frijoles Refritos* (recipe follows).

Frijoles Refritos

Makes about 4 servings

There are as many ways to prepare *Frijoles Refritos* as there are cooks. Some like to fry the beans over high heat until crusty-brown on the bottom; others—and Mrs. Gomez is of this school—like to stir-fry them over gentler heat so that they are creamy.

2 to 3 tablespoons bacon drippings or vegetable oil

4 cups leftover Frijoles (recipe precedes)
Salt and pepper to taste

1.   Heat 2 tablespoons of the drippings in a large heavy skillet over moderately high heat until ripples appear on the surface, add the *frijoles,* reduce heat to moderate and cook, stirring now and then, until steaming hot. If beans seem dry, add 1 additional tablespoon of drippings.
2.   Taste the beans and, if needed, add salt and pepper. Dish up and serve.

Frijoles à la Charra

Makes 6 servings

Next to *Frijoles* and *Frijoles Refritos* (both recipes precede), the Gomez family likes best *Frijoles à la Charra,* piquant beans reddened with tomatoes and flavored with peppers both sweet and hot. If possible, use fresh coriander instead of the ground seeds for seasoning the dish—the flavor is more aromatic.

2 cups dried pinto beans, washed and sorted

5 cups cold water (about)

⅛ pound lean slab bacon, cut in small dice

½ cup minced yellow onion

½ cup minced sweet green pepper

1 large garlic clove, peeled and crushed

2 tablespoons vegetable oil or olive oil

2 medium-sized ripe tomatoes, peeled and chopped (reserve juices)

2 *chiles serranos,* chopped fine, or ¼ to ½ teaspoon crushed dried red chili peppers (depending upon how hot you like things)

1 tablespoon minced fresh coriander leaves, or ¼ teaspoon ground coriander

¼ teaspoon cumin seeds, pulverized

1½ teaspoons salt or to taste

⅛ teaspoon black pepper

1.   Soak the beans in the water overnight in a large heavy kettle. Next day add bacon, bring kettle to a boil over moderate heat, then reduce heat so that liquid ripples gently, cover and cook about 1¼ to 1½ hours or until beans are firm-tender.

2.   Meanwhile, stir-fry the onion, green pepper and garlic in the oil over moderate heat until limp—about 5 minutes. Add the tomatoes and their juices and all remaining ingredients. Reduce heat to lowest point and let mixture mellow until beans have finished cooking.

3.   Stir tomato mixture into beans and simmer uncovered, *very slowly,* about 30 minutes or until mixture is about the consistency of chili (if too thick, thin with a little water). Taste for salt and add more if needed. Dish up and serve as a meat substitute.

Guacamole

Makes about 6 servings

Mrs. Gomez's recipe for guacamole is vastly different from the incendiary appetizer that many of us serve as a cockail dip with corn chips. She serves guacamole as a salad, not as an appetizer. She simply mashes the avocadoes, mixes them with lemon juice to prevent browning, and maybe adds a smidgen of finely grated onion for flavor. The "nip" is in the dressing—called *Salsa Picante*—sort of an all-purpose hot pepper sauce ladled over everything from scrambled eggs to tacos.

3 large soft-ripe avocadoes

2 tablespoons lemon juice

1 tablespoon finely grated onion

½ teaspoon salt

2 cups thinly sliced crisp lettuce

Salsa Picante (recipe follows)

1.   Halve avocadoes lengthwise, twist out seeds, then scoop the flesh into a mixing bowl. Sprinkle with lemon juice, add onion and salt, then mash with a potato masher. Mixture should be lumpy, *not* creamy.

2.   Arrange beds of lettuce on 6 salad plates, mound guacamole on top, then pass the *Salsa Picante* so that everyone can ladle as much as he likes over his guacamole.

Salsa Picante

Makes about 1½ cups

The best peppers to use in making *Salsa Picante* are the small, green *chiles serranos* (they're about the size of your little finger—and fiery). If you must substitute another variety of pepper, adjust the quantity according to the hotness of the pepper—and how hot you can take things. Usually, though not invariably, the smaller the chili, the hotter it is.

2 medium-sized fully ripe tomatoes, peeled and chopped fine
1 small yellow onion, peeled and minced fine
3 *chiles serranos,* chopped fine (use 1 or 2 if you don't like things fiery)
1 tablespoon minced fresh coriander leaves, or 1 tablespoon minced Italian (flatleaved) parsley and a pinch of ground coriander
½ teaspoon salt
3 tablespoons cold water

Mix all ingredients together and serve as a sauce for eggs, meats, tacos or guacamole.

Note:
Resist the temptation to buzz everything up in an electric blender—the mixture will be foamy because of the quantity of air beaten in, and drab in color. A proper *Salsa Picante* should be thick and lumpy, not fluffy. It should also be a nice tomato-red flecked with green.

Flour Tortillas

Makes about 2 dozen

Mrs. Gomez makes two kinds of tortillas—Flour Tortillas, which are made with all-purpose flour, and Masa Tortillas, made with *masa harina,* a floury Mexican corn meal ground out of dried hominy. If you live in a large metropolitan area, you should be able to buy *masa harina* at Spanish or Latin American groceries. To save time, Mrs. Gomez usually rolls all her tortillas out at once, then layers them between sheets of wax paper and stores them in the refrigerator. That way, she has only to brown the tortillas quickly on a griddle. Or, if the family prefers tacos, to deep fat fry the rolled-out dough (see recipe variation for Tacos, which follows).

3 cups sifted all-purpose flour
¾ teaspoon baking powder
¾ teaspoon salt

5 tablespoons lard or vegetable shortening
1 cup hot water

1.   Combine flour, baking powder and salt in a large bowl; cut in lard with a pastry blender until dough has the texture of coarse meal. Pour hot water in a slow stream over the surface, then mix quickly with a fork just until dough holds together. Place in a greased bowl, cover and let stand 1 hour in the refrigerator. Turn dough out on a lightly floured board and knead about 5 minutes or until smooth and elastic.

2.   To shape, pinch off small bits of dough and roll into balls about 1¼ to 1½ inches in diameter. Press flat in a tortilla press or roll out the balls, one at a time, on a floured pastry cloth into circles about 5 inches across. Dough should be very thin—somewhat thinner than piecrust. Layer between sheets of waxed paper and store in the refrigerator until ready to cook.

3.   To cook the tortillas, simply brown quickly—about 30 seconds— on each side on a *very lightly* greased hot griddle. The Gomezes like to eat the tortillas plain or to roll them up around cooked *chorizos* (peppery sausages) or *Machacado* (page 224) or even strips of grilled or barbecued steak.

Tacos

Makes about 2 dozen

The principal difference between tacos and tortillas is texture—tacos are crisp, tortillas limp. What accounts for this difference is the way the dough is cooked. If it is browned on a griddle, it will be limp, if deep-fried, crisp. "The trick in frying tacos," Mrs. Gomez points out, "is that as soon as a taco is browned on one side (but still limp), you must fish it from the deep fat and bend it into a U-shape before finishing the frying." If you wait until the tacos are thoroughly cooked, they will be too crisp to bend. So, if you want to make tacos, simply deep-fry the rolled-out tortillas at between 380° and 400°. When a taco is golden brown on the under side, lift it out, bend into a U-shape, secure edges with toothpicks—not *too* close together because you want to be able to fill the taco—and finish frying until crisp and golden. Drain on paper toweling. What do you fill tacos with? Almost anything you like—Guacamole, for example, or Carne for Tacos (both recipes are included in this chapter).

Masa Tortillas

Makes about 2 dozen

3 cups *masa harina* (obtainable in Latin American groceries)
2½ teaspoons salt

1 tablespoon plus 1 teaspoon lard or vegetable shortening
2½ cups boiling water

1. Combine *masa harina* and salt in a large heatproof mixing bowl. Melt shortening in boiling water, and briskly mix shortening and water into *masa;* beat hard for 8 to 10 minutes.

2. Cover dough and refrigerate for about 1 hour. To shape, pinch off small pieces of dough and roll into 1- to 1¼-inch balls. Press each flat in a tortilla press, or roll flat between floured sheets of waxed paper into circles measuring about 5 inches in diameter.

3. To cook, simply brown quickly on each side on a *very lightly* greased griddle. Serve in any of the ways described for Flour Tortillas (recipe precedes).

Pan de Polvo

Makes about 4 dozen cookies

These short, crisp cookies will have better flavor if you make them with lard instead of vegetable shortening. "We usually cut these into hearts or stars," Albesa Gomez says, "and we serve them a lot at wedding receptions." She adds that the cookies should not be allowed to brown, they should be pale ivory when they are taken from the oven. The baking is more to dry the dough out than to bake it.

1 cup water	¼ teaspoon salt
1 cinnamon stick, broken in several places	1¼ cups lard or vegetable shortening
3 cups sifted all-purpose flour	½ cup sugar mixed with 1 teaspoon cinnamon (cinnamon sugar)
½ cup sugar	

1. Make a cinnamon tea by simmering the water with the cinnamon stick in a small uncovered saucepan 15 minutes; remove from heat and cool to room temperature.

2. In a large mixing bowl, combine flour, sugar and salt. Cut in the lard until mixture is very crumbly and fine-textured. Add ½ to ⅔ cup of the cooled cinnamon tea, just enough to make a moist but stiff dough. Wrap dough in wax paper and chill several hours.

3. Working with about one quarter of the dough at a time, roll on a floured board to a thickness of about ⅛-inch. Cut with a 2¾-inch round cooky cutter (or, if you prefer, with star or heart cutters of approximately the same size).

4. Space cookies about 2 inches apart on lightly greased baking sheets and bake in a moderately slow oven (325°) about 15 to 20 minutes or until firm but not brown. As soon as cookies come from the oven, remove from baking sheets with a spatula and dredge well in the cinnamon sugar. Cool on wire racks before serving.

Buñuelos

Makes about 2½ dozen

"We serve *Buñuelos* mostly around Christmas and New Year's," Mrs. Gomez says of these crispy fritters dusted with cinnamon sugar.

1¼ cups water	½ teaspoon salt
1 cinnamon stick, broken in several places	⅓ cup lard or vegetable shortening
3 cups sifted all-purpose flour	Vegetable shortening for deep-fat frying
¼ cup sugar	½ cup sugar mixed with 1 teaspoon cinnamon (cinnamon sugar)
2 teaspoons baking powder	

1. Simmer the water with the cinnamon stick in a small uncovered saucepan about 15 minutes to make a cinnamon tea; turn off heat and let steep until ready to use.

2. Combine flour, sugar, baking powder and salt in a large mixing bowl; cut in lard with a pastry blender until mixture is the texture of coarse meal. Add about ¾ cup of the hot cinnamon tea and mix briskly with a fork just until mixture holds together—it should be about the consistency of pie dough. If too crumbly, add a bit more cinnamon tea. Cover bowl of dough and chill 1 hour.

3. Turn chilled dough onto a floured board and knead about 5 minutes or until smooth and elastic. Pinch off small pieces of dough and roll into balls about 1 inch in diameter. Let balls of dough stand at room temperature about 30 minutes.

4. Using a rolling pin, flatten each ball of dough on a floured piece of waxed paper into a circle slightly thinner than piecrust. Each should be 4 to 5 inches in diameter.

5. Deep-fry the circles, one at a time, at between 380° and 400° F. until crisp and golden on both sides. As the hot fritters come from the fat, drain on paper toweling and sprinkle both sides of each with cinnamon sugar.

Mrs. Lowell McGraw
of
Finney County, Kansas

WHEN told that she has a reputation for being one of the best cooks in Finney County, Mrs. Lowell McGraw blushes. Like many natural-born cooks, she is modest, doesn't consider the dishes she prepares in any way unusual, and as for the "best cook" reputation, well, surely we must have someone else in mind.

Not at all. Said one friend: "If I know Alma McGraw is going to be making one of her apple pies for a club supper, I'll be sure to be there." And said another, when we went into the County Extension Office to photocopy some of Mrs. McGraw's old-time recipes: "I b'lieve I'll just make me some copies, too. I've been waitin' a long time to get a hold of some of Alma's recipes."

Alma McGraw, who lives on a 1,700-acre grain-and-beef-cattle farm nineteen miles southeast of Garden City, does admit to getting lots of requests for recipes. "Seems like someone's always calling for this recipe or that. My husband Lowell says I've got more recipes than anyone in the county."

It's an impressive collection, sprawling over several rooms of the McGraw's spanking new nine-room house, spilling out of card files, drawers and loose-leaf notebooks. These recipes aren't, for the most part, merely filed and forgotten.

"I like to try out new recipes," says Mrs. McGraw. And she is so good at it that a while back when the Kansas Wheat Commission was looking for "grass roots" cooks to test some of its recipes, Alma Mc-Graw was the one chosen in Finney County.

When did Alma McGraw's love of cooking begin? "I guess when I was a very little girl. I grew up on a farm three and a half miles west of here. We were a big family—six children—and there were harvest crews to feed as well as family. Mama was a good cook but she didn't go in for fancy things. Mostly it was fry meat, potatoes and gravy. I spent a lot of time peeling potatoes, scraping carrots and shelling peas. And when I got to be ten or eleven, I often cooked dinner for my brothers."

Good training, as it turns out, for the life she would later lead as a farmer's wife and mother of four. Even better training, she thinks, were the years she spent as a 4-H Club member (she joined when she was ten) because the 4-H developed in her a more creative approach to food. Mrs. McGraw also credits the 4-H with teaching her much of what she knows about sewing and with interesting her in arts and crafts (today, when she isn't busy cooking or sewing, she likes to paint landscapes in oil, to make candles and corn-husk dolls).

Where did she meet her husband? "I've known him all my life. Lowell and I went through the eight grammar grades together in a one-room school. And we had one year of high school before he had to stop and help his dad. His folks' farm was just three-quarters of a mile north of ours."

While Lowell was busy farming with his dad, Alma Lightner (as she was then) finished high school, then went on and graduated from Garden City Community Junior College. "I expect Lowell and I would have married then if it hadn't been for the Depression. You see, Lowell was my boy friend in grade school. No, he didn't carry my books—we lived in different directions. My brothers and I rode to school till there was too many of us to get on one horse. After that we drove a buggy."

In 1940, when the Depression had eased, Alma Lightner and Lowell McGraw were married on a Sunday morning in her parents' house. "We had only one day to be to ourselves. It was the end of May and we had to get back to farming on the section we'd rented just east of here."

The McGraws stayed on the rented farm for two years, then, shortly after their first son was born, bought a farm directly across the blacktop road from where they live today. By 1949, the family had outgrown the little house that was on the farm when they bought it, so Mr. McGraw, working every spare hour, built an eight-room white stucco house. "Lowell did all the work himself except for the wiring and plumbing, and it took him a year.

"Now this new house, we had a contractor build it and it took him a year, too." Set on the fringe of wheat field, the McGraws' new house is a low and rambling V painted the gold of ripe grain.

Wheat is what the McGraws grow, together with milo, corn and alfalfa. They also raise beef cattle (have about 300 head at the moment), although no dairy cows, hogs or chickens.

It may seem ironic, to say nothing of ill-timed, that the McGraws didn't build their modern house (or that Mrs. McGraw didn't get her dream kitchen) until after the children all had homes of their own. But the children haven't really left home. Every one of them is within hollering distance. All of Mrs. McGraw's brothers and sisters are neighbors, too. "The farthest one away," she says, "is only six miles down the road." The McGraws' children pop in and out of their parents' home every day, as do the nine grandchildren.

They're not likely to find Grandma's cupboard bare. Mrs. McGraw makes sure there's plenty on hand to eat—a fresh-baked carrot-pecan or banana walnut cake (both family favorites), butterscotch cookies or "Pride of Iowa" cookies, doughnuts perhaps (either the cake or the yeast-raised), butter-cream mints or caramel corn.

Mrs. McGraw is constantly being called upon to bake pies or cakes or casseroles for church or club suppers. There are old-fashioned family ice-cream making sessions in summer, plus whopping reunions of both the McGraw and Lightner sides of the family. And there are the dozens of Christmas fruit cakes and cookies that she begins baking along about October to give to family and friends.

Alma McGraw's new dream kitchen is no idle showpiece. It gets a good work-out. "Near 'bout every day."

Beef, Carrot and Green-Bean Stew

Makes 8 servings

Nearly everything needed for this stew is produced on the McGraw farm: beef, carrots, potatoes, onions, green beans—even the wheat from which the dredging flour is milled. Like many "instinctive" cooks, Mrs. McGraw never makes the stew quite the same way twice. Sometimes she will substitute a cup of home-canned tomatoes or tomato juice for one cup of the beef stock, sometimes she will substitute corn or green peas for the green beans.

3½ pounds boned beef chuck, cut in 1-inch cubes
¾ teaspoon salt
¼ teaspoon pepper
½ cup unsifted all-purpose flour
4 tablespoons vegetable oil
1 large yellow onion, peeled and chopped fine
2½ cups rich beef stock or condensed beef broth
1 bay leaf, crumbled
¼ teaspoon dill weed
⅛ teaspoon leaf rosemary, crumbled

6 medium-sized carrots, scraped and cut in 1-inch chunks (halve vertically any chunks that are particularly large)
2 large stalks celery, sliced very thin
½ cup water
12 uniformly small white onions, peeled
12 uniformly small new potatoes, peeled
½ pound fresh green beans, tipped and snapped into 1-inch lengths

1. Spread the cubes of beef out on a large piece of waxed paper; sprinkle with salt and pepper, then toss well so that chunks are evenly seasoned. ("I don't like to mix the salt and pepper with the dredging flour," explains Mrs. McGraw, "because if I do, I never know how much salt or pepper I'm putting in the stew.") Let beef cubes stand at room temperature for about 10 minutes, then dredge a few cubes at a time by shaking in a heavy paper bag with the flour.

2. Heat the oil in a large, very heavy Dutch-oven-type kettle over moderately high heat, then brown the beef cubes well on all sides, doing only a few at a time. As the beef browns, transfer with a slotted spoon to several thicknesses of paper toweling to drain.

3. When all the beef is browned, add chopped onion to kettle, also about ⅔ cup of the beef stock, the bay leaf, dill weed and rosemary, and cook, stirring and scraping up all browned bits on the bottom of the kettle, for about 5 minutes or until stock cooks down to a rich brown glaze. Add remaining beef stock and return beef to kettle. Adjust heat so that liquid barely ripples, cover, and simmer about 1½ hours or until beef is nearly tender.

4. Add carrots and celery, re-cover and simmer slowly for 45 minutes; add water and the onions and potatoes, pushing them down well in the liquid, re-cover and simmer 45 minutes longer. Add beans, pushing them down into stew, re-cover and simmer 20 to 25 minutes longer or until beans are crisp-tender or done the way you like them.

5. Taste for salt and pepper and add more if needed to suit your taste. To serve, ladle the stew into big soup bowls.

Note:
Like most stews, this one is even better if made a day ahead, refrigerated, then reheated just before serving.

Breaded Pork Chops

Makes 6 servings

These breaded pork chops are somewhat like "country-fried" or chicken-fried" steak—that is, they are dipped in crumbs, browned, then cooked in a covered skillet until well done. The crumb coating is not crisp, rather it has more the soft texture of a "stuffing." Plenty of savory juices cook out of the pork chops—enough to spoon liberally over each portion.

6 loin pork chops, cut ¾-inch to 1 inch thick
1 teaspoon salt
¼ teaspoon pepper

2 eggs beaten with 2 tablespoons milk
1½ cups fine soda-cracker crumbs
3 tablespoons vegetable oil

1. Sprinkle both sides of each chop with salt and pepper. Dip chops in egg mixture, then in crumbs to coat evenly. Let chops "dry" on a cake rack at room temperature or 20 to 30 minutes (this helps the crumb coating to stick).

2. Heat oil in a very large heavy skillet over moderately high heat, then brown chops, first on one side and then on the other. Reduce heat to lowest point, cover skillet and let chops braise slowly ¾-hour to 1 hour or until well done. To test, make a tiny slit near the bone; if meat is creamy-white in the center, chops are done.

3. Raise heat under skillet to moderate and let pan juices reduce by about half—3 to 5 minutes. This final cooking also crispens the crumb coating slightly. Serve each chop topped with some of the pan juices.

Scalloped Corn

Makes 6 servings

The McGraws also grow their own sweet corn, and at the end of summer there are bound to be steaming platters piled high with corn on the cob or maybe, as a change of pace, this bubbling casserole of scalloped corn.

8 medium-sized ears fresh corn,
  husked (sweet corn is best)
¾ cup moderately fine soda-cracker
  crumbs
1½ cups milk, at room temperature
1 egg, beaten until frothy
2 tablespoons sugar

2 tablespoons melted butter or margarine
1 teaspoon salt
⅛ teaspoon pepper

Topping:
1 cup moderately fine soda-cracker
  crumbs mixed with 4 teaspoons
  melted butter

1. Parboil the corn 5 minutes in enough boiling water to cover:
drain, quick-chill in cold water, then pat dry on paper toweling. Cut
the kernels from the cob cream-style (the easiest way is to slit down
the center of each row of kernels with a sharp knife, then to scrape all
pulp and milk into a shallow bowl). Measure out and reserve 4 cups
of corn (the 8 ears should yield 4 cups almost exactly).

2. Layer the cracker crumbs and corn into a buttered 8- × 8- ×
2-inch baking dish this way: crumbs, corn, crumbs, corn, using half of
each for each layer. Combine milk, egg, sugar, melted butter, salt
and pepper and pour evenly over corn. Scatter topping over surface.

3. Place baking dish in a large pan, set on middle oven rack, then
pour enough hot water into pan to come halfway up baking dish (this
keeps corn mixture from curdling). Bake uncovered in a moderate
oven (350°) for 1 to 1¼ hours or until mixture is bubbly and topping
lightly browned. Serve piping hot.

Creamed Shredded Cabbage

Makes 6 servings

Another McGraw vegetable favorite.

2 tablespoons butter or margarine
8 cups finely shredded cabbage
  (about 1 small cabbage)
1 teaspoon salt

⅛ teaspoon pepper
Pinch of ground nutmeg or mace
  (optional)
1 cup light cream

1. Melt butter in a large heavy skillet (not iron) over moderate
heat, add cabbage and toss lightly to glaze.

2. Stir in all remaining ingredients, cover, turn heat to lowest
point and let cabbage steam 8 to 10 minutes or until cooked the way
you like it. Stir well and serve.

Kansas Pan Rolls

Makes about 2 dozen rolls

These rich and feathery yeast rolls are one of Mrs. McGraw's specialties.

1 envelope active dry yeast	1 cup scalding hot milk
¼ cup very warm water	1 egg, lightly beaten
⅓ cup sugar	4½ cups sifted all-purpose flour
¼ cup butter or margarine	2 tablespoons melted butter or mar-
1 teaspoon salt	garine (for brushing tops of rolls)

1. Sprinkle yeast over very warm water in a large bowl. (Very warm water should feel comfortably warm when dropped on wrist.) Stir until yeast dissolves.

2. Add sugar, the ¼ cup butter or margarine and salt to hot milk and stir until sugar dissolves and butter or margarine is melted. Cool mixture to 105° to 115°.

3. Add milk mixture to yeast, then beat in egg. Beat in 4 cups of the flour, 1 cup at a time, to form a soft dough. Use some of the remaining ½ cup of the flour to dust a pastry cloth. Knead the dough lightly for 5 minutes, working in the remaining flour (use it for flouring the pastry cloth and your hands).

4. Place dough in a warm buttered bowl; turn greased side up. Cover and let rise in a warm place until doubled in bulk, about 1¼ to 1½ hours.

5. Punch dough down and knead 4 to 5 minutes on a lightly floured pastry cloth. Dough will be sticky, but use as little flour as possible for flouring your hands and the pastry cloth, otherwise the rolls will not be as feathery light as they should be.

6. Pinch off small chunks of dough and shape into round rolls about 1½ to 1¾ inches in diameter. Place in neat rows, not quite touching, in a well-buttered 13- × 9- × 2-inch pan. Cover rolls and let rise in a warm spot until doubled in bulk, 30 to 40 minutes.

7. Brush tops of rolls with melted butter or margarine, then bake in a moderately hot oven (375°) 18 to 20 minutes or until nicely browned. Serve warm with plenty of butter.

Old-Fashioned Kansas Yeast Bread

Makes two 9- × 5- × 3-inch loaves

Bake as conventional loaves or do as Mrs. McGraw often does: shape the bread dough into patties or "slices," butter them well, then bake into Pull-Apart Loaves.

2 envelopes active dry yeast	2 tablespoons butter, margarine or
½ cup very warm water	vegetable shortening
1 cup cold water mixed with 1 cup	1 tablespoon salt
milk	8 cups sifted all-purpose flour
¼ cup sugar	(about)

1.   Sprinkle yeast over very warm water in a large bowl. (Very warm water should feel comfortably warm when dropped on wrist.) Stir until yeast dissolves. Set aside.

2.   Heat water-milk mixture, sugar, butter, and salt to scalding in a medium-sized saucepan, stirring until sugar dissolves and fat melts. Cool to lukewarm.

3.   Add lukewarm milk mixture to yeast. Stir in 4 cups of the flour and beat until very smooth. Mix in 3 more cups of the flour, then turn dough out on a floured board (use some of the remaining flour for flouring the board) and work in enough of the remaining flour to make a soft dough. Knead for 10 minutes, or until dough is satiny and elastic.

4.   Place dough in a greased bowl; turn greased side up. Cover; let rise in a warm place until doubled in bulk, about 1¼ to 1½ hours.

5.   Punch dough down; divide in half. Cover with dry cloth and let dough rest for 10 minutes.

6.   Roll each piece of dough into a rectangle 18 × 9 inches. Roll up from the short side, jelly-roll fashion. Press each end to seal, then tuck ends underneath loaves. Place shaped loaves in two greased 9- × 5- × 3-inch loaf pans, seam sides down. Cover with a dry cloth and let rise in warm place until doubled in bulk, about 1 to 1¼ hours.

7.   Bake in a hot oven (400°) for 25 to 30 minutes or until bread is nicely browned and loaves sound hollow when you thump them with your fingers. Remove from oven, ease loaves out of pans and cool upright on wire racks.

Variation:

Pull-Apart Loaves: Prepare as directed through Step 5. Melt ¼ cup of butter or margarine. To shape each pull-apart loaf, pinch off chunks of dough about 1½ inches in diameter, then roll or flatten into patties measuring about 4½ inches across and ¼ inch thick. You should be able to shape about 16 patties from each half-portion of dough. Brush both sides of each patty liberally with melted butter, then stand the patties on end in greased 9- × 5- × 3-inch loaf pans (16 to each pan). Cover with dry cloth and let rise in a warm place until doubled in bulk, about 1 hour. Bake and cool as directed in Step 7.

Yeast-Raised "Refrigerator" Doughnuts
Makes about 2½ dozen (plus holes)

The beauty of these doughnuts, according to Mrs. McGraw, is that they "rise" in the refrigerator, enabling you to take out small amounts of dough at a time and to roll, cut and fry the doughnuts as needed (the refrigerator dough keeps well 2 to 3 days). If the doughnuts are to be light, the deep fat must be precisely the right temperature, in this case 360°. If the fat is too cool, the doughnuts will become greasy. If it is too hot, they will brown before they cook inside.

¼ cup vegetable shortening
½ cup sugar
1 teaspoon salt
⅛ teaspoon ground mace
1 teaspoon finely grated lemon rind
 (optional, but a nice addition)
1 cup boiling water
1 cup evaporated milk
2 envelopes active dry yeast

½ cup very warm water
2 eggs, lightly beaten
7½ cups sifted all-purpose flour
 (about)
Vegetable oil for frying

Glaze (optional):
1½ cups confectioners (10X) sugar
 blended with ½ cup boiling water
 and ½ teaspoon lemon juice

1. Place shortening, sugar, salt, mace, and lemon rind (if used) in a small bowl and pour in boiling water; stir until sugar dissolves and shortening melts. Mix in evaporated milk and cool until warm (105° to 115°).

2. Sprinkle yeast over very warm water in a large bowl. (Very warm water should feel comfortably warm when dropped on wrist.) Stir until yeast dissolves. Mix cooled shortening mixture into yeast; beat in eggs. Add 4 cups of the flour and beat hard with an electric mixer at high speed 1 to 2 minutes or until smooth. Slowly beat in enough of the remaining 3½ cups flour to make a very soft dough (it will be sticky).

3. Place dough in a large, well-buttered bowl, then turn dough in bowl to grease all over. Lay a piece of buttered waxed paper on top of dough, then cover bowl with a lid. Set dough in refrigerator for 4 to 5 hours or until needed (it will rise as it stands).

4.   Take out whatever amount of dough you need (you will get about 10 doughnuts from one-third of the total amount of dough) and roll out ¼-inch thick on a floured pastry cloth, using a floured stockinette-covered rolling pin. Cut doughnuts with a floured 3-inch doughnut cutter and let them stand at room temperature 15 to 20 minutes.

5.   Meanwhile, pour vegetable oil into a deep-fat fryer to a depth of 3 inches and heat to 360°. Fry the doughnuts, no more than 2 or 3 at a time, in the hot fat, allowing about 1½ minutes per side or until doughnuts are a rich caramel brown. Drain the doughnuts on crumpled paper toweling as they come from the hot fat.

6.   Cool doughnuts almost to room temperature, dip quickly in glaze if desired, then let "drip-dry" on a wire rack set over waxed paper. Or, if you prefer, omit the glaze and simply roll the warm doughnuts in sifted confectioners sugar, granulated sugar, or cinnamon sugar.

Grated-Apple Pie with Streusel Topping

Makes one 10-inch pie

This is the apple pie for which Mrs. McGraw has become famous among friends and neighbors. She developed the recipe herself as a time-saver after she had gotten a new heavy-duty electric mixer with a grinder-grater attachment. "All you have to do is wash the apples, quarter them, core them, and put them through the grater, skins and all," she says. The apples may also be grated in a large rotary manual grater (the kind that clamps to the countertop) or, if need be, on the second-coarsest side of a four-sided grater. Hand-grating the apples is tedious, however, and unless the grater is super-sharp, the skins won't grate at all and will have to be chopped separately with a heavy chopping knife.

Filling:
6 medium to large firm crisp Jonathan or McIntosh apples, washed, quartered, cored (but not peeled) and coarsely grated (grate the skins, too)
½ cup sugar
2 tablespoons flour
1 tablespoon lemon juice
¼ teaspoon cinnamon
⅛ teaspoon salt

Streusel Topping:
½ cup firmly packed light brown sugar
½ cup unsifted all-purpose flour
⅛ teaspoon salt
2 tablespoons butter or margarine, softened to room temperature

Pastry:
1 10-inch unbaked pie shell (use your favorite recipe, or try Alma McGraw's Egg and Vinegar Piecrust; recipe follows)

1. *For the filling:* Mix apples thoroughly with sugar, flour, lemon juice, cinnamon and salt.

2. *For the streusel topping:* Combine sugar, flour and salt, pressing out any lumps of sugar, then, using your hands, rub in the butter or margarine until mixture is crumbly.

3. Spoon apple mixture into unbaked pie shell, then scatter streusel evenly over the top.

4. Bake in a hot oven (400°) for 10 minutes, reduce temperature to moderately hot (375°) and bake 25 to 30 minutes longer, until filling is bubbly and streusel topping dappled with brown.

5. Remove pie from oven and let cool 20 to 25 minutes before cutting.

Alma McGraw's Egg and Vinegar Piecrust

Makes three 8-inch pie shells, or two 9- or 10-inch pie shells, or one 9- or 10-inch double-crust pie

This is the piecrust recipe that Alma McGraw has been using most of her married life. It's an easy pastry to work with and when baked, it's tender with the slightest bit of crunch. Because Mrs. McGraw usually bakes several pies at a clip, this amount of pastry is exactly right for her. But if you prefer to bake pies one at a time, simply shape the balance of the pastry into a pie pan or pans, cover with plastic wrap, freeze, and use another time (thaw the pie shell before filling and baking).

1 cup chilled vegetable shortening
3¼ cups sifted all-purpose flour
¾ teaspoon salt

1 egg, beaten until frothy, then mixed with enough cold water to total ¾ cup
1 teaspoon cider vinegar

1. Cut the shortening into the flour and salt with a pastry blender until mixture has the texture of coarse crumbs; combine the ¾ cup egg-water mixture with the vinegar and add to the flour mixture, a little at a time, mixing briskly with a fork until pastry just holds together. Do not overmix or pastry will be tough.

2. Divide pastry into 3 equal parts (for 8-inch pie shells) or 2 equal parts (for 9- or 10-inch pie shells or a 9- or 10-inch double-crust pie).

3. Roll each section of pastry on a lightly floured pastry cloth with

a lightly floured stockinette-covered rolling pin into a circle 3 inches larger than the pie pan you intend to use. Lay rolling pin across center of pastry circle, lap half of pastry over rolling pin and ease into pie pan. Fit pastry snugly into pan, trim overhang so that it is 1 inch larger all around than the pie pan; turn under and crimp, making a decorative edge. Pie shell is now ready to fill and bake (or to wrap in plastic food wrap and freeze).

Black-Walnut Freezer Ice Cream

Makes about 1 gallon

Ask Mrs. McGraw's husband or her daughter Jolene which kind of homemade ice cream they like best and they will answer straight out, "Black walnut." The walnuts come from "a big old tree" on the Lightner farm just 3½ miles west of the McGraws' where Mrs. McGraw (née Alma Lightner) grew up. *Cook Tip:* To keep the walnuts from sinking to the bottom of the ice cream, add them, as Mrs. McGraw does, after the ice cream has begun to freeze.

2½ cups sugar
3 tablespoons flour
4 eggs, lightly beaten
6 cups milk (about)
1½ teaspoons vanilla
1¼ teaspoons walnut flavoring

3 cups heavy cream
1 cup moderately finely chopped black walnuts (or California walnuts)
Cracked ice (about 30 pounds)
Rock salt (about 3 pounds)

1. In a large, heavy saucepan, blend sugar with flour. Mix in eggs and 1 quart (4 cups) of the milk. Set over very low heat and cook, stirring constantly, until smooth and custard-like, about 8 to 10 minutes. Watch closely and stir all the while lest mixture scorch or curdle. Remove from heat, then quick-chill by setting pan in a large bowl of crushed ice; stir constantly to prevent a skin from forming on the surface of the custard.

2. Stir vanilla, walnut flavoring, and heavy cream into cooled custard. Pour into a 1-gallon freezer canister, then pour in enough additional milk to fill canister to within 3 inches of the top. Insert dasher, snap on lid, set canister into freezer bucket, then layer cracked ice and rock salt into freezer beginning with ice and using about 6 parts of ice to 1 part salt. Attach cranking gear according to manufacturer's

directions; crank steadily and slowly for about 10 minutes or until mixture begins to thicken.

3. Detach cranking gear. Carefully remove ice and salt from top part of freezer, wipe canister with a damp cloth, uncover, being careful not to get any salt into the ice cream; add walnuts, re-cover and reattach cranking gear. Add more ice and salt to cover freezer canister.

4. Continue cranking, adding additional salt and ice, until mixture is too stiff to crank.

5. Remove cranking gear and all ice and salt around top part of canister. Carefully ease canister out, wipe well with a damp cloth, uncover and lift out dasher. Scrape ice cream from dasher back into canister, packing down well (and, of course, give the dasher to children to lick).

6. Re-cover canister of ice cream, making sure the hole in the lid is tightly plugged, then repack in freezer bucket, using 4 parts ice to 1 part salt. Let the ice cream "mellow" for about 30 minutes before serving.

Variation:

Chocolate Chip Ice Cream: Prepare as directed but use 1 tablespoon of vanilla in place of the 1½ teaspoons vanilla and 1¼ teaspoons walnut flavoring. After ice cream has begun to freeze, add 1 cup moderately finely chopped sweet German chocolate instead of the walnuts. Continue freezing until firm. Pack and let "mellow" as directed.

To Freeze the Ice Cream in the Refrigerator: Prepare and cool the custard sauce as directed. Add flavoring, pour into refrigerator trays and freeze until mushy-firm; empty into largest electric-mixer bowl and beat at high speed until fluffy. Whip the cream and fold in along with the walnuts or chopped sweet German chocolate. Return to refrigerator trays and freeze until firm.

Carrot Pecan Cake with Fresh Orange Glaze

Makes one 9-inch tube cake

It's a toss-up as to whether this cake or the Banana-Walnut Cake that follows is No. 1 with the McGraws. Mrs. McGraw makes both often. The Carrot-Pecan Cake is moist and dense, its texture not unlike fruitcake. Be sure it is completely cool before slicing into layers and spreading with glaze.

2 cups sifted all-purpose flour
2 teaspoons baking powder
1 teaspoon baking soda
1 teaspoon salt
½ teaspoon ground cinnamon
¼ teaspoon ground mace
1¼ cups vegetable oil
1 cup granulated sugar
1 cup firmly packed light brown
   sugar

4 eggs
3 cups finely grated raw carrots (do
   not pack the measure—you'll need
   about 4 large carrots)
1 cup moderately finely chopped
   pecans
1 teaspoon vanilla
Fresh Orange Glaze (recipe follows)

1.   Sift flour with baking powder, soda, salt, cinnamon and mace and set aside.

2.   Beat oil and sugars about 5 minutes in an electric mixer, beginning at low speed, then increasing speed to high as mixture creams up.

3.   Sift half of the dry ingredients into the sugar mixture and beat slowly, just enough to mix. Add the remaining half of the dry ingredients alternately with the eggs, beginning and ending with the sifted dry ingredients and adding eggs 1 at a time; mix at low speed. Don't overbeat. Stir in carrots, pecans and vanilla.

4.   Spoon batter into a well-greased 9-inch tube pan and bake in a moderate oven (350°) about 1 hour and 10 minutes, or until cake pulls from edges of pan or until a finger pressed in the surface of the cake leaves an imprint that disappears slowly. Because of the weight of the batter, this cake will not rise the way a conventional butter cake does.

5.   Remove cake from oven, cool upright in pan on a wire rack for 30 minutes, then with a thin-bladed spatula, loosen cake around edges of pan and central tube and invert on a cake rack. Cool completely (overnight if possible) before cutting and spreading with Fresh Orange Glaze.

6.   Slice the cake horizontally into three layers of uniform thickness. Place bottom layer on a cake plate and spread with glaze. Top with second layer and glaze that also. Add top layer and glaze liberally, letting glaze run down the sides of the cake and down into the central hole. Let glaze firm up before cutting the cake—this will take 3 to 4 hours (the glaze has a jellylike consistency, not the hardness of a conventional icing).

Fresh Orange Glaze

Makes about 1⅓ cups

3 tablespoons cornstarch
1 cup sugar
Finely grated rind of 1 orange

1 cup fresh orange juice
Juice of ½ lemon
2 tablespoons butter or margarine

1. In a small heavy saucepan, blend cornstarch and sugar, pressing out all lumps. Mix in orange rind, orange and lemon juices.
2. Set over moderate heat and cook, stirring constantly, until mixture thickens and bubbles 3 minutes. Drop in butter, remove from heat and stir until butter melts. Cool 10 to 15 minutes, stirring often to prevent a "skin" from forming on surface of glaze, then use to glaze Carrot-Pecan Cake as directed in Step 6 (recipe precedes).

Banana-Walnut Cake with Banana Cream Frosting

Makes a two-layer 9-inch square cake

3 cups sifted all-purpose flour
1½ teaspoons baking powder
¾ teaspoon baking soda
½ teaspoon salt
¾ cup vegetable shortening
2¼ cups sugar
3 large eggs

1½ cups mashed ripe bananas
  (about 3 large bananas)
¾ cup buttermilk
1 teaspoon vanilla
1 cup finely chopped walnuts
Banana Cream Frosting (recipe follows)

1. Sift flour with baking powder, soda and salt; set aside.
2. Cream shortening and sugar until fluffy-light; add eggs, 1 at a time, beating well after each addition; beat in mashed bananas.
3. Combine buttermilk and vanilla. Add sifted dry ingredients to creamed mixture alternately with buttermilk, beginning and ending with dry ingredients and beating after each addition only enough to blend. Fold in walnuts.
4. Divide batter equally between two greased-and-floured 9- × 9- × 2-inch baking pans. Bake in a moderate oven (350°) for 40 to 45 minutes or until cakes pull from sides of pans and are springy to the touch.
5. Remove cakes from oven, cool upright in pans on wire racks for 10 minutes, then loosen cakes with a thin-bladed spatula, turn out on

wire racks and cool completely before icing with Banana Cream Frosting.

6. To frost, simply sandwich layers together with a thick layer of frosting, then spread sides and top of cake with frosting, swirling it into peaks and valleys.

Banana Cream Frosting

Makes enough to fill and frost a two-layer 9-inch square or round cake

¾ cup butter or margarine, at room temperature
1 medium-sized ripe banana, peeled and mashed
1 tablespoon lemon juice

1 teaspoon vanilla
1½ pounds (about) confectioners (10X) sugar
3 tablespoons (about) light cream

1. Cream butter or margarine until fluffy; beat in banana, lemon juice and vanilla.

2. Gradually beat in confectioners sugar, adding alternately with the light cream, until fluffy and of a good spreading consistency.

Note:

It's best to make this frosting on a dry, sunny day. In humid weather the frosting will absorb moisture from the atmosphere and will not stiffen up properly.

"Pride of Iowa" Cookies

Makes about 5½ dozen

Mrs. McGraw doesn't know where she obtained the following recipe, only that it has been a family favorite for years. Her late son Leland (killed a little over three years ago in a farm accident) entered a batch of these crunchy cookies at the Kansas State Fair when he was a 4-H Club member and won a prize.

1 cup vegetable shortening
1 cup firmly packed light brown
  sugar
1 cup granulated sugar
2 eggs, beaten until frothy
2 cups sifted all-purpose flour
1 teaspoon baking soda

1 teaspoon baking powder
¼ teaspoon salt
1 teaspoon vanilla
1 cup flaked coconut
½ cup chopped nuts (pecans or
  walnuts are best)
3 cups quick-cooking rolled oats

1. Cream shortening and sugars until fluffy; beat in eggs.

2. Sift flour with baking soda, baking powder, and salt; stir into creamed mixture; blend in vanilla.

3. Mix in coconut, nuts and rolled oats until uniformly blended (mixture will be quite stiff).

4. Roll into 1¼-inch balls and space 2 inches apart on lightly greased baking sheets. Using your fingers, flatten balls into patties about ⅛-inch thick, evening up ragged edges.

5. Bake in a moderately hot oven (375°) 8 to 10 minutes or until pale brown. While cookies are warm, remove to wire racks to cool.

Butterscotch Refrigerator Cookies

Makes about 10 dozen cookies

These crisp cookies are another McGraw family favorite. They're easy to make and can be refrigerated or frozen, then sliced and baked as needed.

4 cups sifted all-purpose flour
1 teaspoon cream of tartar
1 teaspoon baking soda
½ teaspoon salt
¾ cup butter or margarine

2 cups firmly packed light brown
  sugar
2 eggs
1½ teaspoons vanilla
1 cup moderately finely chopped
  pecans or walnuts (optional)

1. Sift the flour with the cream of tartar, soda and salt; set aside.

2. Cream the butter and sugar until light and fluffy; beat in the eggs, 1 at a time, mixing just enough to blend. Stir in vanilla.

3. Add the sifted dry ingredients, 1 cup at a time, beating only until combined. Stir in the nuts if you are using them.

4. Shape the dough into three logs about 10 inches long and 1¾ to 2 inches in diameter (if dough seems too soft to shape, chill several hours until fairly firm). Wrap each log in waxed paper and let "season"

in the refrigerator 4 to 5 hours before slicing and baking. Or wrap each in aluminum foil or plastic food wrap and store in the freezer.

5.   When ready to bake, slice the cookies about ¼-inch thick, space 1½ inches apart on greased baking sheets, then bake in a moderate oven (350°) 10 to 12 minutes or until lightly ringed with brown. Remove from oven, transfer to wire racks and cool before serving.

Caramel Corn

Makes 10 to 12 servings, about 24 popcorn balls

"Now here's a recipe I get lots of requests for," says Mrs. McGraw. *Note:* Pick a dry sunny day for making caramel corn. In humid weather, the syrup will not harden.

5 quarts unseasoned popped corn (about 1½ cups unpopped popcorn)
1 pound light brown sugar
⅓ cup light corn syrup

½ cup (1 stick) butter or margarine
½ teaspoon cream of tartar
½ teaspoon baking soda
1 teaspoon vanilla

1.   Spread popped corn out in your largest roasting pan or in two 13- × 9- × 2-inch pans and set aside.

2.   Mix sugar, corn syrup, butter, and cream of tartar in a large heavy saucepan; set over low heat and heat, stirring, until sugar and butter both melt—about 5 minutes. Insert a candy thermometer and cook over low heat without stirring to the hard-ball stage (250°).

3.   Remove from heat, mix in soda and vanilla. Pour syrup slowly and evenly over popped corn, tossing to mix. Serve as is, or, if you prefer, shape while still warm into tennis-ball-sized balls.

Easy Butter-Cream Mints

Makes about 12 dozen 1-inch round candies

Mrs. McGraw made hundreds of these buttery mints for her daughter Jolene's wedding reception. They are uncooked and quick to mix. But for best results, make the mints on a cold, sunny, dry day.

½ cup melted butter or margarine
⅓ cup heavy cream
9 cups (about) unsifted confectioners (10X) sugar
1 egg white

2 to 3 drops oil of peppermint
  (available at drugstores)
2 to 3 drops red or green food coloring (optional)

1. Beat butter, cream and 5 cups of the sugar in an electric mixer at medium speed until smooth; beat in egg white. Add the remaining sugar and a little bit more if needed to make a very stiff mixture (about the consistency of a stiff cooky dough). Add oil of peppermint to taste and, if you like, food coloring to tint mixture pale pink or green. Blend until evenly flavored and colored.

2. Working with about half of the mixture at a time, roll with a rolling pin between two sheets of waxed paper to a thickness of about ¼ inch. Cut into rounds, using a 1-inch round candy or truffle cutter; if you have neither, use the top of a twist-cap bottle. Reroll scraps and cut.

3. Arrange mints on waxed-paper-lined baking sheets, cover loosely with waxed paper and refrigerate several hours, or until firm, before serving. Store in refrigerator or freezer.

Mrs. Lorenzo Gonzales
of
San Ildefonso Pueblo, New Mexico

SHE didn't learn to cook as a child, or even as a bride. But once she did learn, Mrs. Lorenzo Gonzales, an American Indian who lives on the San Ildefonso Pueblo near Santa Fe, New Mexico, made up for lost time.

Time—or rather the lack of it—is one reason Dolores Gonzales did not discover her knack for cooking earlier. But an even more important reason, perhaps, is that when she moved to the Pueblo in 1946 as a twenty-year-old bride, she was surrounded by in-laws—excellent cooks all. Dolores had recently graduated from boarding school in Santa Fe (it was through friends there that she met her husband), but being a Winnebago from Nebraska, she did not know how to prepare any of the Pueblo chilies or hominy stews or rough yeast breads with which her husband had grown up.

"The in-laws," Dolores says, "looked out for us. They were very good to me and I'll always be grateful because I didn't have any of my own family nearby."

Life on the Pueblo was primitive in those days. There was little electricity, even less running water. Jobs were scarce and money scarcer. What Lorenzo earned at odd jobs, Dolores tried to supplement by doing Winnebago beadwork.

"But," she remembers, "you couldn't even give it away at that time. All people were interested in were the Southwestern crafts"—hand-woven rugs, silver and turquoise jewelry, pottery, which Lorenzo made in his spare time.

By 1955 Dolores and Lorenzo had five children and little income. So they pulled up stakes and moved to Waukegan, Illinois, where

Lorenzo found work. Two more children came along. In addition to raising her family, Dolores studied accounting, then took a job to help make ends meet. Cooking was something she had little time for or interest in.

"There was a while there," she admits, "when I bought a whole lot of canned soup. And I served it 'most every day. But finally Lorenzo protested. 'What?', he would say. 'Not *a-g-a-i-n!*' So I decided I was a big girl. It was time I knew how to cook."

That was in 1962. "Our older children were getting into their teens," Dolores continues, "and Lorenzo and I wanted them to grow up among their friends at San Ildefonso." So they packed up and moved back to the Pueblo.

The Pueblo dishes are what Dolores first learned to cook, "because," she explains, "I figured that this is where we were going to stay the rest of our lives." They were also economical recipes and, for the most part, still are: beef or pork stews stretched to the limit with squash and/or corn and/or tomatoes; dried pinto beans slow-simmered with salt pork and eaten either plain or topped with Green Chili; ears of sweet corn roasted in the husk; a pudding made out of toast, raisins and snippets of sharp cheese, the lot sweetened with caramelized sugar syrup; rustic round loaves of yeast bread, crisp of crust and chewy-firm inside.

Today Dolores no longer confines herself to the Pueblo specialties and "the different things she makes" are the talk not only of her own children, but of their husbands and wives as well. Her five oldest children are now married, all of them to Pueblo Indians. Jeanne and Linda, the two children born in Waukegan, are teenagers. They live at home and attend the Pojaoque High School just down the highway from the Pueblo.

"When the older children married and began bringing their in-laws here to eat," Dolores says, "the in-laws were surprised that I would serve such things as lasagne or spaghetti. But they would try them, and now, if they are coming to dinner, they will request them."

There is good reason for what Dolores Gonzales's family and friends call her "exotic tastes." Unlike many Pueblo Indians, she has spent as much time off the reservation as on it. She was born on the Winnebago Reservation in eastern Nebraska and given, as was the custom, both an Indian name (Good Eagle Voice) and a European name (Dolores because she was born on a Sunday, the day of the Seven Sorrows, or Dolores).

Her father died when she was a baby, and her mother, in order to be near Red Wing, an aunt to whom she was especially close, moved to New York City, taking Dolores and her older sister with her. These were WPA days and there was work for Indians in New York. Red

Wing, who had starred in silent movies (notably Cecil B. DeMille's epic *The Squaw Man*) was active in Indian affairs, serving as a cultural entertainer. Thanks to her, Dolores and her mother both became artists' models soon after their arrival in New York.

So Dolores spent her early childhood in New York, most of it on West 67th Street where, she remembers, "The Irish lived on one end, the Indians in the middle, and the Italians on the other end." It was here that she developed a fondness for lasagne and spaghetti, which she makes today, adding chili for a Southwestern touch.

In New York, her mother met and married Ernest Naquayouma, a Hopi entertainer from Arizona. Dolores took her stepfather's name ("he was the only father I ever knew") and remains close to him today (her mother has died).

Today Santa Fe is "home" for Dolores Gonzales. Or rather the San Ildefonso Pueblo twenty-three miles north of it is. Like the other Pueblo homes clustered around a large central plaza, their house is adobe, with walls so thick that even on blistering summer days it remains cool inside. Dolores and Lorenzo have enlarged the old house, adding a studio for Lorenzo, a bedroom for the girls, and a huge kitchen for Dolores, which extends the depth of the house. It's the biggest room in the house, and with windows front and back it is cheerful and bright. Cupboards and counters line the walls, punctuated by a modern range, refrigerator and sink, and it is the room where family and friends drop by to visit, to chat, and more than likely, see what's cooking.

Lorenzo is semiretired now and once again hand-shaping and polishing the traditional black-on-black and polychrome pottery for which San Ildefonso is famous. Dolores works as counselor at the Institute of American Indian Arts in Santa Fe, a school attended by several hundred young Indian artists representing tribes from all over the United States. She is active, moreover, in Pueblo affairs and takes part in the ceremonial dances, as do all the other members of the family—even her five young grandchildren.

But she is proudest, perhaps, of the fact that she herself now cooks for the feast days, spreading out on her long kitchen table a smörgasbordian array of Pueblo stews and chilies and breads and sweets.

"It's not that the feasts are fancy," she says, "but that you have to prepare food in such quantity."

She never knows quite how many will be coming, simply that she must be prepared for the dozens of friends and relatives who will drop in and out of her kitchen all day long. Appetites are invariably ravenous, particularly among the ceremonial dancers who perform non-stop for an hour or more, then arrive breathless—and in costume—and devour everything in sight.

Dolores cooks every day, too, but "being a working mother," she explains, "I like things that I can put together fast. And things that are not expensive. Mostly it's just plain old cooking that I do."

Her family and friends might disagree, for she frequently surprises them with a non-Indian recipe that she has picked up from friends or relatives in New York or Chicago or New England or California.

"The people of the Pueblo," she points out, "are mostly within the Pueblo. I like to think that I am bringing to them a little taste of the outside world."

Red Chili

Makes 4 to 6 servings

"I like to cut my meat up real small for chili," says Mrs. Gonzales. "It seems to go farther that way." Her Red Chili is much closer to the "bowl of red" Texans consider true chili than to the conglomerations of hamburger, kidney beans, onions, sweet green peppers, and tomatoes that most of us think of as chili. The Gonzaleses like their chili hot (for this recipe Mrs. Gonzales would use ½ cup chili powder). But half that amount—¼ cup chili powder—makes a peppery chili by most standards. We suggest starting out with 2 tablespoons chili powder, then upping the amount until the chili is as hot as you like it.

1 pound boned beef chuck or pork shoulder, cut in ¼-inch cubes (or, if you prefer, ½ pound each beef and pork)
4½ cups cold water
1 clove garlic, peeled and crushed
2 to 4 tablespoons chili powder, blended to a paste with ¼ cup broth (in which you are cooking the meat) or ¼ cup water

6 medium-sized Irish potatoes peeled and cut in ½-inch cubes, or 4 cups fresh or frozen whole-kernel corn (you will need about 4 large ears of sweet corn for 4 cups fresh whole-kernel corn)
1¼ teaspoons salt (about)

1. Place meat, water, and garlic in a large heavy kettle, bring to a simmer over moderate heat, adjust heat so that water bubbles very gently, cover and simmer slowly about 1½ hours. Blend in chili powder paste, re-cover and simmer about 1 hour longer, until meat is very tender.

2. Add the potatoes or, if you prefer, the whole-kernel corn, and

the salt, cover and simmer 35 to 45 minutes until potatoes or corn are tender. Taste for salt and add more, if needed. Ladle into soup bowls and serve as a main dish.

Green Chili

Makes 6 servings

Green Chili is served on Feast Days at San Ildefonso, "green" meaning that green chili peppers instead of red are used to prepare it. Fresh green chilies are incendiary, and to temper their hotness Pueblo women roast them in a moderate oven for about 45 minutes, then skin, seed, and mash them. "I always put the chilies in toward the end of cooking," says Mrs. Gonzales, "because they seem to get hotter and hotter as they cook." Because fresh green chilies are not widely available across the country, we have taken the liberty of substituting canned green chilies. They are milder than the fresh—two of them, seeded and minced, will make a nippy but not torrid chili. The Pueblo way to serve Green Chili is with pinto beans. The two are spooned into separate bowls, each person helps himself first to beans, then ladles a spoonful or two of Green Chili on top of them much as we would ladle gravy over mashed potatoes.

1 pound hamburger meat
1½ cups chopped onions
1 clove garlic, peeled and crushed
1 can (1 pound) tomatoes (do not drain)
1½ cups water

1 teaspoon salt
2 to 4 drained canned green chili peppers (from a 4-ounce can), depending upon how hot you like things

1. Brown the hamburger meat lightly in a large heavy skillet over moderate heat; add onions and garlic and stir-fry about 10 minutes until lightly browned.

2. Add tomatoes, water and salt, turn heat down very low and simmer, uncovered, stirring now and then, about 1¼ hours or until mixture is fairly thick (about the consistency of spaghetti sauce) and flavors are well blended.

3. Seed the green chilies, mince, then add to the skillet and simmer 10 to 15 minutes. Serve as a sauce for pinto beans (recipe follows).

Pueblo-Style Pinto Beans

Makes 6 servings

"Pinto beans are the staff of life of the Pueblo," says Mrs. Gonzales. "And the longer they cook, the better." Now that she has one of the new electric crock-type slow cookers, she lets the beans simmer in it most of the day. "Slow cooking gives them a delicious flavor," she says.

1 pound dried pinto beans, washed and sorted
6 cups cold water (about)

¼ pound salt pork, cut in ¼-inch cubes
⅛ teaspoon freshly ground black pepper

1. Place pinto beans in a large bowl, add 6 cups of the cold water and soak overnight.
2. Next day, transfer beans and their soaking water to a large heavy kettle, add just enough additional cold water to cover the beans, and bring to a simmer over moderate heat. Add salt pork and pepper, turn heat down very low—the liquid should ripple very gently—cover and simmer, stirring now and then, 6 to 7 hours or until beans are very tender and liquid has cooked down to the consistency of a cream soup. If, toward the end of cooking, the beans seem too soupy, cook uncovered for the last 1 to 2 hours. But watch the pot closely, and add a little additional cold water if beans threaten to cook dry.
3. Serve the beans plain or accompanied by Green Chili (recipe precedes).

Skillet Squash, Corn, Tomatoes and Beef

Makes 4 to 6 servings

Squash and corn are the Gonzaleses' favorite vegetables. They used to be grown at the Pueblo, but aren't anymore because there is rarely enough water to keep them alive. Rain can never be counted upon and the Pueblo's own water system is insufficient for irrigation. So like most of the other Pueblo women, Mrs. Gonzales now shops at the supermarket, buying those fruits and vegetables that she once grew. She likes skillet-cooked vegetables best—either cooked singly or mixed together as in this combination of squash, corn, tomatoes, and beef.

1 pound boned beef chuck or stew meat, cut ½-inch cubes
2 tablespoons lard or bacon drippings
1½ cups chopped onions
1 clove garlic, peeled and crushed
1 can (1 pound) tomatoes, drained (reserve juice)
¾ cup water
¾ teaspoon oregano (optional)
1 teaspoon salt (about)
⅛ teaspoon pepper (about)
2 cups fresh or frozen whole-kernel corn (for 2 cups fresh whole-kernel corn, you will need 2 large ears; to cut from the cob, simply hold ear perpendicular to cutting board and with a small sharp knife, cut down along cob, freeing kernels)
3 medium-sized zucchini or yellow squash, trimmed and sliced ½-inch thick

1. Brown beef well on all sides in lard or bacon drippings in a very large heavy skillet over moderately high heat; reduce heat to moderate, add onions and garlic and stir-fry about 5 minutes until they are limp. Add juice drained from tomatoes, water, oregano (if you like), and salt and pepper. Adjust heat under skillet so that liquid barely ripples, cover and simmer very slowly about 1½ hours or until meat is nearly fork-tender.

2. Stir in drained tomatoes and the corn, re-cover and cook 35 to 40 minutes longer until corn is tender and no longer tastes raw.

3. Add zucchini or yellow squash, toss lightly to mix, re-cover and cook 20 to 30 minutes, until squash is cooked the way you like it—after 20 minutes it will still be somewhat crisp; after 30 minutes, more well done. Because her family likes their vegetables "soft," Mrs. Gonzales may let the squash simmer slowly as long as 40 to 45 minutes.

4. Toss skillet mixture lightly, taste for salt and pepper and add more if needed to suit your taste. Serve hot as a main dish, accompanied, if you like, by fresh chunks of Adobe Oven Bread (page 261).

Italian Spaghetti American Indian Style

Makes 6 servings

Because she spent part of her childhood in New York City, Mrs. Gonzales was introduced early to such European dishes as lasagne, spaghetti and Swedish meatballs. She cooks them today for her family and for friends in the Pueblo, although at first, she says, people were wary of such non-Indian foods and would say, "Golly, how come?" Soon, however, they began to request them—especially the spaghetti.

1 pound hamburger meat
1½ cups chopped onions
1 clove garlic, peeled and crushed
1 teaspoon leaf oregano, crumbled
½ teaspoon leaf basil, crumbled
1 bay leaf, crumbled
4 teaspoons chili powder
¼ to ½ teaspoon crushed dried red chili peppers (¼ teaspoon makes a fairly mild sauce, ½ teaspoon a pretty peppery one. Mrs. Gonzales often adds a whole teaspoon, which makes a hotter sauce than most nonsouthwesterners like)

1 can (6 ounces) tomato paste
1 can (1 pound, 12 ounces) tomatoes (do not drain)
1 cup water
¾ teaspoon salt
¼ cup minced fresh parsley
1 to 2 teaspoons sugar (if needed to mellow the tartness of the tomatoes)
1 pound thin spaghetti, cooked by package directions and drained
Grated Romano or Parmesan cheese (topping)

1.   Brown hamburger lightly in a large heavy skillet over moderate heat; add onions, garlic, oregano, basil, bay leaf, chili powder, and crushed dried chili peppers and stir-fry about 5 minutes until onions are limp.

2.   Turn heat to low, blend in tomato paste, tomatoes, water and salt and simmer, uncovered, stirring now and then, about 1½ hours, until sauce is quite thick and flavors are well blended. Mix in parsley and simmer 10 minutes longer. Taste sauce, and if it is too tart, add sugar to mellow the flavor.

3.   Pile cooked spaghetti on a large deep platter, ladle the sauce on top and sprinkle with grated Romano or Parmesan cheese.

Fried Spinach and Onions

Makes 6 servings

"A long time ago there used to be a natural spinach that we'd find out here—in the yard, anywhere," says Mrs. Gonzales. "It was sort of a flat green leaf. We'd wash it, fry it in bacon drippings or lard with some diced onion and, oh, that was delicious. But I don't see the natural spinach much anymore. It's another thing that seems to have disappeared." Mrs. Gonzales says you can prepare regular spinach the same way. It's quick, easy, inexpensive, and good although it hasn't quite the same flavor as the wild spinach.

4 tablespoons bacon drippings or lard
1½ cups chopped onions
1¼ pounds (two bags, 10 ounces each) fresh spinach, washed well and trimmed of coarse stems

¾ teaspoon salt
⅛ teaspoon freshly ground black pepper

1.   Melt bacon drippings or lard in a large heavy kettle over moderately high heat, add onions and stir-fry 8 to 10 minutes until lightly browned.

2.   Add spinach (it will almost fill the kettle at first) and fry, tossing constantly 3 to 5 minutes until wilted and lightly glazed with drippings or lard. Add salt and pepper, toss well again and serve.

Oven-Roasted Sweet Corn in the Husk

Makes 6 servings

The Gonzaleses' favorite way to prepare corn is to roast it in the husk in the outdoor adobe oven. Mr. Gonzales usually does it, first building a fire in the oven and then when the oven is uniformly hot, scraping out the coals and sealing the openings at the top of the oven. He piles the ears in the oven, slides a metal slab in front of the door, and lets the corn roast in the retained heat. In rainy weather, Mrs. Gonzales will roast corn the same way in her modern indoor oven.

6 medium-sized ears fresh sweet   Salt (optional)
   corn, in the husk   Pepper (optional)
Butter (optional)

1.   If corn husks seem dry, sprinkle lightly with cool water. Lay ears one layer deep in a large shallow roasting pan and roast, uncovered, in a hot oven (400°) for 45 to 50 minutes or until kernels are tender; to test, peel husks back on one ear and pierce a kernel with a small metal skewer—if no milky juices run out, corn is done. Or, if you prefer, cut several kernels from the tip of the cob and taste. They should be firm-tender and taste faintly nutlike but not raw.

2.   Remove ears from oven, husk and remove silks, then serve hot with butter, salt, and pepper, if you like (the Gonzaleses use no seasonings at all).

Adobe Oven Bread

Makes two 7-inch round loaves

This hard-crusted yeast bread resembles the round peasant loaves of Europe and, like them, owes its chewy texture to a high proportion of flour and to energetic kneading. Pueblo women make it in hundred-pound lots—that is, using as much as a hundred pounds of flour at a time. It is the traditional feast-day or ceremonial bread, baked in *hornos*, beehive-shaped outdoor adobe ovens. It can be baked in modern indoor ovens, and is, on those rare rainy days when the outdoor ovens cannot be fired. Pueblo Indians prefer the *horno*-baked bread, however, because of its woodsy-smoky flavor.

2 packages active dry yeast
1¾ cups very warm water
1 tablespoon sugar
3 tablespoons melted lard or vegetable shortening (lard is what Mrs. Gonzales prefers)

1¼ teaspoons salt
5½ cups sifted all purpose flour (about)

1. Sprinkle yeast over ½ cup of the very warm water in a large bowl. (Very warm water should feel comfortably warm when dropped on wrist). Stir until yeast dissolves.
2. Stir in sugar, 2 tablespoons of the melted lard or vegetable shortening, the salt and the remaining 1¼ cups very warm water.
3. Beat in the flour, 1 cup at a time. You will only be able to beat in about 4 cups of the flour with a spoon because the dough becomes quite stiff. When you have stirred in as much flour as possible, flour a board or pastry cloth with about ½ cup of the remaining 1½ cups of flour, turn the dough out onto the floured board, flour your hands well, and knead the flour in thoroughly. Knead in the remaining 1 cup of flour the same way, working in about ½ cup at a time. The dough will be very stiff, but this is as it should be. Knead the dough hard for 5 minutes until satiny and elastic. You'll find this tiring because of the dough's stiffness but keep at it and don't shortcut the kneading time because kneading is what gives the dough its springy-chewy texture.
4. Shape the kneaded dough into a smooth round ball, place in a warm, greased, large bowl; turn dough in bowl to grease all over. Cover with a clean dry cloth and let rise in a warm place, away from draft, until doubled in bulk, about 1 to 1¼ hours.
5. Punch dough down, turn onto a lightly floured board and again knead hard for 5 minutes, adding only what flour is necessary to keep the dough from sticking to the board or your hands.

6.   Divide dough in half and shape each half into a ball—don't flatten balls on top, but make them as spherical as possible. Place each ball of dough in a lightly greased 8-inch round layer cake pan and brush the tops lightly with a little of the remaining 1 tablespoon of melted lard or vegetable shortening. Cover with cloth and let rise in a warm place, away from draft, until doubled in bulk, about 40 to 45 minutes.

7.   Bake the loaves in a moderate oven (350°) for about 1 hour and 15 minutes or until loaves are golden brown on top and sound hollow when thumped with your fingers. Remove loaves from oven and brush with remaining lard or vegetable shortening. Lift loaves to wire racks and cool upright to room temperature before serving.

8.   To serve, tear the bread into large chunks (the Indian way), or, if you prefer, cut into wedges with a sharp serrated knife. The Indians like the bread plain—without butter—and often use it to get up the last bit of meat or vegetable juices on their plates.

Capirotada (*Indian Bread Pudding*)

Makes 4 to 6 servings

This dessert, made with toast and raisins, caramelized sugar and sharp cheese, is a feast-day specialty at many of the Rio Grande Indian Pueblos.

1 cup sugar
2⅓ cups water
1 teaspoon ground cinnamon
¼ teaspoon ground cloves
8 slices lightly buttered crisp dry toast, broken into about 1-inch pieces

1 cup seedless raisins
1½ cups coarsely shredded sharp Cheddar cheese (Mrs. Gonzales would use Longhorn, a nippy local cheese, but any aged Cheddar works well)

1.   Melt the sugar in a medium-sized heavy skillet over moderate heat until liquid and the color of butterscotch—this will take only 3 to four minutes, so watch closely and stir often with a wooden spoon lest the sugar burn. Slowly pour in the water—it will sputter at first and the sugar will harden into brittle. Continue heating and stirring until the brittle dissolves. Add the cinnamon and cloves, turn heat to low and keep warm while proceeding with the pudding.

2.   In a lightly buttered 2-quart casserole, make a layer of toast,

then one of raisins, and finally one of cheese, using only about one-fourth of each ingredient. Repeat three more times, layering the same way, until all ingredients are used up. Pour the hot sugar syrup over all and toss lightly to mix.

3. Bake uncovered in a moderate oven (350°) 20 to 25 minutes—just until cheese is melted and the toast has absorbed the liquid. Serve hot. You may want to top each portion of pudding with a trickle of light cream, but this is not the Indian way.

Prune or Apricot Pies

Makes 20 individual-sized square "pies"

Another favorite feast-day dessert: crisp, sweet pastry filled with spicy prune or apricot puree. Mrs. Gonzales usually bakes the pies in big round pans—pizza pans, for example—but since they are traditionally cut into squares, we tried rolling them in rectangles and baking them on cooky sheets—easier somehow. Besides, there's less waste. Though called "pies," these really are more like filled cookies. The prune filling is the more traditional, but for variety Mrs. Gonzales will often make an apricot filling. You can, if you like, simply make up half the recipe of each flavor, then fill half the pastry with prune filling and the remaining half with apricot.

Prune Filling:
1 pound prunes, pitted
1½ cups water
½ cup sugar
¾ teaspoon ground cinnamon
¼ teaspoon ground cloves

Apricot Filling:
1 pound dried pitted apricots
1½ cups water
1½ cups sugar

½ teaspoon ground cinnamon
¼ teaspoon ground cloves

Sweet Pastry:
3 cups sifted all-purpose flour
⅓ cup sugar
1 teaspoon baking powder
¼ teaspoon salt
1 cup lard or, if you prefer, vegetable shortening
⅔ cup cold water (about)

1. *Prepare the filling first:* Make either the prune or the apricot, or if you prefer, half the recipe of each. Both are made the same basic way: Place prunes or apricots in a heavy medium-sized saucepan, add water and bring to a simmer over moderately low heat. Cover and simmer slowly 25 to 30 minutes until fruit is quite soft. Uncover, and if there is still a lot of visible liquid, simmer uncovered until it has evaporated. But watch the pot closely lest the fruit scorch. Puree fruit

through a food mill, or press through a fine sieve. Mix in sugar, cinnamon and cloves and stir until sugar dissolves. Set aside to use in Step 4.

2. *To make the sweet pastry:* Combine flour, sugar, baking powder and salt in a large shallow mixing bowl. Cut in lard or vegetable shortening with a pastry blender until mixture is crumbly—about the texture of uncooked oatmeal. Add cold water, a few tablespoons at a time, scattering evenly over surface of mixture and tossing mixture briskly with a fork. Continue adding and forking in the water just until mixture holds together to form a soft pastry.

3. Divide pastry in half (this is a very tender pastry, so handle it gently). Roll out half of the pastry on a lightly floured pastry cloth with a floured stockinette-covered rolling pin into a rectangle about 15 inches long, 10 inches wide and ⅜-inch thick—slightly thicker than you would roll a piecrust. Keep the margins as even and the corners as "square" as possible. Using a ruler to guide you and a sharp knife dipped in flour, halve the pastry rectangle the short way so that you have two pastry rectangles measuring about 7½ inches by 10 inches.

4. Ease one of the pastry rectangles onto an ungreased cooky sheet (it's simple if you fold it gently over the rolling pin, then lift it to the cooky sheet). Spread with a thick (about ¼-inch thick) layer of Prune or Apricot Filling, spreading well to the edges. Ease the second pastry rectangle on top of the filling (again using the rolling pin for support), and press the top "crust" gently into the filling. With a sharp knife, square up uneven edges.

5. Roll remaining pastry the same way, transfer to a second ungreased cooky sheet, then cut, fill and trim as directed in Step 4.

6. Bake "pies" in a hot oven (425°) about 20 minutes or until they are lightly browned and pastry feels firm to the touch. Remove from oven and while quite warm, cut into large squares (about 2½ inches) or, if you prefer, rectangles (about 2 inches by 3 inches). While "pies" are still warm, use a pancake turner to transfer them to wire racks to cool.

Biscochitos

Makes 6 to 7 dozen cookies

"This is my favorite cookie recipe," says Dolores Gonzales. "And I always try to keep some on hand because the family likes them as well as I do. They're crunchy and not too sweet but they have a delicious, delicate spice flavor."

6 cups sifted all-purpose flour
3 teaspoons baking powder
½ teaspoon salt
1½ cups sugar
2 cups vegetable shortening
1 tablespoon whole anise seeds

2 eggs
½ cup water

Cinnamon-Sugar Topping:
½ cup sugar mixed with 1 teaspoon ground cinnamon

1. Sift flour, baking powder, and salt together and set aside.

2. Cream the sugar with the shortening until light and fluffy, then beat in the anise seeds and the eggs. Continue beating until fluffy.

3. Mix in the sifted dry ingredients, then the water to make a stiff dough.

4. Roll out about one-fourth of the dough at a time to a thickness of about ¼ inch on a lightly floured pastry cloth. Cut with a round 2- to 2½-inch cooky cutter.

5. Space cookies about 1 inch apart on ungreased cooky sheets and bake in a hot oven (400°) for about 10 minutes or until pale tan.

6. Remove cookies at once from cooky sheets, coat both sides with cinnamon-sugar, then let cool well before eating.

The West and Mountain States

Mrs. Ennis Woffinden
of
Utah County, Utah

"YOU want to know how good a cook my wife is?" Ennis Woffinden asks (he has just come in from the corn fields and caught us mid-interview discussing old-fashioned Utah recipes). "Here, look at this," he continues, patting his stomach. "There's your proof!"

Bea smiles. She's a pretty woman in her late fifties with fair skin, blue eyes, curly, close-cropped dark-brown hair. "We both have to watch our weight," she adds, although she, like her husband, looks just about the right weight. "I guess I work it off," she explains, "up to the school." She has just been named lunchroom manager at the Spanish Fork Complex School a few miles away and as such is responsible (along with a staff of fifteen) for feeding a thousand children a substantial hot lunch each day.

No small task, and considering the fact that she must be up and out of the house well before sun-up, one wonders that she has any inclination to cook when she returns home in mid-afternoon.

"Well," Bea says, "I've always loved to cook. Ever since I was a little girl. What I wanted to be when I grew up was a teacher of cooking and sewing. I studied home ec in high school and I had a year of home ec at Brigham Young University. Then I fell in love and got married."

Born Bernice Harmer in the town of Springville just a few miles away, Bea met Ennis Woffinden while visiting her uncle in the north end of Utah County. "Ennis's father worked for the sugar company there and so did my uncle." Bea was only a high school sophomore then (Ennis had already finished school), but within five years they were married and starting a family of their own (two sons, both now married, who have provided four grandchildren, and a daughter, who is still in college).

Like the majority of families in Utah County, the Woffindens are Latter Day Saints, or Mormons, and as such a particularly warm and close-knit family. The day of our interview, in fact, the phone seemed to ring nonstop. Bea would answer it, chat awhile, then return saying, "That was my father. He and my stepmother are coming down to supper tonight." Or, "That was my son. He's coming to pick sweet corn and I've asked him to stay to supper. Wouldn't *you* like to stay, too? I don't know what I'll cook, but I'll think of something."

"Thinking of something" spur-of-the-moment is as effortless to Bea Woffinden as breathing. First of all, she's an old hand at cooking and menu planning. Second, like most Mormons, she keeps on hand at least a full year's supply of food.

The Woffinden's fifty-five-acre "mostly grain" farm, nestled in a green valley between the Wasatch Mountains on the east and Utah Lake on the west, makes them virtually self-sufficient. "It's funny," Bea says. "Ennis and I neither one grew up on a farm. And we're the only ones of all our brothers and sisters who live on a farm today. Ennis Woffinden doesn't farm full time; he works as a maintenance man at Brigham Young University in Provo.

He is plainly proud of his farm, however. He says, "If you want to see the most beautiful meal in the world, I'll show it to you." He is speaking of his big vegetable garden and patch of sweet corn (people come from miles around to load up on fat, succulent ears at fifty cents a dozen).

Both Ennis and Bea have been active as leaders in the 4-H Club. "I've been a leader for twenty-nine years," Bea says. "Doing cooking, sewing, knitting, home improvement, and safety projects. We've sent about twelve or fourteen kids to the National 4-H Club Congress in Chicago and we've had National Winners in safety and swine."

Although Bea is a busy lady, she is not one to brag about her accomplishments. It took several hours of interviewing to pry out of her the fact that in 1975 she was named "The Outstanding Food Service Woman of the Year for the State of Utah."

"My kids say that's why I got this new job as lunchroom manager at the Spanish Fork Complex School," she continues. "I've been in school lunch for fourteen years. I started out as a main-dish cook, then I went into baking. Five years ago I became manager of the Park School hot lunch in Spanish Fork. It's a small elementary school . . . only three hundred and fifty children.

"After I won the award, the Park School came and got me and took me back there to a surprise party. Every child had written me a letter, they made me a crown, and a train out of kitchen towels clothespinned together. I was Lunch Queen for the Day and marched up and down the auditorium while the kids sang songs they had written. Oh, it was a lot of fun!"

Mushroom-Smothered Swiss Steak

Makes 6 servings

The Woffindens raise their own beef (Herefords and Charolais) as well as lambs and hogs. "One beef a year will about do us," Mrs. Woffinden says. The family likes steak best ("pink but not raw"). As for the less-than-tender cuts, Bea Woffinden makes them into soup, stew, or Swiss steak. "Ennis loves *this* Swiss steak," she continues, "because mushrooms are a favorite of his."

1 blade, arm or round steak cut about 2 inches thick (3 to 3½ pounds)	¾ pound mushrooms, wiped clean and sliced thin
2 tablespoons butter, margarine, or bacon drippings	6 tablespoons flour
	1 cup beef broth
	1 cup milk
1 medium-sized yellow onion, peeled and chopped	½ teaspoon salt (or to taste)
	⅛ teaspoon pepper (or to taste)

1. Brown the steak on both sides in the butter in a large heavy frying pan over moderately high heat ("I brown it *real* good," Bea Woffinden says). Transfer to a roasting pan that is only slightly larger than the steak.

2. In the drippings sauté the onion and mushrooms over moderate heat about 5 to 8 minutes until limp and lightly browned. Blend in flour well, add broth, milk, salt and pepper, and heat, stirring constantly, until thickened and smooth—about 3 minutes.

3. Pour mushroom sauce over steak, cover pan snugly with aluminum foil, and bake in a moderate oven (350°) about 1½ hours or until steak is fork-tender.

Sausage and Rice Casserole
Makes 6 servings

The sausage Mrs. Woffinden would use for this casserole is likely to be made out of home-grown pork. You can, of course, use any good commercial sausage meat.

1 pound bulk sausage meat
1 cup diced celery
½ cup chopped onion
½ cup chopped green pepper

½ cup toasted slivered almonds
1 cup uncooked converted rice
2 cups chicken broth

1.   Brown the sausage in a large heavy skillet over moderately high heat, then with a slotted spoon transfer to a 2½-quart casserole. Drain all but 3 tablespoons drippings from skillet, or if sausage is lean and drippings seem skimpy, add a little bacon drippings, butter, or margarine to skillet.

2.   Sauté the celery, onion and green pepper in drippings over moderate heat about 5 minutes or until limp and lightly browned. Transfer to casserole. Add almonds, rice and broth and stir well. Cover casserole snugly.

3.   Bake in a moderate oven (350°) about 1½ hours or until rice is fluffy-tender.

Note:

Because most sausage is highly seasoned, you will not need to add salt or pepper to this recipe.

Green Beans with Mushrooms and Bacon
Makes 6 servings

"We do a lot of Sunday-night suppers around here, and these beans are everybody's favorite," says Bea Woffinden. We might add that the beauty of this bean recipe is that the beans can be "held" successfully for about an hour—simply spoon them into a large casserole, cover with foil, and set in a very slow oven (300°). They are best, of course, served straight away.

4 slices bacon, snipped crosswise into julienne strips
1 medium-sized yellow onion, peeled and minced fine
¾ pound mushrooms, wiped clean and sliced thin
5 tablespoons flour

1¾ cups milk or light cream
1 teaspoon salt
⅛ teaspoon pepper
2 pounds green beans, washed, tipped, then boiled about 10 to 12 minutes in lightly salted water until crisp-tender

1. Brown the bacon in a large heavy skillet over moderately high heat; with a slotted spoon, lift out crisply browned bits of bacon and drain on paper toweling. Pour all drippings from skillet, then measure out 4 tablespoons and return to skillet.

2. Sauté onion and mushrooms in drippings over moderate heat 5 to 8 minutes—until limp and lightly browned. Off heat, blend in flour. Add milk, salt, and pepper, return to moderate heat and cook, stirring constantly, until thickened and smooth. Lower heat and let sauce mellow, stirring now and then, for about 10 minutes.

3. Drain beans well, then mix with mushroom sauce and reserved bacon crumbles and serve.

Stuffed Tomatoes

Makes 6 servings

"Now this recipe goes back to my mother," Bea Woffinden explains. "It was a family favorite then and it's a favorite of ours, now. Why, I made it just last night."

6 medium-sized to large vine-ripe tomatoes
½ cup finely minced onion
6 tablespoons butter (about)
Tomato pulp (scooped out of tomatoes)
1 cup water

½ teaspoon salt (or to taste)
⅛ teaspoon pepper (or to taste)
1 teaspoon sugar (if needed to mellow the tartness of the tomatoes)
2 cups dried bread cubes (about ¼-inch cubes)

1. With a sharp knife, slice off the top one-fourth of each tomato (reserve tops). Loosen pulp from tomato walls with the knife, then with a teaspoon scoop out all pulp. Put tomatoes upside-down on several thicknesses of paper toweling and let drain while you prepare the filling. Chop tomato pulp and press through a fine sieve to remove seeds.

2.   In a large heavy skillet sauté the onion in 2 tablespoons of the butter about 5 minutes or until limp. Add tomato pulp, water, salt and pepper and simmer uncovered about 30 minutes until mixture has reduced considerably and is about the consistency of pasta sauce. Taste and add sugar, if needed, also a bit more salt and pepper. Add bread cubes and toss to mix, then stir in 2 more tablespoons of the butter (or as Bea Woffinden says, "a good big chunk of butter").

3.   Fill tomato shells with stuffing (don't pack it in), dot top of stuffing with remaining 2 tablespoons of butter, then replace tomato tops. Stand tomatoes close together in a 7- or 8-inch layer-cake pan ("they'll help hold one another up," Bea says), then bake uncovered in a moderate oven (350°) for 20 to 25 minutes—just until good and hot.

Chicken, Vegetable and Macaroni Salad

Makes 8 to 10 servings

"Not everybody likes raw cut-up onions in a salad," Mrs. Woffinden begins, "so what I do is grate the onion up real fine and mix it with the dressing." Her chicken salad, unlike many, contains cooked peas, carrots, and macaroni as well as big chunks of chicken.

3 cups diced cooked chicken
1½ cups finely diced celery
1½ cups cooked drained elbow
   macaroni
1 cup cooked diced carrots, well
   drained
1 cup cooked green peas, well
   drained
4 hard-cooked eggs, peeled and
   diced

Dressing:
1½ cups mayonnaise (preferably
   homemade)
3 tablespoons milk or light cream
½ medium-sized yellow onion,
   peeled and grated very fine
½ clove garlic, peeled and crushed
1 tablespoon spicy brown prepared
   mustard
¼ teaspoon ground nutmeg
1 teaspoon salt
¼ teaspoon pepper

1.   Place all salad ingredients in a large bowl and toss lightly to mix.

2.   Whisk together all dressing ingredients until smooth, pour over salad and toss well to mix.

3.   Cover and refrigerate until ready to serve.

Potato and Egg Salad

Makes 8 to 10 servings

"My mother always made a good potato salad, and I make it the way she did. One trick I've learned," Bea Woffinden continues, "is that if you cook the potatoes the day before, peel them, cut them up, and then sprinkle them with salt, the salt will really sink into the potatoes."

8 large potatoes, cooked in their skins until tender, peeled and cut in about ¾-inch cubes
2 teaspoons salt
6 hard-cooked eggs, peeled and diced
2 cups cooked diced carrots, well drained (optional)

Dressing:
1 cup mayonnaise (preferably homemade)
1 medium-sized yellow onion, peeled and grated very fine
1 tablespoon spicy brown prepared mustard
¼ teaspoon pepper
¾ cup heavy cream, whipped

1.   Place potato cubes in a large bowl, sprinkle with salt and toss to mix. Cover and refrigerate overnight.

2.   Next day, add eggs and, if you like, the carrots, and toss lightly.

3.   *For the dressing:* Blend mayonnaise with onion, mustard, and pepper, then fold in whipped cream.

4.   Pour dressing over salad, toss well, then cover and let marinate in the refrigerator several hours before serving.

Bulgur Bread

Makes two 8½- × 4½- × 2½-inch loaves

Here's a bulgur wheat recipe Mrs. Woffinden obtained through the Utah Extension Service. "Bulgur makes a real good bread," she says. We think so, too. The bread is coarse of texture, chewy and, with its hard crust, much like the peasant breads of Italy, Spain, and Portugal.

¼ cup bulgur wheat
1 cup water
¾ cup milk
2 teaspoons salt
3 tablespoons sugar

3 tablespoons vegetable shortening or oil
1 package active dry yeast
½ cup very warm water
4½ cups flour (about)

1.   Simmer (do not boil) bulgur in the water in a covered saucepan 20 minutes or until bulgur is tender and almost all water is absorbed; do not drain. Cool to 105° to 115°.

2.   Scald milk with salt, sugar, and shortening and cool to 105° to 115°.

3.   Sprinkle yeast over very warm water in a large bowl (very warm water should feel comfortably warm when dropped on wrist). Stir until yeast dissolves. Add cooled milk mixture, then cooled bulgur.

4.   Add the flour, 1 cup at a time, beating hard after each addition. The 4½ cups should make a soft yet manageable dough, but if not, add slightly more flour.

5.   Turn dough out on a floured board (dough will be sticky at first) and knead hard about 10 minutes or until dough is smooth and elastic ("You'll know you've kneaded the dough enough when it blisters," Mrs. Woffinden points out).

6.   Place dough in a warm buttered bowl; turn greased side up. Cover with a clean dry cloth and let rise in a warm, draft-free spot until doubled in bulk—about 1 to 1½ hours.

7.   Punch dough down and let rest 10 minutes. Knead again lightly for 2 to 3 minutes, then divide dough in half and shape into two loaves.

8.   Place loaves in greased 8½- × 4½- × 2½-inch loaf pans, cover with dry cloth and again let rise in a warm spot until doubled in bulk—about 1 hour.

9.   Bake the loaves in a hot oven (400°) for 35 to 40 minutes or until loaves are nicely browned and sound hollow when thumped with your fingers. Remove loaves from oven, lay pans on their sides on wire racks and let bread cool 15 minutes. Remove loaves from pans and cool upright on wire racks.

Mother's Parker House Rolls

Makes about 2½ dozen rolls

"Everybody remembers my mother for her rolls," says Mrs. Woffinden. "Anytime anybody got sick, my mother would always take them some hot rolls. Her recipe is the one I use today—for Parker House Rolls, for Caramel-Walnut Rolls, for all kinds of rolls."

1 package active dry yeast
½ cup very warm water
1 cup milk
3 tablespoons butter or margarine
3 tablespoons sugar

3 eggs, lightly beaten
1 teaspoon salt
5 cups (about) sifted all-purpose
    flour
3 tablespoons melted butter

1. Sprinkle yeast over very warm water in a large bowl (very warm water should feel comfortably warm when dropped on wrist). Stir until yeast dissolves.

2. Combine milk, butter and sugar in a saucepan and heat just enough to scald the milk and melt the butter. Remove from heat and cool mixture until 105° to 115°.

3. Add milk mixture to yeast, then beat in the eggs, the salt and 1 cup of the flour. "I just beat the batter until it looks like cake batter," says Bea Woffinden. Mix in the remaining 4 cups flour, 1 cup at a time, to make a soft but manageable dough. "Depending upon the humidity," says Mrs. Woffinden, "you may need a little bit less flour or a little bit more."

4. Turn dough out on a floured board (dough will be sticky at first) and knead well 5 to 10 minutes—until dough is smooth and elastic.

5. Place dough in a warm buttered bowl; turn greased side up. Cover with a clean dry cloth and let rise in a warm, draft-free spot until doubled in bulk—about 1½ hours.

6. Punch dough down and divide in half. Roll out one half into a circle about ¼-inch thick, then cut into rounds, using a floured 2¾-inch biscuit cutter. Spread a little of the melted butter across the center of each round, then fold in half, stretching and tucking the top edge of dough down over the bottom edge, sealing the butter in (this way, the rolls will not open up as they rise and bake). Roll, cut and shape the remaining dough the same way.

7. Space rolls about 1½ inches apart on ungreased baking sheets, cover with a clean cloth and let rise in a warm spot until doubled in bulk—about 35 to 40 minutes.

8. Bake in a moderately hot oven (375°) 15 to 20 minutes or until rolls are a rich golden brown. Serve hot with plenty of butter.

Caramel-Walnut Rolls

Makes about 2 dozen rolls

"My daughter Sharlene took a batch of these rolls over for a county 4-H exhibit," says Mrs. Woffinden. "And when we went back the next morning, there were only two of them left."

1 recipe dough for Mother's Parker House Rolls (recipe precedes)	⅓ cup firmly packed light brown sugar
½ cup butter	¾ teaspoon cinnamon (about)
	1 cup finely chopped walnuts

1. Prepare the dough for Mother's Parker House Rolls through Step 5.

2. Meanwhile, warm butter and sugar in a heavy saucepan over low heat, stirring occasionally, about 15 minutes or until sugar is no longer granular. Set aside and keep warm.

3. When dough has risen sufficiently, punch down and divide in half. Roll half into a rectangle about 16 inches long, 11 inches wide and ¼-inch thick. Spread half the brown sugar mixture over dough, leaving about a 1-inch margin along one of the 16-inch edges. Sprinkle with about half of the cinnamon, then scatter half the nuts on top.

4. Beginning with one long edge of dough (not the one with the unbuttered margin), roll up snugly jelly-roll style so that you have a roll of dough about 16 inches long. Make sure that the unbuttered margin of dough is on the bottom. Roll and fill the remaining dough the same way.

5. Cut rolls of dough into 1-inch slices and place, spiral sides up, in greased muffin-pan cups. Cover with a dry cloth and let rise in a warm, draft-free spot until doubled in bulk—about 35 to 40 minutes.

6. Bake the rolls in a moderately hot oven (375°) 15 to 20 minutes or until nicely browned. Serve hot.

Raisin Tea Ring

Makes two 9-inch tea rings

Of all the yeast breads Mrs. Woffinden bakes, this breakfast sweet bread is probably the family favorite.

1 recipe dough for Mother's Parker House Rolls (page 276)
¼ cup butter, at room temperature
1 recipe Raisin Filling (recipe follows)

Orange Glaze:
1 cup confectioners (10X) sugar
1 tablespoon orange juice

1 tablespoon softened butter
Water (just enough to make a spoonable glaze—about 1 tablespoon)

Optional Decoration:
Sliced glacéed cherries (about 2 tablespoons)
Chopped walnuts (about ⅓ cup)

1. Prepare the dough for Mother's Parker House Rolls as directed through Step 5.

2. Punch dough down and divide in half. Roll half into a rectangle about 16 inches long, 11 inches wide and ¼ inch thick. Spread half the butter over dough, then spread with half of the Raisin Filling. Beginning with one long edge of dough, roll up snugly jelly-roll style so that you have a roll of dough about 16 inches long with the seam on the bottom. Transfer to an ungreased baking sheet, bend into a ring, inserting one end of dough into the other and pinching well to seal. With a sharp knife, cut about two-thirds of the way through the ring at 1-inch intervals, then twist slices outward so that they lie flat, slightly overlapping. Roll, fill, and shape the remaining dough the same way.

3. Cover the rings with clean dry cloths, then let rise in a warm, draft-free spot until doubled in bulk—about ¾ to 1 hour.

4. Bake in a moderately hot oven (375°) about 20 to 25 minutes or until rings are nicely browned and sound hollow when thumped with your fingers. Remove from oven.

5. *For the orange glaze:* Blend 10X sugar with orange juice and butter until smooth, then add just enough water to make a thin glaze (about the consistency of thin white sauce). Spoon over the tea rings while they are still warm. If you like, decorate tops of rings with sliced glacéed cherries and chopped nuts.

Raisin Filling

Makes about 1½ cups

When making this filling, be sure that the raisins you use are nice and plump and soft.

1 cup seedless raisins
1 cup hot water
1 cup sugar blended with 2 tablespoons cornstarch

1 teaspoon lemon juice
1 teaspoon vanilla

1.   Combine all ingredients in a small heavy saucepan, set over moderate heat and cook and stir until thickened and clear—about 3 minutes.

2.   Turn heat to lowest point and let mixture simmer very slowly—uncovered—about 35 to 40 minutes or until quite thick. Cool 35 to 40 minutes before using.

3.   Use in making Raisin Tea Ring (recipe precedes).

Rocky Road Cake

Makes one 13- × 9- × 2-inch loaf cake

This is one of the most tender crumbed chocolate cakes you will ever eat. No wonder it has won blue ribbons for the Woffindens at the Utah County Fair. You'll note as you finish mixing the cake that the batter seems unusually thin. Don't be alarmed; the finished cake will be exceptionally fine and feathery.

½ cup butter
½ cup cooking oil
1 cup water
2 cups sifted all-purpose flour
1¾ cups sugar
1 teaspoon salt
¼ cup cocoa (not a mix)
2 eggs
½ cup buttermilk blended with 1 teaspoon baking soda
1½ teaspoons vanilla

Rocky Road Frosting:
¼ cup cocoa (not a mix)
⅓ cup buttermilk
½ cup butter
3½ cups (about) confectioners (10X) sugar (you'll need enough to make the frosting a good spreading consistency)
⅔ cup finely snipped marshmallows, or, if you prefer, ⅔ cup miniature marshmallows
½ cup coarsely chopped walnuts
1 teaspoon vanilla

1.   In a small saucepan, bring butter, oil, and water to a boil; remove from heat and let cool 10 minutes.

2.   Combine flour, sugar, salt, and cocoa in a large mixing bowl, pressing out all lumps. Pour in butter-oil mixture and beat just until smooth. Beat in the eggs, then stir in the buttermilk-soda solution and the vanilla.

3.   Pour batter into a well-greased 13- × 9- × 2-inch loaf pan and bake in a moderate oven (350°) for 30 to 35 minutes or until cake begins to pull from sides of pan and a finger pressed into center of cake leaves an imprint that vanishes slowly.

4.   Remove cake from oven and cool upright in its pan on a wire rack at least 25 minutes before frosting.

5.   *To make the frosting:* Heat and stir cocoa, buttermilk, and butter in a small heavy saucepan over low heat until butter melts and mixture is smooth. Transfer mixture to a mixing bowl, then beat in 10X sugar until mixture is satiny and of a good spreading consistency. Stir in marshmallows, nuts, and vanilla.

6.   Frost the cake right in its pan, swirling the frosting into peaks and valleys. Let frosting "set," then cut cake into squares and serve.

Mrs. George McKamey
of
Cascade County, Montana

IT takes some time (plus skillful navigation) to reach the McKamey Ranch, a 25,000-acre sheep-and-cattle spread that sprawls for miles along the lush Missouri River valley of west-central Montana. "Big Sky Country," they call this, with good reason. You feel as if you're at the top of the world.

From the country road that meanders past the McKamey Ranch, only the front gate and a red barn are visible. The snug, one-story white ranch house (built in 1947) lies well beyond sheltering hills in a green valley shaded by willows and box elders. "We really amount to a little village," Mrs. McKamey says of the ranch. It is jointly operated by her husband (who has managed the ranch since he was twenty-five), his two brothers, and his oldest son, all of whom live on the land.

"We are the very last of the large sheep ranchers in Cascade County," Ada McKamey continues. "And would you believe that what's driving people out is the coyote? Don't let anyone—not even Walt Disney—tell you that coyotes don't eat sheep because they do."

Ada McKamey came to this sheep ranch forty years ago at the age of twenty when she married George McKamey. ("I'd met him at a dance in Cascade near where my family lived," she explains.)

"I'm not from Montana originally," she continues, "although George is. I was born in Canada (Alberta Province), but my people, the Turners, moved to Montana when I was nine and I grew up on a farm eight miles outside Cascade."

Turning to things culinary, she says, "No, I didn't do much cooking as a child, maybe because I was the youngest of seven children, maybe because my mother was such a good cook. Oh, I knew how to bake cakes and things like that. But my husband laughs and says that all he got the first few months we were married was potato salad. And I don't think I even made a very great potato salad.

"You know," she continues, "George is an *excellent* cook. I've learned a lot about cooking from him. And his mother taught me a lot. Of course, I've saved my mother's recipes because she was also an excellent cook.

"Today I do most of the cooking. I'm not like a lot of women in Montana who work outside with the machinery. That's something I never *did* do. Well, I had five children to raise." (The McKameys' two girls and three boys now range in age from the mid-thirties down to the late teens; two are married and have, between them, six children). "So," Ada McKamey reemphasizes, "it was *my* lot to do the cooking."

She might also have added tending the vegetable garden and preserving its harvest each year. Like many other Mormons, Ada McKamey is a great one for "putting food by." The ranch, of course, also provides all the beef and lamb the family can eat, not to mention chicken and venison, even trout pulled from nearby streams.

Because of such a surfeit of good food, Ada discovered to her chagrin that she had been gaining weight steadily in recent years. "But," she says proudly, "I've joined Weight Watchers and lost twenty pounds."

Although she insists that she still needs to lose weight, Ada McKamey seems trim. She's a handsome woman of medium height with short-cut wavy brown hair, delicate features, and warm brown eyes.

Before she became diet-conscious, Mrs. McKamey made lots of cakes and cookies. "And *pies*," she says. "Pies were always the main dessert with us, especially fruit pies." She still makes all of her own breads and rolls; in fact she grinds her own wheat, using that grown on her older daughter's wheat ranch just east of Great Falls. She ferments her own yogurt and even makes her own cheese—a nippy golden Cheddar as well as cottage cheese.

She is delighted that her younger daughter Ruth, now a high school senior, has inherited her love of cooking. The two of them spend many hours in the big country kitchen together—cooking in tandem, improvising, having fun.

"I really think," Ada McKamey says, obviously pleased, "that Ruth is going to be a better cook than I am."

Broiled Avocado-Stuffed Mushrooms

Makes 10 to 12 appetizer servings or 8 vegetable servings

Here's a recipe that Mrs. McKamey's teenage daughter, Ruth, made for me the day I was visiting the ranch. Ruth says you can serve these mushrooms either as appetizers or as a vegetable. She adds that the avocado filling can also be used to stuff hollowed-out cherry tomatoes or mounded onto artichoke bottoms.

2 pounds medium-sized mushrooms (they should be of as uniform size as possible)
1 large ripe avocado, halved and pitted
1 tablespoon lemon juice
1 tablespoon finely grated onion (optional)

2 cups moderately fine soda-cracker crumbs
½ cup grated Parmesan cheese or finely grated sharp Cheddar
⅓ cup melted butter or margarine
½ teaspoon salt
⅛ teaspoon black pepper or, for more nip, cayenne pepper

1.   Wipe mushrooms clean with a damp cloth. Twist stems out of caps; reserve the caps and save the stems to use later in soups or stews.
2.   Scoop avocado pulp into a bowl, add lemon juice and, if you like, the grated onion and mash well with a potato masher. Blend in remaining ingredients.
3.   Fill mushroom caps with avocado mixture, mounding it up. Arrange mushroom caps on a broiler pan and broil 6 inches from the heat about 5 to 6 minutes or until lightly browned. Serve hot.

Lamb Soup

Makes 8 to 10 servings

Because they raise and butcher their own lambs, the McKameys have on hand plenty of bony cuts as well as the choicer chops and roasts. "We like lamb soup better than stew," Mrs. McKamey says, adding that she makes Venison Soup precisely the same way (see Variation). Because lamb contains a lot of hard, brittle, not very digestible fat, Mrs. McKamey recommends cooking the lamb one day, refrigerating overnight, then lifting off the layer of solidified fat before proceeding with the soup.

2 pounds lamb riblets
10 cups cold water
1 bay leaf, crumbled
3 large yellow onions, peeled and chopped
4 medium-sized carrots, peeled and sliced thin
3 large celery ribs, washed and sliced thin

4 teaspoons salt (or to taste)
¼ teaspoon pepper (or to taste)
⅛ teaspoon crumbled leaf rosemary (optional)
2 tablespoons minced parsley
6 medium-sized potatoes, peeled and cut in ½-inch cubes

1. Simmer lamb riblets in the water with the bay leaf 2½ to 3 hours in a large covered kettle or until lamb is very tender. Cool to room temperature, then refrigerate, covered, overnight.

2. Next day, lift off and discard the fat that has risen to the top of the broth. Add all remaining ingredients except the potatoes, cover and simmer very slowly about 3 hours. Add potatoes and simmer 1 to 2 hours longer—if you keep the burner heat low enough, it really doesn't matter how long you simmer the soup because the vegetables do not seem to overcook. The soup, moreover, gathers flavor with the long, slow simmering.

3. Taste soup for salt and pepper and add more, if needed, then ladle soup into large bowls and serve.

Variation:

Venison Soup: Prepare as exactly as you would the Lamb Soup except substitute 2½ pounds bony cuts of venison (neck slices, shanks, rib ends, etc.) for the lamb.

Curried, Fricasseed Lamb Riblets

Makes 4 to 6 servings

"We like lamb better this way than almost any other," Ada McKamey says of this fricassee that she devised herself. "It's such an easy recipe."

4 pounds lamb riblets, cut in serving-sized chunks
2 tablespoons cooking oil
1½ cups chopped yellow onions
1 bay leaf, crumbled
1 tablespoon curry powder (or to suit your taste)

1½ cups water
1 teaspoon salt (or to taste)
⅛ teaspoon pepper (or to taste)
4 tablespoons flour blended with ¼ cup cold water (to thicken gravy)

1. Brown the lamb riblets, a few at a time, in the oil in a very large heavy kettle over high heat. As riblets brown, remove to paper toweling to drain.

2. When all riblets are nicely browned, drain all but 1 tablespoon drippings from kettle. Reduce heat to moderate, add onions and stir-fry 8 to 10 minutes or until lightly browned. Add bay leaf and blend in curry powder. Let mellow 2 to 3 minutes, then mix in water, salt and pepper.

3. Return riblets to kettle, pushing down into mixture, cover and simmer slowly about 2½ hours or until very tender. Rearrange ribs in kettle once or twice as they simmer so that all will absorb the curry flavor.

4. When riblets are tender, remove from kettle and pile onto a large platter. Taste kettle liquid and, if needed, add more salt and pepper. Quickly whisk in the flour-water paste and heat, stirring constantly, until gravy is thickened and smooth—about 3 minutes. Return riblets to kettle, pushing them down into gravy, cover and simmer very slowly about 15 minutes longer. Serve hot with potatoes or rice.

Bacon-Draped Roast Venison

Makes 8 servings

"We allow hunting by permission on our ranch," says Mrs. McKamey. "And one year alone two hundred deer were taken here. We usually kill one each year for ourselves. And sometimes we get an elk or a moose as well, which I prepare the same way. Venison," she explains, "is a pretty dry meat, so when I roast it, I drape it well with bacon."

1 loin or saddle of venison, weighing 5 to 6 pounds	¼ teaspoon crumbled leaf rosemary (optional)
1 teaspoon salt	½ pound sliced bacon
¼ teaspoon freshly ground pepper	

1. Rub the roast well with salt and pepper and, if you like, the rosemary. Stand in a shallow roasting pan, letting roast rest on its rib ends so that you do not need to use a rack. Drape bacon slices over the roast, covering it completely. Insert a meat thermometer so that it rests in the meat, not touching bone.

2. Roast uncovered in a moderate oven (350°) allowing 15 to 20 minutes per pound for rare meat (125° to 130° on the meat thermometer) and 25 minutes per pound for medium (140°). The McKameys like their venison "pink."

3.   Remove roast from oven and let rest at least 10 minutes before carving—this is to allow the juices to settle and the meat to firm up. If you like, make a gravy with the pan drippings, thickening with a flour-and-water paste (2 tablespoons flour blended with 3 tablespoons cold water should be about right).

Baked Walnut-Stuffed Onions

Makes 6 servings

An inveterate recipe collector, Mrs. McKamey doesn't recall where she got this particular recipe. But she does know she's had it a long time and that the family likes it.

6 medium-sized Spanish onions (they should be about the size of navel oranges)
1 cup unseasoned boiled rice
⅔ cup finely chopped walnuts
1 egg, beaten slightly

½ cup minced fresh mushrooms lightly sautéed in 2 tablespoons butter
1 teaspoon salt
⅛ teaspoon pepper
¼ teaspoon crumbled leaf thyme

1.   Peel the onions, then slice off the top fourth of each. Parboil the onions in about 1 inch of water in a covered kettle 15 to 18 minutes, or until they are almost tender and the insides can be scooped out easily. Drain onions well, then very gently remove all but the outer two layers of onion so that you have onion "cups" with walls about ¼-inch thick. If you have any difficulty removing the centers, an apple corer is the best implement to use.

2.   Finely chop enough of the scooped-out onion to measure 1 cup and reserve; the remainder of the onions can be saved to use in soups or stews later. Mix the rice and walnuts and egg, stir in the reserved 1 cup of chopped onion, the sautéed mushrooms, salt, pepper, and thyme. Toss lightly.

3.   Fill the onion "cups" with the mixture, packing it in gently and mounding it up on top.

4.   Arrange in a pie pan and bake uncovered in a moderate oven (350°) for 30 to 35 minutes or until stuffing is lightly browned.

100-Percent-Whole-Wheat Honey Bread

Makes two 9- × 5- × 3-inch loaves

The ultimate in "back-to-scratch" cooking must be to grind your own flour, which is precisely what Mrs. McKamey does, using an electric unit that is slightly larger than a heavy-duty mixer (the grinder is, in fact, a combination grinder-kneader-mixer). She and her family like rough whole-grain breads best, especially this one made altogether with whole-wheat flour. It is a heavy, close-textured bread, but its flavor is superb.

2 packages active dry yeast
½ cup very warm water
1 teaspoon sugar
⅔ cup cooking oil
⅔ cup honey
3 cups warm (105° to 115°) potato water (water in which peeled potatoes have been cooked)

1 tablespoon salt
10½ to 11 cups unsifted whole-wheat flour (or enough to make a stiff but pliable dough. "The consistency," Mrs. McKamey explains, "should be about like 'play dough,' or modeling clay.")

1. Sprinkle yeast over very warm water in a small mixing bowl (very warm water should feel comfortably warm when dropped on wrist). Stir in sugar. Cover mixture, set in a warm draft-free place and let stand until yeast begins to bubble and work, forming a sponge that is about twice the volume of the original mixture. This will take about 30 minutes.

2. In a large mixing bowl (if you have one of the heavy-duty mixers that is sturdy enough to knead bread, use the mixer mixing bowl) place the oil, honey, potato water, and salt. Mix in the yeast sponge, add about 4 cups of the flour and beat, with the mixer set at medium speed, for 5 minutes.

3. Work in the remaining flour, about 1 cup at a time, adding just enough flour to make a dough stiff enough to hold its shape. The dough should not be so thin that a small amount of it, spooned onto a plate, flattens out. Nor should the dough be sticky. The amount of flour you add, it should be stressed, will vary according to the humidity—the more humid the day, the more flour you will need to add.

4. Beat the dough hard in the mixer at medium speed for 5 minutes. Turn onto a lightly floured board and knead vigorously for 10 to 12 minutes—this is exhausting work because the dough is so stiff, but persist. Kneading is essential to develop the gluten (protein) in the dough, which provides the bread's framework.

5. Shape dough into a round ball, place in a large well-greased

bowl and turn greased side up. Cover with a dry cloth, set in a warm draft-free spot and let rise until doubled in bulk—about 2 hours or more because of the heaviness of the dough.

6. Punch dough down and let rest 10 minutes. Again turn onto a floured board and knead lightly 3 to 5 minutes. Divide dough in half and shape each half into a loaf. Place in well-greased 9- × 5- × 3-inch loaf pans, cover pans with cloth and again let rise until doubled in bulk—about 1 hour.

7. Bake the loaves in a moderate oven (350°) for 40 to 45 minutes or until they are nicely browned and sound hollow when thumped with your fingers.

8. Remove loaves from oven and cool in their pans (the pans should be turned on their sides on wire racks) about 15 minutes. Loosen loaves from pans, using a thin-bladed spatula, turn loaves out onto wire racks and cool upright to room temperature before slicing and serving.

Steamed Suet Pudding

Makes 6 to 8 servings

"My mother-in-law and I worked out this recipe during World War II," says Ada McKamey, "using honey as the sweetener." The pudding's texture and flavor are much like those of the old English plum pudding and like plum pudding, it is best served with a sauce of some sort. We recommend Mrs. McKamey's Cider Sauce (recipe follows).

1 cup moderately finely grated raw carrots
1 cup moderately finely grated raw potatoes
½ cup fairly finely chopped suet
1 egg, beaten slightly
½ pound seedless raisins or snipped pitted dates, or ¼ pound of each
½ cup apple cider
½ cup honey
½ cup fairly fine dry breadcrumbs
½ cup finely chopped pecans or walnuts
1 cup sifted all-purpose flour
½ teaspoon baking soda
¼ teaspoon salt

1. Mix carrots, potatoes, suet, egg and raisins or dates. Stir in cider and honey, then mix in breadcrumbs and nuts. Combine flour with soda and salt and mix in at the end, stirring just enough to mix.

2. Spoon into a well-oiled 1-quart steamed-pudding mold, snap on cover, then steam for 3 hours on a rack in a large covered kettle—there

should be about 1 inch of boiling water in the kettle. Check water level from time to time and add more boiling water if kettle threatens to boil dry. Otherwise, keep kettle tightly closed.

3. When pudding has steamed 3 hours, lift from kettle—with the cover still on the pudding mold—and let cool upright on a wire rack for 15 minutes.

4. Uncover mold, loosen pudding by running a thin-bladed spatula around edge of mold and central tube, then turn pudding out on a dessert plate and let cool another 15 minutes before slicing.

Cider Sauce

Makes about 2 cups

"This is one of my mother's recipes," Mrs. McKamey says, "and I told you she was a good cook."

½ cup firmly packed light brown
   sugar
½ cup granulated sugar

1 cup (2 sticks) butter, at room
   temperature
3 large eggs, beaten slightly
3 to 4 tablespoons apple cider

1. In the top of a double boiler combine brown sugar, granulated sugar, butter, and eggs. Whisk lightly to mix.

2. Set over simmering water and cook and stir about 5 minutes or until thickened. Remove from heat and cool to room temperature, then cover and chill several hours or until quite thick.

3. Beat well, then add the apple cider, 1 tablespoon at a time, until the sauce is about the consistency of butterscotch sauce. Keep refrigerated until ready to use, and beat well just before serving.

Spicy Sour-Cream Pie

Makes one 9-inch single-crust pie

"I grew up on this pie," Ada McKamey says, adding that her mother used heavy cream that had soured rather than the commercial sour cream available today. "It might work with the commercial sour cream," Mrs. McKamey says, "but I have always used soured cream."

1½ cups soured heavy cream
2 eggs, lightly beaten
1 cup sugar
½ teaspoon ground cinnamon
¼ teaspoon ground cloves
¼ teaspoon ground nutmeg
4 tablespoons flour
1 teaspoon vanilla
½ cup plump, moist seedless raisins
1 9-inch unbaked pie shell

1. Combine cream and eggs; also combine sugar with cinnamon, cloves, nutmeg, and flour. Stir egg mixture into dry ingredients, stirring just enough to mix. Stir in vanilla.

2. Sprinkle raisins across bottom of pie shell, then pour in filling.

3. Bake in a moderate oven (350°) for 35 to 40 minutes or until filling is golden brown and just set—it should quiver slightly when you nudge the pie pan. Remove pie from oven and let cool to room temperature before cutting.

Note:
In hot weather, store pie in the refrigerator.

Open-Face Dutch Pear Pie

Makes one 9-inch single-crust pie

"The game warden was out here once and I served him this pie," Ada McKamey says. "He claimed it was the best apple pie he ever ate. And I said, 'Well, *this* apple pie just happens to be made with *pears.*'"

6 cups sliced, peeled pears (Bartletts make a particularly good pie; for 6 cups of sliced pears, you will need 6 large Bartletts)
1 9-inch unbaked pie shell with a high fluted edge (use your favorite recipe or try Mrs. McKamey's Leavened Hot-Water Pastry recipe, which follows)
1 cup sugar
6 tablespoons flour
¼ teaspoon freshly grated nutmeg (Mrs. McKamey always grates her own nutmeg—"It makes all the difference in flavor.")
Pinch of salt
1 cup heavy cream

1. Place a layer of sliced pears in pie shell; combine sugar, flour, nutmeg, and salt and sprinkle liberally over pears. Continue adding layers of pears and sprinkling with sugar mixture until pie is filled. Drizzle in the heavy cream.

2. Bake pie in a moderate oven (350°) for about 1 hour or until crust is lightly browned and filling is set. Remove pie from oven and let cool at least 30 minutes before serving.

Leavened Hot-Water Pastry

**Makes two 9- or 10-inch pie shells or one 9- or 10-inch
double-crust pie**

This excellent short piecrust can be made ahead of time, then stored
in the refrigerator until you are ready to roll it.

1 cup lard (hog lard), at room temperature
½ cup boiling water

3 cups sifted all-purpose flour
1 teaspoon baking powder
1 teaspoon salt

1. Combine lard and boiling water and stir until lard is completely
melted. In a large mixing bowl, combine flour, baking powder and
salt. Make a well in the center of the dry ingredients, pour in the hot
lard mixture, and stir briskly to mix (pastry will seem quite soft).
2. Wrap pastry in waxed paper or plastic food wrap and chill several hours before rolling.
3. Divide pastry in half and roll on a lightly floured pastry cloth
with a lightly floured stockinette-covered rolling pin into a circle 3
inches larger than the pie pan you intend to use. Lay rolling pin across
center of pastry circle, lop half of pastry over rolling pin and ease into
pie pan. Fit pastry snugly into pan, trim overhang so that it is 1 inch
larger all around than the pie pan; turn under and crimp, making a
decorative edge. Pie shell is now ready to fill and bake.

Scotch Shortbread

Makes about 2 dozen 2-inch squares

The McKameys are of Scottish descent, so one of their favorite sweets,
appropriately, is Scotch Shortbread. This recipe is a very old one and
possibly the shortest shortbread we have ever eaten. The trick in baking it is merely to dry the dough out, not to brown it—hence the 325°
oven temperature and the long baking time.

1 pound lightly salted butter, at
   room temperature

1½ cups unsifted confectioners
   (10X) sugar
4 cups sifted all-purpose flour

1. Cream butter hard until very smooth, then beat in confectioners sugar. Add flour, 1 cup at a time, beating after each addition until smooth.

2. Spread dough out ½-inch thick on an ungreased baking sheet. The dough will virtually cover the sheet. Make sure that the dough is as uniform in thickness as possible (otherwise the thinner portions will bake faster than thicker portions) and also that the surface of the dough is as smooth as possible.

3. Bake in a moderate oven (325°) for 1¼ to 1½ hours or until shortbread is the color of old ivory and fairly firm to the touch.

4. Remove from oven and while shortbread is still hot, cut into 2-inch squares. Cool to room temperature before serving. Store in airtight canisters.

Mrs. Leroy Losey
of
Yakima County, Washington

"I think I learned more about cooking as a child than my mother ever knew because she just wasn't interested," says Mrs. Leroy Losey, reminiscing about her childhood in South Dakota where, as Nellie Van De Brake, she grew up in a Dutch family on a small farm near Aberdeen.

"Mother had seven children" (Nellie was the second oldest child and the oldest girl) "and she had a lot of work to do. She had also had a heart attack when she was quite young and wasn't able to use her arms much. So as soon as I was able, she taught me how to make bread. I was about ten and she would put the pan of dough on a chair because I was too short to knead it at the table. That is my first memory of responsibility.

"From then on," she continues, "I baked all the bread for the family. If we had store-bought bread, we thought it a very special treat. Of course, we didn't get to the store so often. We lived six miles from one small town and five miles from another, and we had to travel by horse and buggy. Kids today have missed the pioneering and the hard times, but just *think* what they're living through in this age of technology!"

Mrs. Losey is not at all certain she'd like to change places with her own three children (a girl and two boys who grew up in the 1940s and 1950s). Or with her ten young grandchildren. "Things are just happening so fast today," she says. "It's hard to keep up."

This applies especially to chemistry, Mrs. Losey's major at Jamestown, a small Presbyterian college in Jamestown, North Dakota. "I expect I would have majored in home economics if Jamestown had offered it," she adds, "because I have always been so fond of cooking and sewing."

Her years at Jamestown, it turns out, were to change the course of her life because it was here that she met Leroy Losey. "He left school two years before I did," Mrs. Losey says, "because he had always looked forward to being a fruit rancher. He had an uncle here in Yakima growing fruit, and he worked for him for a while before setting out on his own."

It was in the spring of 1931 that Mrs. Losey graduated from Jamestown and in the fall of the same year that she came west to Yakima and married Leroy Losey. "I've lived here for forty-five years now. And I love it. It's such wonderful country."

Indeed it is, especially as seen from the Loseys' rambling hilltop home (built in 1954), which looks across miles of fruit orchards toward Mount Adams, a distant, snow-clad peak that seems to have been painted on the sky.

"Our orchard isn't as big as it once was," Mrs. Losey continues. "We originally had twenty-five acres, but we've sold some of them off. Today we have ten acres in fruit and five acres in pasture. "We keep a few beef cattle—Hereford-Charolais crosses mostly—which we fatten up and slaughter. We also used to have our own milk cow until the state passed a law saying you couldn't sell unpasteurized milk."

Mrs. Losey still plants a garden each year and in a patch about the size of a tennis court raises bumper crops of carrots, corn, beets, potatoes, winter squash, peas, beans, onions, and asparagus. "Asparagus grows wild in the orchard," she says, "so we just transplant it." As for fruit, Mrs. Losey grows (in addition to apples and pears) peaches, grapes, and raspberries.

What fruits and vegetables she and her husband cannot eat fresh, or share with family and friends, Mrs. Losey will freeze and can, averaging about 300 quarts a year. She has been canning ever since she was a little girl and is so proficient at it that she is frequently called upon to judge the 4-H entries at the county fair.

Baking, however, is what Mrs. Losey enjoys most. "I bake all of our own bread, and I enjoy making fancy Christmas breads."

Now that her children are grown up and have homes of their own, Mrs. Losey helps satisfy her yen for cooking by preparing quantity meals at their local Presbyterian church. "This way I get to do lots of baking," she says. "It's rare when we have a dinner that I bake less than twelve dozen rolls. Usually it's more like twenty dozen. I bake them ahead and freeze them so that all we have to do is warm them up at the church.

"I also like to try new recipes—casseroles and main dishes that I clip out of magazines. I guess I always have. I remember when I was a little girl I was always trying new things that I had read about in magazines. I don't think my mother had but one cookbook in the house, so I was always experimenting and making things up. My family would make fun of me, but still they would eat almost anything I cooked."

It would be difficult these days to find a woman more genuinely devoted to cooking than Nellie Losey, or a woman more creative about it. Or, for that matter, a more inveterate recipe collector. Her files overflow with favorites—the old Dutch recipes of her childhood, including such things as Buttermilk Soup ("it was really a thin oatmeal porridge"), recipes from friends, recipes that have won blue ribbons at the county fair, and, of course, recipes that she herself has worked out.

"What I'm most interested in today," she says, "is doing things the easy way." This is not to be interpreted as using packaged foods; Nellie Losey rarely does. What she does do, whenever possible, is to short-cut time-consuming or difficult techniques. "Take my yeast breads, for example. I just beat them all up in a mixer.

"I don't believe in doing things the hard way anymore," she concludes. "Besides, the more simply you do things, the better they are."

Pheasant Fricasseed in Soured Cream

Makes about 6 servings

"You never know when you get a pheasant how old the bird is or how gamy," says Mrs. Losey. "I find that if I disjoint the bird and cook it in sour cream—not the commercial sour cream but heavy cream that has gone sour—it tenderizes the bird and takes away the wild taste."

2 pheasants (about 2½ pounds each), cleaned, dressed, and disjointed
¾ cup *unsifted* flour
2 teaspoons salt
½ teaspoon pepper
¼ cup bacon drippings

2 medium-sized yellow onions, peeled and chopped
1 cup diced celery
2 tablespoons butter or margarine (optional)
2½ cups soured heavy cream

1. Dredge the pieces of pheasant by shaking in a brown-paper bag with the flour, salt, and pepper. Shake excess flour off each piece.
2. Brown the pheasant, a few pieces at a time, in the bacon drippings in a very large shallow Dutch-oven-type kettle over moderately high heat. As pheasant browns, transfer pieces to several thicknesses

of paper toweling to drain. If drippings in kettle seem burned after all pieces are browned, pour out, wipe kettle out with paper toweling, and use butter for browning the onions and celery. If drippings do not seem unduly dark, they may be used for browning.

3. Sauté onions and celery in either the drippings or butter about 5 to 8 minutes over moderate heat until vegetables are limp and lightly browned. Push to one side of kettle. Return pieces of pheasant to kettle, spooning onions and celery over them. Pour in the soured cream, cover and simmer *very* slowly about 1 to 1½ hours or until pheasant is fork-tender. Serve with boiled potatoes (there will be plenty of rich pheasant gravy in the kettle).

Sausages with Sauerkraut, Onions and Apples

Makes 6 servings

"This is one of my favorite apple main dishes," says Mrs. Losey. To make it she uses sauerkraut that she has "put down" herself and Golden Delicious apples from her orchard and onions from her garden. In the old days she might even have used homemade sausage and ketchup. "It's an easy recipe," she continues. "I do it all in my electric skillet."

1 pound sauerkraut, rinsed well in cool water and drained thoroughly
2 Golden Delicious apples, peeled, cored and sliced thin
1 large sweet onion, or 2 medium-sized yellow onions, peeled and sliced thin
1 cup condensed beef broth
¼ cup ketchup
2 tablespoons brown sugar
6 knackwurst or bratwurst or frankfurters
Salt and pepper (optional)

1. Place sauerkraut in the bottom of a large heavy skillet; layer apples and onions on top. Blend beef broth with ketchup and sugar and pour evenly over all. Arrange knackwurst or other sausages on top, pressing down gently.

2. Cover and simmer over moderately low heat about 45 to 50 minutes or until sausages are done and flavors well blended.

Note:

Because of the saltiness of the kraut and the spiciness of the sausages, you will probably not need to add any salt or pepper. Taste first and add only if necessary.

Salmon Steaks Baked with Onion, Lemon and Parsley

Makes 4 servings

One of the advantages of living in the Pacific Northwest is having at hand an abundance of fresh salmon. Although salmon do sometimes swim as far upriver as the Yakima Valley to spawn, it is not these fish that Mrs. Losey cooks. "They aren't good to eat after they spawn," she says. This and the following are her two favorite salmon recipes.

2 cups minced onion	4 fresh salmon steaks, cut about 1½
4 tablespoons butter or margarine	inches thick
¼ cup minced parsley	½ teaspoon salt
2 tablespoons lemon juice (or to	⅛ teaspoon pepper
taste)	

1.   Sauté the onion in the butter in a medium-sized skillet over moderate heat about 5 minutes or until golden and limp; mix in parsley and lemon juice (taste and add more lemon juice if mixture is not tart enough to suit you).

2.   Sprinkle the salmon steaks well on both sides with salt and pepper, then place in a shallow roasting pan just large enough to accommodate the steaks.

3.   Spread onion mixture on top of each steak, dividing total amount evenly. Cover pan snugly with foil.

4.   Bake in a moderate oven (350°) for 10 minutes, then uncover and bake 15 to 20 minutes longer or just until fish will flake at the touch of a fork.

Sautéed Corn-Meal-Dredged Salmon Steaks

Makes 4 servings

If these salmon steaks are to be properly moist and tender, you must keep the heat under them low and serve them the minute the flesh will flake at the touch of a fork. Too high a heat will toughen them, as will too long a cooking time.

4 fresh salmon steaks, cut 1 inch thick

1½ teaspoons salt (about)

⅛ teaspoon freshly ground black pepper (about)

½ cup stone-ground corn meal

1½ tablespoons butter or margarine

1½ tablespoons cooking oil

4 large lemon wedges

1.   Sprinkle each side of each steak with salt and pepper; spread corn meal out on a piece of waxed paper and press steaks gently into meal so that they are lightly dredged on each side.

2.   Brown the steaks lightly on one side, then on the flip side, in the butter and oil in a very large heavy skillet set over moderately high heat. As soon as the steaks are browned, reduce heat to low, cover skillet and cook 12 to 15 minutes or until a steak, gently probed with a fork, will flake without showing any signs of translucence (the meat will be quite moist).

3.   Dish up the salmon steaks and serve with large wedges of lemon.

Stir-Fried Cabbage, Onion, Green Pepper and Celery

Makes 4 to 6 servings

"I like cooked cabbage to be just wilted and still crisp," says Mrs. Losey. "And I also like nutmeg on my cabbage." This recipe—cabbage shredding aside—is quick and easy.

3 tablespoons butter, margarine, or vegetable oil

3 cups finely shredded cabbage

¼ cup minced onion

½ cup minced green pepper

½ cup thinly sliced celery

1 teaspoon salt (or to taste)

⅛ teaspoon pepper

⅛ teaspoon ground nutmeg

1.   Melt butter or margarine or heat oil in a very large heavy skillet over moderately high heat. Add cabbage, onion, green pepper, and celery and stir-fry 5 to 6 minutes or just until vegetables are crisp-tender.

2.   Add salt, pepper, and nutmeg, tossing well to mix. Taste and add more salt if needed. Serve the cabbage straight away, or if you prefer cabbage more well done, cover skillet, turn heat to low and let mixture steam about 5 minutes or until cabbage is cooked the way you like it.

Mashed Potato Dinner Rolls

Makes about 4 dozen rolls

"I've been making these rolls for twenty-five years or more," Mrs. Losey says. "The dough is quite soft and does not shape well for fancy rolls, but it has excellent flavor." We would also caution you to pick a dry day for making these rolls. In humid weather, the dough requires more flour than usual, which will make the rolls heavy.

½ cup butter or margarine, at room temperature
1 cup hot unseasoned mashed potatoes
⅔ cup sugar
2 teaspoons salt

1 package active dry yeast
2 cups very warm milk
2 eggs, lightly beaten
9 to 10 cups sifted all-purpose flour (enough to make a soft but manageable dough)

1. Combine butter, mashed potatoes, sugar and salt and stir until butter melts; cool mixture to 105° to 115°.

2. Sprinkle yeast over very warm milk in a large mixing bowl (very warm milk should feel comfortably warm when dropped on wrist). Stir until yeast dissolves.

3. Add mashed-potato mixture to yeast; beat in eggs. Add the flour about 2 cups at a time, beating well to blend. Add only enough flour to give you a soft but workable dough—it should not be so sticky that you cannot knead it.

4. Turn dough onto a floured board and, with well-floured hands, knead about 5 minutes or until soft and springy.

5. Turn dough into a buttered bowl and brush the surface with melted butter. Cover with a clean dry cloth and let the dough rise in a warm, draft-free spot until doubled in bulk—about 2 hours. (This dough takes somewhat longer than usual to rise because it contains only 1 package of yeast.)

6. Punch dough down and let rest about 10 minutes. Turn onto a lightly floured board and knead lightly again—about 2 to 3 minutes.

7. Pinch off bits of dough and roll into balls about the size of golf balls. Arrange one layer deep, in concentric rings, in three well greased 9-inch layer-cake pans, spacing the rolls so that they do not quite touch one another (they will after they have risen). Cover pans with clean dry cloth, set in a warm, draft-free spot and again let rise until double in bulk—about 1 hour or slightly longer.

8. Bake the rolls in a very hot oven (450°) for 10 minutes or until

rolls are nicely browned and sound hollow when thumped with your fingers. Serve hot with plenty of butter.

Note:

Any rolls not eaten right away can be cooled to room temperature, then wrapped in foil (do not separate rolls) and frozen to enjoy later.

Rich Sweet Dough

Makes enough for two 12-inch coffee or tea rings

Mrs. Losey begins baking sweet breads early in the fall as Christmas gifts, then keeps them frozen until the holiday season. This basic sweet dough is the one she likes best.

2 packages active dry yeast
¼ cup very warm water
1 cup milk, scalded
½ cup sugar
½ cup butter or margarine, at room temperature

2 teaspoons salt
6 cups sifted all-purpose flour (about)
3 eggs
½ teaspoon ground cardamom or anise

1. Sprinkle yeast over very warm water in a large bowl (very warm water should feel comfortably warm when dropped on wrist). Stir until yeast dissolves.

2. Combine scalded milk with sugar, butter and salt, stirring until sugar dissolves and butter melts. Cool mixture to 105° to 115°.

3. Add milk mixture to yeast, then beat in 1 cup of the flour. Mix the eggs in, 1 at a time, beating well after each addition. Blend in the spice.

4. Mix in the remaining 5 cups of flour (or just enough to make a soft but kneadable dough), 1 cup at a time.

5. Turn dough out on a floured board and knead, keeping hands floured, for about 5 minutes or until dough is smooth and elastic.

6. Place dough in a warm buttered bowl, turn greased side up. Cover with a clean dry cloth and let rise in a warm, draft-free place until doubled in bulk—about 1¼ to 1½ hours.

7. Divide the dough in half. Use for making Apple Coffee Ring (recipe follows) or any of your own favorite sweet breads.

Apple Coffee Ring

Makes two 12-inch coffee rings

Mrs. Losey makes a variety of coffee and tea rings—cinnamon, raisin, nut—but one of the most unusual is this one filled with shredded Golden Delicious apples. "One trick I've learned in making yeast breads," she says, "is that if you *don't* punch the dough down after it's risen, it will be easier to shape. You're punching it down as you roll it anyway." When making this particular recipe, you will note that considerable liquid oozes out of the filled ring as it rises. It's best to blot up this seepage with paper toweling before you bake the ring, so that the ring will be easy to remove from the baking sheet and the sheet will be easier to wash.

1 recipe Rich Sweet Dough (recipe precedes)
4 tablespoons butter or margarine, at room temperature
1 cup firmly packed light brown sugar mixed with 2 teaspoons cinnamon (cinnamon sugar)

4 cups peeled and coarsely shredded Golden Delicious apples (2 large apples, if shredded on the second-coarsest side of a four-sided grater, will yield 4 cups)

1. Prepare Rich Sweet Dough, divide the dough in half.
2. Roll half the dough on a lightly floured pastry cloth into a rectangle about 22 inches long and 12 to 14 inches wide. The rolled-out dough should be between ⅛- and ¼-inch thick.
3. Spread the sheet of dough with 2 tablespoons of the softened butter, sprinkle with half of the cinnamon sugar, then scatter 2 cups of the shredded apples evenly on top. Roll the dough up snugly jelly-roll style, beginning at one long side so that you have a roll about 22 inches long. Make sure that the seam is on the bottom of the roll.
4. Transfer roll to a lightly greased baking sheet, then bend into a ring, tucking one end into the other and pinching seam well to seal. With a sharp knife, cut about three-fourths of the way through the ring at 1-inch intervals, then twist slices outward so that they lie flat, slightly overlapping. Roll, fill, and shape the remaining dough the same way, using remaining filling ingredients.
5. Cover the rings with clean dry cloths, then let rise in a warm, draft-free spot until doubled in bulk—about 1¼ hours.
6. Bake in a moderately hot oven (375°) for about 30 minutes or until rings are richly browned and sound hollow when thumped with your fingers. Remove from oven and let cool about 10 minutes before cutting into wedges and serving.

Fresh Apple Torte

Makes one 9-inch torte

"This torte has no shortening," Mrs. Losey points out, "and we think it's excellent." Top it with whipped cream or, if you prefer, a scoop of vanilla ice cream.

1 egg, well beaten
¾ cup sugar
½ cup sifted all-purpose flour
½ teaspoon baking powder
Pinch of salt

1¼ cups fairly finely chopped, peeled apples
½ teaspoon vanilla
½ cup chopped walnuts

1. Beat egg and sugar in a mixer at high speed until mixture is thick and the color of mayonnaise. Combine flour with baking powder and salt and mix in alternately with the chopped apples. Stir in vanilla and walnuts.

2. Spread batter in a well-greased-and-floured 9-inch pie pan and bake in a moderate oven (350°) for about 30 minutes or until torte is lightly browned and springy to the touch.

3. Remove from oven and let cool about 20 minutes before cutting into wedges and serving.

Golden Delicious Pie

Makes one 9-inch double-crust pie

"We're very conscious of apple pies out here," says Nellie Losey, who has judged many of them at county fairs. "Nothing gripes me more than to get a piece of pie that has no more'n a quarter inch of apples in it. When you bake apples, they do shrink quite a bit. I've found that if I cook the apples in a skillet first—just let them wilt a bit with the other filling ingredients—that I will always get a good full pie. You can also be sure that the apples will be properly cooked—in so many pies they are half raw."

7 cups peeled and sliced Golden Delicious apples (you may substitute a tarter apple if you like, but Mrs. Losey prefers Golden Delicious—no doubt because her husband grows them)
¾ cup sugar
1 tablespoon fine, quick-cooking tapioca

1 teaspoon cinnamon
2 tablespoons butter or margarine, melted
2 tablespoons apple juice or cider
¼ cup firmly packed light brown sugar
1 recipe Lemon Pastry (recipe follows), or use any favorite pastry for a double-crust pie

1.   Place apples in a large heavy skillet; combine sugar with tapioca and cinnamon and sprinkle over apples, tossing to mix. Add butter and cider, cover and cook over low heat about 5 minutes or just until apples are limp and have reduced slightly in volume. Raise heat and let mixture bubble gently until juices have cooked down to a nice thick syrup—about 5 to 10 more minutes. Cool 15 minutes.

2.   Fit pastry for bottom crust into a 9-inch pie pan, sprinkle brown sugar over it, spoon in apple filling, mounding it up, then fit top crust into place. Trim pastry overhang so that it is 1 inch larger than the pie pan all around. Roll top and bottom crust overhangs together up onto rim of pie pan, then crimp, making a high decorative edge. With a sharp knife, cut decorative steam vents in top crust.

3.   Bake in a hot oven (400°) for 20 to 25 minutes or until pastry is nicely browned and filling bubbly. Remove pie from oven and let cool about 20 minutes before cutting.

Lemon Pastry

Makes two 9- or 10-inch pie shells or one 9- or 10-inch double-crust pie

"One of our 4-H Cherry Pie Contest winners used this piecrust recipe," says Mrs. Losey. "It's really a good one." It's also very short, so you have to handle the pastry gently.

2¼ cups sifted all-purpose flour
1 tablespoon sugar
1 teaspoon salt
¾ cup vegetable shortening

1 egg yolk
¼ cup milk
1 tablespoon lemon juice

1.   Place flour, sugar, and salt in a large mixing bowl and stir to mix. Cut in shortening, using a pastry blender, until mixture is crumbly and the texture of coarse meal.

2.   Combine egg yolk and milk, beating lightly with a fork, then drizzle over flour-shortening mixture, mixing briskly with a fork. Drizzle in lemon juice, forking up lightly.

3.   Divide pastry in half and roll one half on a lightly floured pastry cloth with a lightly floured stockinette-covered rolling pin into a circle 3 inches larger than the pie pan you intend to use. Lay rolling pin across center of pastry circle, lop half of pastry over rolling pin and

ease into pie pan. Fit pastry snugly into pie pan and trim overhang so that it is 1 inch larger than the pie pan all around. Roll edge under and crimp, making a decorative edge. Repeat with remaining pastry. Pie shells are now ready to fill and bake. Or fill a pastry-lined pan, add a top crust, and bake as individual pie recipes specify (see Mrs. Losey's Golden Delicious Pie, recipe precedes).

Mrs. Charles A. Volpi
of
Napa County, California

JUST a few miles south of the little town of St. Helena, the Volpis' drive bounces off the blacktop Route 29, sweeps for two hundred yards or so through a double row of olive trees, then swings behind the low-lying house nestled in the middle of a thirty-five-acre vineyard. As befits the Napa valley, the vineyards contain wine grapes, not table grapes. And the Volpis can see, from any room in their home, vineyards herringboning the gentle hills and marching, east and west, toward the rumpled mountain ranges that shelter and contain their valley.

Charles Volpi is a vineyard man and has been ever since he and his wife moved to this valley in 1931 from Contra Costa County where they had begun married life fourteen years earlier.

"When we married," Adele Volpi says, "Charlie was working in a refinery at Martínez. But then we moved here and got into grapes. I felt right at home because my father had been a big vineyard man near Martínez. My people were Italian—from Bologna" (her maiden name was Ferrarini) "and they have worked with grapes ever since they came to California." That was in the late nineteenth century.

So for Adele Volpi, a first-generation American, wine is not merely something to sip with meals. It is as integral to her old-fashioned Italian family recipes as basil and tomatoes. Her pasta sauces are often laced with wine, as are her succulent veal stews. She even makes anise-and-almond-scented cookies that are dunked, doughnut style, in wine before they are eaten. "Wine sticks, we call them."

Adele Volpi grew up in a family of good Italian cooks and learned at an early age how to knead and roll pasta, how to slow-simmer the accompanying sauces, taking care not to brown the onions or meat that went into them. The oldest of four children (two brothers and a sister), she was encouraged in her kitchen ventures by her grandmother as well as her mother.

"Then I married an Italian whose mother was an excellent cook. Charlie's people are from Tuscany and before his mother came to this country, she worked in the kitchens of rich families and picked up a lot of fine recipes."

Although Mrs. Volpi says that she knew "the fundamental part of cooking" when she married Charles in 1917 at the age of twenty, she credits her mother-in-law with teaching her many of the techniques and recipes that are family favorites today. Family includes a daughter who lives near enough to visit fairly often and two unmarried granddaughters. The Volpis' only son was killed during World War II.

Almost family is a doctor friend, who recently bought the Volpis' vineyard and who comes "pretty near every Wednesday to eat because he loves my cooking. He says," Adele Volpi continues, "'If you get tired of me, tell me.'"

Not likely. Mrs. Volpi enjoys cooking for company, especially appreciative company. "When it's just the two of us, it's not so easy to cook the fancy things."

By "fancy things" she means Italian White Bean or Lentil Soup, Ossobuco or Pasta alla Bolognese, Sausage-Stuffed Zucchini or Baked Spinach Balls smothered with tomato sauce, all of which she makes with no assist whatever from packaged foods. Adele Volpi doesn't even use bottled herbs; she grows her own—basil (great clumps of it tuft her garden), rosemary, sage, marjoram, oregano, and thyme. "Fresh herbs make all the difference," she says. She also grows her own tomatoes, which ripen so fast under the California sun that she sometimes has to pick them twice a day, her own green beans, zucchini, cucumbers, onions, even garlic. She cans and freezes the surplus, making sure to have on hand plenty of pasta sauces that she need only thaw and heat.

Mrs. Volpi's kitchen, bigger than most living rooms, is that of a born cook. She designed it herself, and although it was built in 1953, it looks brand-new and up to the minute. One end, faced with old brick, is the cooking center—a huge wall oven set into the brick, together with a gas cooktop. Natural pine cupboards line the walls, and for kneading and shaping pasta, there's a central work island topped with rock maple. The far end of the kitchen—opposite the oven—is the dining area, which overlooks an immense bay tree. "When we designed the kitchen," she says, "we angled the dining ell around this way so that we wouldn't have to cut that tree down."

The kitchen, plainly, is Adele Volpi's favorite room in a house filled with big, airy rooms. "Cooking," she explains, "is what I like to do best. I'm always fussing around in the kitchen. If I don't have anything better to do, I'll bake a batch of cookies.

"Italian food," she continues, "is the most tasty. I watch Julia Child doing those French things on TV. Ye gods, she puts the cream and the butter in by the gobs. If I cooked like that, I'd be as big as a balloon."

Adele and Charles Volpi are both astonishingly trim and agile. And both look a good twenty years younger than they are (early eighties). Clearly Adele's cooking agrees with them.

"I've always been very careful when I cook," she says. "I always take time and try to do things right. I start from scratch with everything. I'm not like my daughter Eleanor or so many other younger cooks who are always trying to do things in a hurry. You can't," she concludes, "hurry the old-fashioned Italian recipes."

Italian White-Bean Soup

Makes 6 to 8 servings

Here's a lusty legume soup made the old-fashioned way with garlic, fresh sage, onion, and tomato to season.

2 cups dried navy or pea beans, washed, sorted, and soaked overnight in just enough cold water to cover
2 quarts (8 cups) cold water
2 tablespoons olive oil
2 tablespoons butter
1 large branch of fresh sage, or 1½ teaspoons crumbled leaf sage
2 large garlic cloves, peeled and bruised

1 medium-sized yellow onion, peeled and chopped
1 large ripe tomato, peeled, cored, chopped and seeded (reserve juice)
½ cup any small pasta (Mrs. Volpi uses *ditalini*)
1 tablespoon salt (or to taste)
¼ teaspoon pepper (or to taste)

1. Drain soaking water from beans; place beans in a large heavy kettle, add 2 quarts cold water, cover and boil gently about 2 hours or until beans are quite tender.

2. Meanwhile, heat olive oil and butter in a second large heavy kettle over moderate heat, add sage, garlic, and onion and sauté slowly, stirring, about 10 minutes or until onion is limp and golden—do not allow to brown. Remove sage branch, if used, also garlic cloves,

and discard. Add tomato, turn heat to lowest point and allow mixture to mellow until beans are done.

3. Spoon 2 heaping ladlefuls of beans into the tomato mixture, also pour in all the liquid in which the beans cooked. Bring to a boil, add pasta, salt, and pepper, cover and cook 10 to 15 minutes—just until pasta is tender.

4. Mash the remaining drained beans well with a potato masher, then mix into soup. Taste for salt and pepper, adjusting if necessary, then serve piping hot.

Lentil Soup

Makes 6 to 8 servings

"You eat this," Adele Volpi says of her Lentil Soup, "and that's really all you need for a meal. My husband just loves it." It's unlike the more familiar lentil soup (made with ham) because it contains "a good handful of fresh chopped basil," another of parsley and another of Swiss chard.

2 cups lentils, washed and sorted
2 quarts (8 cups) cold water
2 tablespoons olive oil
2 tablespoons butter
1 medium-sized Spanish onion, peeled and chopped
½ cup chopped parsley
½ cup chopped fresh basil

1 large very ripe tomato, peeled, cored, and chopped (reserve all juice but discard some of the seeds)
1½ cups diced celery ("the more celery the better," says Mrs. Volpi)
1 cup diced Swiss chard leaves or escarole
1 tablespoon salt (or to taste)
¼ teaspoon pepper (or to taste)
⅓ cup uncooked converted rice

1. Place lentils and water in a medium-sized heavy kettle, cover and simmer until lentils are quite tender, about 40 to 45 minutes.

2. Meanwhile, heat olive oil and butter in a large heavy kettle over moderate heat, add onion, parsley, and basil and sauté, stirring, about 10 minutes just until onion is limp and golden ("you don't want to *brown* the onion," Adele Volpi cautions). Add tomato and its juice, celery, chard or escarole, salt and pepper, turn heat to low and just let mixture warm all the while the lentils cook.

3. When lentils are tender, spoon 2 ladlefuls of them into the tomato mixture; also drain all the lentil cooking liquid into the mixture.

Bring to a boil, add the rice, cover and cook about 20 minutes or until rice is tender.

4.   While rice cooks, put remaining drained lentils through a food mill to puree. When rice is tender, smooth pureed lentils into the soup and heat and stir just until mixture is steamy hot. Taste for salt and pepper and add more, if needed. Ladle into soup bowls and serve.

Note:

The beauty of this soup is that, once made, it can be set over lowest heat and allowed to stand the better part of the morning or afternoon—the flavors mellow and intensify and the soup will taste even better. It also freezes well.

Adele Volpi's Ossobuco

Makes 6 servings

"I use herbs in almost everything," says Adele Volpi, as she dictates her way of making *Ossobuco* (braised veal shanks), which she seasons with fresh basil, marjoram, rosemary, and parsley. "The veal shanks should be tied around with string," she points out, "so that the meat will hold together during cooking. And you should stand the shanks on end in the kettle to keep the marrow in the bone."

6 veal shanks, 2 to 2½ inches thick
¾ cup unsifted flour
4 to 5 tablespoons olive oil
1½ teaspoons salt (or to taste)
⅛ teaspoon freshly ground black pepper (or to taste)
2 medium-sized yellow onions, peeled and chopped
2 garlic cloves, peeled and minced
2 tablespoons finely chopped fresh basil
2 tablespoons finely chopped parsley (preferably the flat-leafed Italian parsley)

2 teaspoons finely chopped fresh marjoram, or ½ teaspoon crumbled dried leaf marjoram
1 teaspoon finely chopped fresh rosemary, or ¼ teaspoon crumbled dried leaf rosemary
1 large vine-ripened tomato, peeled, cored and coarsely chopped (reserve juice but remove some of the seeds)
1¼ cups dry white wine

1.   Dredge the veal shanks well in the flour on all sides; shake off excess flour. Brown the veal shanks nicely in 4 tablespoons of the oil in a large heavy kettle. You'll only be able to brown about half of them at a time. Add the additional tablespoon of olive oil, if needed. As

shanks brown, transfer them to paper toweling to drain and season well with salt and pepper.

2.   In the drippings remaining in the kettle, sauté the onions, garlic, basil, parsley, marjoram, and rosemary over very low heat, stirring occasionally, until mixture is limp—this will take 15 to 20 minutes. "*Do not brown the mixture*," Adele Volpi cautions, "because that will alter the flavor." Add the tomato and its juice and let simmer, covered, about 10 minutes.

3.   Stand the browned veal shanks in the kettle, spooning some of the tomato mixture on top of them. Pour in the wine, adjust heat so that mixture bubbles very gently, cover and simmer slowly 3½ to 4 hours or until veal very nearly falls from bones. Taste for salt and pepper and add more, if needed.

4.   To serve, stand veal shanks up on a large platter and spoon some of the kettle juices on top.

Homemade Pasta

Makes about ¾ pound, enough for 4 servings

"My greatest desire as a little girl was to learn how to make pasta—you know, by hand," says Adele Volpi. "Little by little I mastered it. About three or four months ago, some of the women around here were eager to learn how to make pasta. So we had a party here. About twelve women came and they all watched me make pasta the old-fashioned Italian way. I do *everything* by hand although I know that a lot of women like to use the pasta machine."

2 cups sifted all-purpose flour	2 teaspoons olive oil
2 eggs	2 tablespoons water (about)

1.   Mound the flour on a large dough board and make a well in the center. Break eggs into well, then add olive oil and water. Mix with a fork just to combine ingredients. If mixture seems too crumbly, add a bit more water. Knead hard with your hands until the dough is the right consistency to roll. "The dough should be satiny," Mrs. Volpi says. "And it should not stick to your hands or be too hard."

2.   Divide dough in half and shape each half into a mound; cover each with a turned-upside-down bowl and let stand for at least 30 minutes. Roll the dough, half at a time, on a lightly floured board, using

a rolling pin and considerable pressure. "You'll also have to help shape the dough with your hands," says Mrs. Volpi. The trick is to roll it as thin as possible. "They say you can really roll it thinner with a rolling pin than you can with a pasta machine, although I don't know," she continues. "I've never operated a pasta machine."

3. Let the rolled-out dough stand, uncovered, at room temperature for at least 1 hour (if the weather is humid, you will have to let the dough stand longer). "The point," Mrs. Volpi explains, "is to let the dough stand until it is no longer sticky, so that it can be rolled up and sliced without sticking to itself."

4. Roll a sheet of dough up jelly-roll style, then slice as thin or thick as you want—⅛-inch for thin pasta, ¼-inch for medium, and ½-inch for broad. The same pasta, of course, may be used for making ravioli or tortellini or other fancy-shaped pasta. "I cut the dough maybe an hour before I cook it," Mrs. Volpi says. "Then it won't get too dry."

5. Cook the pasta in plenty of salted water just until *al dente*. Begin testing a strand of it after 4 to 5 minutes, then watch closely and drain pasta the instant it is tender but still offers slight resistance between the teeth. "I never use oil in the cooking water to keep the pasta from sticking," Adele Volpi says. "If you use enough water and keep it boiling hard, you don't need any oil. I also don't put any cold water on the pasta after I drain it. I just add the sauce and toss it all up like a salad so that the pasta is well coated."

Pasta alla Bolognese (*Pasta with Meat Sauce*)
Makes 4 to 6 servings

When making a Bolognese (meat) sauce for spaghetti, Adele Volpi likes to use equal parts ground beef, pork, and chicken. "I save chicken gizzards and hearts and often grind them up for my Bolognese sauce," she says. You may, of course, make the sauce with beef only, but it won't have quite the flavor of the three-meat sauce. One of Adele Volpi's tricks in making the sauce is to simmer it slowly—*very slowly*—over lowest heat. "You don't want to brown the meat," she says. "And you don't want to brown the onions, either." She puts no garlic in her Bolognese sauce. "I know a lot of people do," she says. What she does add are mushrooms that she has gathered and dried herself. "They make all the difference," she explains. The best dried mushrooms to use are the European ones, carried by many specialty food shops. The dried Japanese or Chinese mushrooms are too gelatinous when reconstituted to create the proper effect.

1 ounce dried European mushrooms
2 cups boiling water
2 tablespoons olive oil
1½ tablespoons butter
1 large yellow onion, peeled and chopped
2 large celery ribs, washed and finely diced
½ cup finely chopped fresh basil
½ cup finely chopped parsley (preferably the flat-leafed Italian parsley)

¾ pound ground raw meat (preferably ¼ pound each lean ground beef, pork, and chicken or chicken giblets)
1 quart (4 cups) puréed drained canned tomatoes (Mrs. Volpi would use those that she has canned herself)
1 teaspoon salt (or to taste)
⅛ teaspoon freshly ground black pepper (or to taste)
1 pound hot cooked and drained fine spaghetti
Freshly grated Parmesan cheese

1.   Place the dried mushrooms in a bowl, pour in the boiling water, cover and let stand about 1 hour. Drain the mushrooms, then chop fine and reserve.

2.   In a very large heavy skillet set over low heat, warm the olive oil and butter—just until butter melts. Add the onion, celery, basil, and parsley and let sauté very slowly, stirring occasionally, about 20 minutes—just until mixture is quite soft. Do not allow to brown. Add the meat, breaking up clumps, cover and let simmer slowly about 15 to 20 minutes; again, do not allow mixture to brown.

3.   Stir in the reserved mushrooms, the tomatoes, salt, and pepper, adjust heat so that mixture barely bubbles, cover and simmer 1½ to 2 hours or until flavors are well blended. Taste for salt and pepper and add more if needed. If you keep the heat under the skillet at the lowest point, you can simmer the sauce as long as 3 to 3½ hours—in fact, its flavor and texture will be better if you do. But do check the skillet often to make sure that the sauce is *barely* simmering—not boiling and reducing too much.

4.   To serve, place the hot drained pasta in a large bowl, pour in the sauce and toss well to mix. Transfer to a platter or individual plates and put out plenty of freshly grated Parmesan. "A lot of people would pile the pasta on a platter and then pour the sauce on top," says Adele Volpi. "But I like to mix it all up—like a salad."

Pesto Sauce
(*Fresh Basil and Garlic Sauce for Pasta*)

Makes 4 to 6 servings,
enough to dress 1 pound of cooked spaghetti

"My husband is not fond of pesto sauce," Adele Volpi admits, "but I am." To make it, you need a big bunch of *fresh* basil, preferably on the verge of blooming because that is when basil is the most aromatic. The old-fashioned Italian way of making pesto sauce is to crush the garlic, basil and parsley in a mortar with a pestle until all is reduced to a thick paste. To shorten the job, use an electric blender, or better still, one of the new high-powered food processors such as the Cuisinart. "Some women," says Adele Volpi, "grind *pignoli* (pine nuts) into their pesto sauce. But I never do."

¼ cup butter, at room temperature
3 tablespoons olive oil
2 garlic cloves, peeled and diced
½ cup finely minced fresh basil

½ cup finely minced parsley (preferably the flat-leafed Italian parsley)
¾ teaspoon salt

1.   Place all ingredients in an electric blender cup or in a food processor fitted with a chopping blade. Buzz at high speed until mixture is uniformly thick and creamy.

2.   Scoop mixture into a small bowl, cover, and let stand several hours before serving.

3.   To serve, spoon pesto sauce over 1 pound of *hot* cooked well-drained thin spaghetti and toss well to mix. Put out plenty of freshly grated Parmesan so that people can spoon as much as they like over the pasta.

Sausage-Stuffed Zucchini

Makes 6 servings

"People just gobble these things up," Mrs. Volpi says of her Sausage-Stuffed Zucchini. "Even my husband, who doesn't like zucchini, loves these—or at least he loves the stuffing. You can serve them as finger food or you can serve them as a main dish." Mrs. Volpi says that she worked the stuffing recipe out herself, adding sweet Italian sausage to keep the stuffing moist. Mrs. Volpi does not cook the sausage before she mixes it into the stuffing, but to make sure that the sausage cooks completely as the zucchini bakes, we recommend sautéing it lightly before combining it with the remaining stuffing ingredients.

6 medium-sized zucchini, washed and trimmed of stem ends
1 quart (4 cups) lightly salted water (for parboiling the zucchini)
½ pound sweet Italian sausages
1 medium-sized yellow onion, peeled and minced fine
⅓ cup chopped fresh basil
¼ cup chopped parsley (preferably the flat-leafed Italian parsley)
¼ teaspoon crumbled leaf marjoram
½ cup freshly grated Parmesan cheese
¼ cup moderately fine dry bread-crumbs
1 large egg
½ teaspoon salt
Pinch of pepper

1. Halve the zucchini lengthwise, then parboil in the lightly salted water about 10 to 12 minutes, just until barely tender. (The easiest way to do this and the best way to keep the zucchini halves from breaking is to arrange them one layer deep in a shallow roasting pan, pour in the water and set over two burners. Use a baking sheet to cover the pan while the zucchini parboils.) When zucchini is crisp-tender, drain well, then scrape out the central seedy portions, leaving zucchini shells with walls ⅛- to ¼-inch thick. Chop the scooped-out zucchini very fine and reserve.

2. Slit the casings on the sausages, scoop the meat into a large heavy skillet set over low heat and break clumps up well with a spoon. Sauté very slowly about 5 to 8 minutes, just until no traces of pink remain in the meat. Do not brown the meat but do continue breaking it up with a spoon so that it is uniformly fine and crumbly. Add onion, basil, parsley, and marjoram, turn heat to lowest point, cover and let simmer slowly 5 to 8 minutes, or until onions are limp.

3. Remove from heat and mix in reserved chopped zucchini, Parmesan cheese, breadcrumbs, egg, salt, and pepper. Mix briskly and lightly with a fork.

4. Fill zucchini shells with the stuffing mixture, dividing it evenly among the 12 zucchini halves and mounding it up slightly in the center. Arrange the filled zucchini—one touching another so that they will help support one another as they bake—on an ungreased baking sheet.

5. Bake uncovered in a moderate oven (350°) for 30 minutes, just until stuffing is hot and lightly browned.

Baked Spinach Balls

Makes 4 to 6 servings

To those who think they don't like spinach, we recommend Adele
Volpi's Baked Spinach Balls smothered with Tomato-Wine Sauce and
predict that it will win applause.

1 medium-sized yellow onion, peeled
and minced fine
2 garlic cloves, peeled and minced
2 tablespoons butter
2 cups finely chopped cooked spinach that has been pressed as dry as
possible in a sieve (you'll need
about 1½ pounds fresh spinach or
4 10-ounce packages of frozen
chopped spinach)

½ teaspoon salt
⅛ teaspoon pepper
¼ cup moderately fine dry breadcrumbs
⅓ cup freshly grated Parmesan
cheese
1 large egg
1 recipe Tomato-Wine Sauce (recipe follows)

1. In a large heavy skillet sauté the onion and garlic in the butter
over moderately low heat about 15 minutes until very limp—do not
brown. Mix in the spinach, salt, and pepper, cover, turn heat to lowest
point and steam 15 minutes.

2. Remove from heat and blend in breadcrumbs, cheese and egg.
Chill several hours or until firm enough to shape. Shape into 1-inch
balls and arrange one layer deep in a buttered 9- × 9- × 2-inch flameproof baking dish.

3. Bake uncovered in a moderate oven (350°) for 30 minutes.
Spoon into a vegetable dish or onto individual plates and serve topped
with a generous ladling of Tomato-Wine Sauce.

Tomato-Wine Sauce

Makes about 1 quart, enough for 4 to 6 servings

This is the sauce that Mrs. Volpi would serve over her Baked Spinach
Balls, but it is also very good over pasta.

1 medium-sized yellow onion,
peeled and minced fine
1 garlic clove, peeled and minced
fine
2 tablespoons olive oil
2 teaspoons minced fresh sage, or
1 teaspoon crumbled leaf sage

1 quart (4 cups) tomato sauce
(Mrs. Volpi would use that which
she has canned herself)
½ cup dry white wine
Salt and pepper (optional)

1. In a large heavy skillet, sauté the onion and garlic in the olive oil over moderately low heat about 15 minutes until very limp—do not brown. Add the sage and sauté about 5 minutes longer.

2. Blend in the tomato sauce and wine and simmer, uncovered, about 10 minutes, then cover and simmer 1 to 1½ hours or until flavors are well blended. Depending upon the seasoning of the tomato sauce you are using, the sauce may or may not need additional salt and pepper.

Marsala Peach Pie

Makes one 9-inch single-crust pie

"I make a fresh peach pie that is out of this world," says Adele Volpi not in the least boastfully. "You can use the same recipe for blackberries and strawberries, only you leave the Marsala wine out."

½ cup plus 1 tablespoon sugar
2 tablespoons cornstarch
1 teaspoon unflavored gelatin
½ cup orange juice
½ cup water

7 cups sliced, peeled and pitted very ripe freestone peaches (about 6 to 8 large peaches)
¼ cup Marsala wine
1 9-inch baked pie shell
1 cup heavy cream, whipped

1. In a small heavy saucepan blend the ½ cup sugar, cornstarch and gelatin, pressing out any lumps. Stir in orange juice and water, set over moderate heat and cook and stir until mixture bubbles 3 minutes. Remove from heat and chill until mixture becomes syrupy.

2. Meanwhile, mix peaches with the remaining 1 tablespoon sugar and the Marsala wine and let marinate until gelatin mixture has thickened. Combine with gelatin mixture and chill, covered, until almost set.

3. Spoon into baked pie shell and chill until set. Just before serving, "frost" with whipped cream.

Date Bars

Makes about 5 dozen cookies

These are quite unlike the date bars with which most of us are familiar. First of all, they are not baked in a loaf pan and cut into bars. They are shaped into long rolls, sprinkled with granulated sugar, and baked just until firm. Then, while the rolls are still hot, they are sliced—on the bias—into long thin strips. The result is that the bars are crisp rather than chewy.

1 cup butter, at room temperature	¼ teaspoon ground cloves
2 cups sugar	¼ teaspoon salt
3 eggs	1 package (8 ounces) pitted dates,
1 teaspoon baking soda blended	snipped fine with scissors
with 2 teaspoons cold water	1 cup moderately finely chopped
4½ cups sifted all-purpose flour	walnuts
1 teaspoon ground cinnamon	2 tablespoons sugar (for sprinkling
1 teaspoon ground nutmeg	on top of bars)

1. Cream the butter and sugar until fluffy-light; beat in the eggs, 1 at a time. Blend in the soda mixture.

2. Combine flour with cinnamon, nutmeg, cloves and salt and blend into the creamed mixture to form a soft dough. Fold in dates and walnuts. Divide dough into 3 parts, wrap in waxed paper, foil or plastic food wrap and refrigerate overnight or until firm enough to shape.

3. Shape each section of chilled dough into a roll about 7 or 8 inches long and 1 inch in diameter. Arrange rolls of dough, crosswise, on lightly greased baking sheets, spacing at least 2 inches apart as the dough will spread as it bakes. Sprinkle top of each roll lightly with sugar.

4. Bake in a moderate oven (350°) for about 25 minutes or until rolls are a nice golden brown and seem fairly firm to the touch.

5. Remove from oven and with a very sharp knife, slice the rolls crosswise and on the bias at ½-inch intervals.

Note:

"You must slice the bars while they are hot," cautions Mrs. Volpi. "Otherwise, they will shatter." Transfer bars to wire racks to cool, then store in airtight canisters.

Wine Sticks

Makes about 5 dozen cookies

"The way to eat these," explains Mrs. Volpi, "is to dunk them in wine. Any kind of wine. It doesn't have to be sweet. I often serve these as dessert," she continues, "and a doctor friend who comes often to dinner thinks they are just the best things ever."

½ cup butter, at room temperature
1 cup sugar
3 eggs
3 cups sifted all-purpose flour
3 teaspoons baking powder

½ teaspoon salt
1 teaspoon anise extract
1 cup moderately finely chopped *unblanched* almonds

1. Cream the butter and sugar until light and fluffy; beat in the eggs. Combine flour, baking powder, and salt and mix in. Stir in anise extract and almonds.

2. With floured hands, shape dough into rolls about 7 or 8 inches long and 1½ inches in diameter. Space the rolls of dough crosswise and about 2 inches apart on lightly greased baking sheets.

3. Bake in a moderate oven (350°) for about 20 minutes or until rolls are fairly firm to the touch—they will not have browned much but will be a pale ivory color.

4. Remove from oven and while rolls are still hot, slice crosswise and on the bias at ½-inch intervals. Separate the sticks, then arrange upside-down on ungreased baking sheets and toast in a hot oven (400°) about 2 to 3 minutes or just until crisp and lightly browned. Remove from oven, cool to room temperature, then store in airtight canisters.

Index